1964
YEAR OF
TRIUMPH
AND
TRAGEDY

1964

YEAR OF TRIUMPH AND TRAGEDY

Thomas Brennan

REGENT PRESS
Berkeley, California

Paperback
ISBN 13: 978-1-58790-347-2
ISBN 10: 1-58790-347-4

E-book:
ISBN 13: 978-1-58790-348-9
ISBN 10: 1-58790-348-2

Library of Congress Control Number: 2016931478

First Edition

0 1 2 3 4 5 6 7 8 9 10

Manufactured in the United States of America

REGENT PRESS
www.regentpress.net
regentpress@mindspring.com

CONTENTS

INTRODUCTION

FOR many, the 1960s represents a decade of historic change not experienced before or since. America entered a brutal and drawn-out war that divided a nation and created a generation of cynics. The world was introduced to a new kind of sports icon, one who was not afraid to speak out against what he believed was fundamentally wrong with America. The leader of the free world was gunned down in Dallas, Texas, and his alleged assassin was later murdered on live television. The civil rights movement flourished and grew more powerful, but not without serious repercussions. Many young, innocent blacks were murdered and its leader was assassinated in Memphis, Tennessee, while trying to settle a black union grievance. And a small rock band from England would stun the world and captivate a generation and future generations with its innovative and influential style of music.

In 1964 several events occurred that would change America and the world forever. On February 9, the Beatles played to a television audience of over 73 million viewers. Their long hair, tight dark suits, and foreign sounding accents captivated America's youth and terrorized their parents. America's media blasted the band as no-talents, but the kids kept buying their albums anyway. Soon, established recording artists discovered just how great the Beatles actually were and began covering many of their songs. To capitalize on the band's new-found fame, the movie, *A Hard Day's Night*, cemented their fame, even among many parents, and Beatlemania in America was born.

On February 25, Cassius Marcellus Clay, the decided underdog, soundly defeated the nearly invincible Sonny Liston to become the new world heavyweight champion. So unbelievable was the outcome that most boxing fans believed the fight was fixed. Clay soon announced to the world that he had become a Muslim and demanded that he be referred to as Muhammad Ali. Boxing fans and the press criticized Ali for worshiping this odd, foreign religion. In time, sports fans and the press alike would grow to respect Ali the man and the sports hero.

In July the Civil Rights Act of 1964 would become the law of the land. The new legislation would now make it unlawful to deny any American citizen access to public accommodations such as public schools, universities, restaurants, and public restrooms. No longer could an American citizen be beaten and thrown in jail for exercising his or her federally protected rights without legal recourse. Martin Luther King, Jr., the leader of the civil rights movement, would also deservedly receive the Nobel Peace Prize for his important role in the civil rights movement.

In August North Vietnamese torpedo boats, on two separate occasions, reportedly fired upon U.S. destroyers in the Gulf of Tonkin. Based on these reports, President Johnson asked and received from Congress a special resolution which effectively allowed him to escalate the war in Vietnam. The alleged second attack by the North Vietnamese has been called into question by many who have reviewed all the available evidence. It was after the alleged second "attack" that Johnson asked for what would become known as the Tonkin Gulf Resolution. This would mark the first stage in which America would aggressively engage the enemy.

In September the Warren Commission Report, as it is commonly referred to, would be released to the American public. The report basically attempted to explain who assassinated President Kennedy and why. Immediately upon its release, critics blasted the Commission's findings as preposterous. Nowhere in the report, according to the critics, was there anything significant about the possibility of a conspiracy. More specifically, the critics wondered how the president's frontal wounds could have been initially described by surgeons as entry wounds, but then were later referred to as exit wounds. There continues to be too many unexplained circumstances regarding Kennedy's murder, and so over the last several decades, authors have offered their theories regarding the most written about assassination in the history of the world.

Part One

BEATLEMANIA

CHAPTER 1

THE EARLY YEARS

JOHN LENNON first became infatuated with rock and roll music when he heard Elvis Presley's version of "Heartbreak Hotel" in 1956. His Aunt Mimi recalled that "I never got a minute's peace. It was Elvis Presley, Elvis Presley, and Elvis Presley. In the end, I said, 'Elvis Presley is all very well, John, but I don't want him for breakfast, dinner, and tea.'" Amazingly, the BBC did not allow rock and roll music to be broadcast. Radio Luxembourg was the only station that provided this kind of music via the airwaves. John and thousands of rock and roll fans became avid fans of newcomers like Little Richard, Bill Haley and the Comets, and Buddy Holly. Aunt Mimi finally gave in to John's pleadings and bought him his first guitar. John would lie in bed for hours and strum chords his mother, Julia, had taught him. His aunt often scolded John about wasting time learning to play the guitar. "The guitar's all very well, John, but you'll never make a living out of it," she'd warn him.

John formed a skiffle band and called it the Quarry Men. The band members included Peter Shotton, Eric Griffiths, Colin Hanton, Nigel Whalley, and Ivan Vaughn. John was the dominant member of the band and he played a mean guitar. It wasn't unusual for John to break a guitar string and quickly switch to playing a banjo during a performance. Initially, the band played skiffle favorites such as "Cumberland Gap," "Rock Island Line," and "Don't You Rock Me, Daddy." John insisted, however, on playing rock and roll music and belted out hits like "Blue Suede Shoes." John got in the habit of singing his own words to current hits because he couldn't afford to buy the records and learn the lyrics.

Paul McCartney grew up in a home filled with the sound of music. His father, Jim, led a band called the Jim Mac Jazz band. In the living room sat a piano that Jim would play when he wasn't busy working. Paul's mother, Mary, died when Paul was very young. His father took over all the domestic chores his wife once performed. Paul decided he wanted to play guitar after having watched a performance by Lonnie Donegan. His father gladly bought his son a guitar and immediately began teaching him chords to play. Paul sat for hours trying to practice playing the instrument without much progress. Paul eventually realized that although he was right-handed, he could only play the guitar left-handed. The guitar was taken back to the music shop in order to have the strings reversed.

Paul quickly learned enough chords to be able to play many of the skiffle hits. He eventually got bored with skiffle and began learning how to replicate rock and roll guitar solos. He played his favorite Elvis Presley record, "All Shook Up" over and over again along with hits by Little Richard and Carl Perkins. He would sing along with these rock and roll giants, trying to learn the secret of their mesmerizing style of singing. A little later he became a huge fan of the Everly Brothers with their low keyed, smooth vocals.

On July 6, 1957, John and his Quarry Men played at a garden fete in Woolton. John vigorously shouted out the lyrics to "Cumberland Gap," "Railroad Bill," and "Maggie May," a Liverpool waterfront song supposedly about a loose woman. Luckily for the band, no one in charge of the festival could make out what the song was about. Witnessing this performance was Paul and his friend Ivan Vaughn.

After the performance, Paul and John were introduced to each other. They exchanged pleasantries, but that was about it until John discovered that Paul knew how to tune a guitar. John and the rest of the band had never learned this simple, necessary function because they were always able to find someone who could tune their stringed instruments. John was further impressed by Paul's knowledge of all the lyrics to several rock and roll songs. John was haunted by his inability to remember words to songs.

To further impress John, Paul grabbed a guitar and began singing several of Little Richard's songs, such as "Tutti Frutti," and "Long Tall Sally." John was duly impressed by Paul's passionate singing and guitar work. He closely studied the way Paul's fingers glided up and down the neck of his guitar. Paul may not have realized it at the time, but his "audition" did not go unnoticed. Even after his impressive display of musicianship and vocal expertise,

Paul was not asked to join John's band. It's possible that he may even have been too polished for the Quarry Men and that is why he was not immediately asked to join. After about a week, Paul was indeed asked to join up with John and his band mates. Apparently, John may have been thinking more about the importance of strengthening the band rather than continuing to be its sole leader.

Shortly after Paul became a member of the band, Pete Shotton's tenure with the group abruptly ended when John smashed a washboard over his head at a party. Pete took this as a sign that his duties as a washboard player were no longer required. Pete later recalled that "All of us were pissed and larking around. It didn't hurt me. I just sat there, framed by the washboard, with tears of laughter running down my face. I'd known for a long time that I was no good at music. I was only in the group through being a mate of John's. I was finished with playing, but I didn't want to say so, nor did John. This way let me out and it let John out."

Paul sat with John for hours every day teaching him new chords and different strumming techniques. The other members of the Quarry Men did not care for Paul's so called cockiness. Paul began complaining about not receiving a bigger share of the money earned by the band. He also criticized the drummer, Colin, for not playing better. Paul would constantly ask Colin to play the drums a certain way depending on the arrangement of a song. He would even sit at the drums and show Colin exactly how he wanted them played.

Circumstances were beginning to cause unwelcome and unexpected changes with the Quarry Men. One by one band members began leaving the group for one reason or another. Nigel Whalley came down with tuberculosis and the bass player, Len Garry, contracted meningitis. Rod Davis was too busy working and so he stopped playing banjo for the band. Skiffle bands were also out of style by 1957 and rock and roll was now the in thing in Liverpool. Music acts like the Most Brothers, Marty Wilde, and Russ Hamilton were England's answer to America's Elvis Presley, Bill Haley and the Comets, and the Platters.

Sitting in the audience at many of the shows that featured the Quarry Men was a friend of Paul's. He was very quiet and unassuming. No one would ever take him for a guitar player at first glance. His name was George Harrison and Paul thought he would make a fine addition to the band. George did not come from a musical family, but he did have an insatiable desire to learn how to play the guitar. Learning to play the instrument was an agonizing experience for young George. He did not seem to have a natural ability to play the guitar as Paul did. In time, however, George and his brother, Peter, formed a band and called themselves the Rebels.

George was introduced to the members of the Quarry Men in late 1957. The meeting took place at a club called the Morgue. The club was located in a cellar beneath an old seedy house. The band members stood around George while he played songs like "Raunchy" and "Guitar Boogie Shuffle." George may not have impressed the band as Paul did because he was not asked to join the Quarry Men. Undeterred, George followed the band to all their shows. Occasionally, he would be asked to sit in if a band member failed to show up for a gig.

John was not overwhelmed by George's talent as a

guitarist and would often tease him about it. John did, how-ever, value something important about George. The band was allowed to rehearse quite often at George's house while his father was away working. In the meantime, George was playing a lot more guitar for the band. One reason for this was that Eric Griffiths, one of the band's founders, was unceremoniously tossed out.

On July 15, 1958, John's mother, Julia, had paid a visit to Aunt Mimi. After leaving Aunt Mimi's house to return home, she was struck and killed by a car driven by an off-duty policeman. John was grief stricken by his mother's tragic death, but he was determined not to show his true state of mind. John started to drink more and more and his friends began to worry about his safety. He became extremely difficult to be around because of his abusive lan-guage and temper tantrums. A girl he had been seeing had had enough of his insults and shouted at him, "Don't take it out on me, just because your mother's dead."

The Quarry Men changed their name to Johnny and the Moondogs, evidence that John was still the band's supreme leader. The band basically went nowhere, playing at birthday parties and small events. Sometimes the band appeared for a show calling themselves whatever name struck them at the time. One night they all appeared in dif-ferent colored shirts and called themselves the Rainbows. Often they played without a drummer. Such was the state of the band through the end of 1958.

Pete Best, now eighteen, lived with his family in a large Victorian house in Hayman's Green. His father, Johnny Best, had been a boxing promoter in nearby Liverpool. Pete's mother, Mona, was of Anglo-Indian decent. Pete's father and mother had been recently separated and so Mona was in charge of caring for her two sons, Pete and Rory, and her invalid mother. Pete was attending Liverpool Collegiate Grammar School and he excelled in scholastics and sports. He was handsome, reserved, and not very assertive.

The house the Best family lived in had a huge cellar. Pete and Rory were allowed to turn part of the cellar into a den so that they could invite their friends over. So many friends hung out in the den that Mona Best thought perhaps the cellar could be renovated and turned into a club. Benches and a counter were installed and a large dragon was painted on the ceiling. The club was called the Casbah, the name evidently inspired by the film, *Algiers*, starring Charles Boyer.

George had heard that Mona Best was looking for a band to play on club nights. George toured the club, but was unimpressed. He decided to come back for another look, but this time he brought along John and Paul. John and Paul thought the club could perhaps be a regular venue for the band. John even tried to help the Best brothers paint the walls, but made a mess of things because of his poor vision and his refusal to wear glasses.

The Casbah Coffee Club was an immediate hit with the teenagers. Mona Best sold coffee, soft drinks, and snacks to her young, eager customers. Mona Best also chose John, Paul, George, and Ken Browne to play all the club dates. There was no drummer in the band and only one ten-watt amplifier was used during their performances. In time, the band took a strong liking to the reserved Pete Best. But there was no discussion about Pete joining the band. In fact, Pete was seriously considering becoming a teacher.

One night Ken Browne arrived at the Casbah with a bad head cold. He was not feeling well enough to play and so John, Paul, and George performed without him. After the show Mona Best paid John, Paul, and George 15 shillings each. They asked Mona Best for the other 15 shillings. When they were told that she had paid 15 shillings to Ken Browne, they forcefully voiced their dissatisfaction to her. John, Paul, and George argued with Ken Browne until Browne could take the bickering no longer. He told the three he was done with the whole lot of them and they stormed out of the club shaking their heads.

The band desperately needed a drummer and so John asked a business acquaintance, Allan Williams, for help. Williams introduced the band to a transient drummer named Tommy Moore. Although Moore was busy playing with other bands, he agreed to audition for Johnny and the Moondogs. Moore was thirty-six and worked in the Garston Bottle Works as a fork lift operator. The band was willing to overlook the age disparity between Moore and the band members after hearing the drummer play for them. Paul, in particular, was more than satisfied with Moore's drumming technique.

Allan Williams arranged for Johnny and the Moondogs to play at a club called the Jacaranda. John and Paul were constantly trying to outdo each other with their onstage antics. George would quietly stand off to the side playing his guitar while John and Paul competed with one another. Stu Sutcliffe, who had recently joined the band, was hardly noticeable on stage as he fumbled with the bass strings. He stood broodingly in the dark behind the others, wearing sunglasses and looking aloof. The other band members occasionally teased

Sutcliffe about his lack of musicianship, hoping perhaps their good-natured ribbing would cause him to learn how to play bass properly. It was to no avail, however.

Larry Parnes, a fairly successful local promoter, was in search of Liverpool musicians willing to back up some of his "star" singers, most notably, Billy Fury. Parnes asked for Allan Williams' help in this endeavor. Williams provided the names of bands that had performed at the Jacaranda and who he thought would be sufficient back up bands for Parnes' solo singers. He enlisted popular local favorites like Rory Storm and the Hurricanes, Cass and the Casanovas, and Johnny and the Moondogs. He forwarded Johnny and the Moondogs name with some trepidation because he felt they might not be experienced enough.

Parnes did not like the name, Johnny and the Moondogs, and strongly suggested a name change immediately. He wanted the band to change their name to something much catchier. He thought, for example, that the band should have a name similar to Buddy Holly's Crickets. When Stu Sutcliffe heard of Parnes' complaint, he jokingly suggested a name like the "beetles." Surprisingly, the other band members liked Sutcliffe's tongue-in-cheek suggestion. John, always keen on word changes, changed "beet" to "beat" and the name "Beatles" was born.

Allan Williams, sensing that customers at the Jacaranda were very unhappy with the name change, suggested that the band come up with something better. He was, after all, afraid that business at the club would drop off due to the odd, unpopular sounding name. Cass, of Cass and the Casanovas, was evidently a big fan of the book *Treasure Island*, because he suggested the band should be called Long John and the Silver Beatles. John was aghast at calling himself "Long John" and so the name Silver Beatles was decided on instead.

The audition was held in a small men's club near the Jacaranda. Parnes arrived at the club with the biggest pop music star in all of England, Billy Fury. The Silver Beatles felt totally out-classed by the competition. The other bands, like Derry and the Seniors, looked and acted professional. Moreover, the bands were already established, popular acts. Also on hand was none other than the Hurricanes' very popular drummer, the dour-faced Ringo Starr, then known as Ritchie Starkey. Ringo sported a beard and looked quite dapper. John and Paul, however, did not appreciate the drummer's appearance. Perhaps he was not bohemian enough for them.

Derry and the Seniors and Rory Storm's band went over quite well with Parnes. He thought they exhibited a lot of power and excitement. The Silver Beatles, on the other hand, were only adequate. Parnes did not like their jeans and black sweaters. To make matters worse, their drummer, Tommy Moore, was a no show because he was too busy searching for assorted drum equipment at the last minute. Another drummer reluctantly sat in for Moore. The fill-in drummer, Johnny Hutch, hurt the Silver Beatles chances of passing the audition because he looked utterly bored.

Eventually, Parnes offered the Silver Beatles a chance to go on a two-week tour in Scotland as a backup band for one of Parnes' singers, the one and only Johnny Gentle, a former merchant seaman. The band was promised 18 pounds a week for their efforts. The Silver Beatles went into hysterics when they heard the news. The opportunity, however, presented problems. Each band member needed to temporarily put aside regular responsibilities at home. Paul, for example, was attending school and exams were coming up. Somehow he got his father to agree with the notion that a brief break from the constant grind of homework would do him some good. Tommy Moore explained to his girlfriend that lost wages as a fork lift operator would be more than compensated by the money he earned while on tour.

Complications from the tour were many. Chief among them involved Johnny Gentle. Gentle, who suffered from stage fright, took to drinking to steady his nerves. Early in the tour he drove the van into a parked car. Inside the Ford Poplar car sat two elderly ladies who, fortunately, were not seriously injured. Tommy Moore was badly crushed by the luggage and equipment that slid on top of him during the collision. He was rushed to the hospital where he was administered pain medication for his concussion and badly loosened teeth. He was not able to perform for several days. The rest of the band, however, could not do without a drummer for very long. One night they quietly lifted him from his hospital bed, threw him into the van, and sped off for a scheduled gig. Moore played the drums while he was still very groggy from the medication. He also sported a huge bandage on his head.

The Silver Beatles were getting a great deal of favorable reaction from audiences everywhere. They were so popular with the Scottish fans that Johnny Gentle advised Parnes to sign the band up immediately. Parnes refused because he thought solo singers were hard enough to manage, let alone a five-member band. The band travelled all the way to Inverness where they had to wait for the hotel to open because they arrived much too early. Disgusted, Tommy Moore decided to quit the band. The only band member he could tolerate to any degree was Stu Sutcliffe.

Allan Williams was now taking the Silver Beatles a lot more seriously after receiving positive feedback about the band during their Scottish tour. He booked them in several new venues this time, not just the Jacaranda. Some of the venues, unfortunately, introduced the band to extreme forms of violence. One night at the Grosvenor Ballroom in Wallasey, a fight broke out. A local gang of thugs, or "Teds" as they called themselves, battled with some outsiders from New Brighton. At another gig, a sixteen-year old boy was kicked to death during a performance by the band. Quite often the band had to protect themselves and their guitars from flying bottles and other debris. Luckily, the band members remained relatively unscathed during most of these violent episodes.

Allan Williams booked the band for a show at Litherland Town Hall in Liverpool. During the show certain members of the audience became infuriated by something someone from the band had either said or insinuated. After the show the band was ambushed by a gang of thugs as they made their way to the van. During the attack, Stu Sutcliffe was thrown to the ground and kicked repeatedly. Blood poured from a wide gash in his head. John fought off the assailant and managed to carry Sutcliffe to safety. When Sutcliffe arrived home, his mother was horrified to see her blood soaked son. Surprisingly, he refused medical attention.

By the summer of 1960, the Silver Beatles were still without a drummer. This made it virtually impossible for them to get bookings from dance promoters. They were able, however, to play at a strip club on Upper Parliament Street, near Liverpool. They were paid ten shillings each day to play back up music for a dancer named Janice. The stripper determined what music to play, and so the band had to strum to songs like "Moonglow" and "The Gypsy Fire Dance." Around this time the band decided to call themselves the Beatles.

Allan Williams received word from his business contacts that Hamburg, West Germany, was fast becoming a mecca for music acts. Initially, he wanted to send his favorite bands like the Hurricanes, and Gerry and the Pacemakers, but they had business obligations in England, and therefore could not make the journey. He decided to send the Beatles instead. George, only seventeen, received the least amount of protest from his folks. His family boasted a tradition of world travelers. His sister, for example, married an American and was currently living in St. Louis, Missouri. In retrospect, Germany did not seem to be that far away after all.

There was one huge fly in the ointment, however, regarding this unusual opportunity. The Beatles badly needed a drummer. Allan Williams advised the band that a drummer was essential in order to be allowed to play at an influential venue like the Indra Club. Williams did not care that the Beatles had been frantically searching for a drummer. This time he wanted results and no excuses. He warned them that another band would go in their place if they did not fulfill this last requirement of the contract he agreed to with Herr Koschmider.

With no new prospects on the horizon, the Beatles decided to return to the club they had walked out on, the

Casbah Club. They had been known as the Quarry Men the last time they performed there. To their amazement, the club was bringing in a lot of business. Ken Browne was the leader of a very popular band called The Black Jacks. They were also surprised that Pete Best was the band's drummer. Best had decided to drop any aspirations of becoming a teacher and threw himself wholeheartedly into becoming a rock and roll star. His mother even helped him raise the deposit money for a set of new drums.

The Black Jacks soon disbanded, however, when Ken Browne decided that he had had enough of Liverpool. Unfortunately for Pest Best, no other band was keen on hiring him. To make matters worse, Best was not very assertive. He just hung around his mother's house waiting for his luck to change. Occasionally, he would come down to the club at night and check out some of the bands. Pete Best had experienced a taste of the kind of world he so desperately craved. Now he was on the outside looking in.

One day Pete Best received a telephone call from Paul. He explained to Pete that the Beatles were interested in offering him a job as their drummer. As a caveat, he would have to agree to go on a two-month booking in Hamburg, Germany. Pete Best agreed to the arrangement immediately. After all, there was nothing else going on in his life at this point. As for the Beatles, not only did they finally find a drummer they so desperately needed, they were now the proud owners of a brand new set of drums.

The Beatles' first experience performing at the Indra was a huge disappointment for them. The club was located inside a dark and dingy cellar. There were only a handful of miserable looking customers who couldn't have cared less for Chuck Berry or Buddy Holly covers. It was here where they were expected to play for over four hours each weeknight and even more hours on weekends. They also had to sweat out an old tenant who lived above the club and who constantly complained to the police about the loud music emanating from the club each night.

It was at the Indra where the Beatles began to really put on emotionally charged performances night after night. John in particular would stomp his feet loudly to the beat and occasionally scream "Sieg Heil!" John was fond of imitating popular rock and rollers jumping and twisting erratically while shouting barely audible words to songs. Soon, other musicians came to the club to witness the band everyone was suddenly raving about. Fans began providing the Beatles with all the free beer and liquor they could possibly swallow without passing out on stage.

After months of playing in Hamburg, the band was back at it again at the Casbah. They played with much more energy and showmanship than ever before. Their experience in Hamburg had definitely transformed the group into a powerhouse rock and roll band. One evening, Mrs. Best spoke to the owner of the Cavern Club. She raved to him about how great the Beatles were. The band was subsequently hired, but when they arrived at the club for their first performance, they were warned not to wear jeans. The Beatles told the owner to get stuffed. The band was hired anyway and soon scores of young girls flocked to the club to hear this new phenomenon just back from Germany.

All was not well within the band, however. Paul absolutely detested Stu's bass playing and insisted he could play a lot better than Stu. On more than one occasion Paul's taunts led to a physical altercation between the two band mates. Stu's headaches grew worse and sometimes drove him into uncontrollable fits of rage. He eventually quit the band and Paul immediately assumed the role as bass player. Paul was allowed to play Stu's Hofner President guitar until he could afford his own bass. Curiously, Stu occasionally returned to the band and played bass alongside Paul.

On October 28, 1961, a teenager named Raymond Jones entered a little music shop and asked the man standing behind the counter for a single called "My Bonnie" by the Beatles. Brian Epstein was surprised that this regular customer didn't ask him about the latest Carl Perkins release. He had never heard of the Beatles and the single didn't ring a bell with him either. Later in the afternoon, some girls asked Epstein if he carried "My Bonnie." It was odd that Epstein had never heard of the Beatles because their name appeared frequently in the *Mersey Beat* newspaper. Epstein had been writing a column for the newspaper for some time. Also, the Cavern was very close to his shop. Curiosity got the better of Epstein because the Beatles represented a local band that had released a record his customers were inquiring about. He decided to find out more about this band with the peculiar name.

On November 9, 1961, Brian visited the Cavern around lunchtime to check out the Beatles. Strangely, he wore a dark suit and carried a briefcase for the occasion. At twenty-seven, he felt totally out of place among all the screaming teenagers. He was appalled by the cramped, dark archways of the cellar and the odor the walls emitted. He was mesmerized not so much by the Beatles' music, but how they presented themselves on stage. He seemed particularly interested in John's persona. After their session, Brian approached the band and introduced himself. George turned to him and asked, "What brings Mr. Epstein here?" During his short discussion with the Beatles, he was surprised to discover that they had only played as a backup band called the Beat Brothers on "My Bonnie."

By the end of November, the Beatles had established themselves as a local band to be reckoned with. They were the number one draw at the Cavern, they had played abroad, released a single, and they were a regular feature in the *Mersey Beat.* Bands were copying their style of music and the way they appeared on stage. For all the attention they were getting, however, the Beatles were still broke. In the meantime, Brian had ordered two-hundred copies of "My Bonnie" to sell at his shop and he advertised the record in the *Mersey Beat.* The single was a moderate success. Brian began entertaining the idea of managing the band. The Beatles agreed to meet with Brian to discuss the idea. The Beatles arrived very late at the appointed location. Brian presented the idea of managing them and they responded with a very lukewarm, "We'll see." Many of Brian's business associates warned him about managing the Beatles. The five of them met again at the NEMS music shop and once again Brian asked them if he could manage the band. After a brief pause, John replied "Yes." Paul asked if the band would have to change their type of music. Brian assured him that their music would be determined solely by the band. After another pause, John declared, "Right then, Brian. Manage us."

Brian Epstein believed from the very beginning that he would have no trouble getting the Beatles a recording contract. He had developed connections through the years as the owner of a NEMS affiliated record shop. Brian contacted Decca and asked them to listen to a live performance of his band. Decca agreed and sent a young A & R type named Mike Smith to the Cavern to watch the Beatles perform. The band was very impressed when they received word that a Decca representative was coming to see them. Decca, after all, had signed Buddy Holly, Little Richard, and the Everly Brothers. Smith was impressed by the Beatles, but he hesitated in signing them up. Instead, he invited the band to audition at the Decca studios in London.

The band arrived in London on New Year's Eve during a horrible blizzard. The next morning the Beatles played fifteen numbers that were mostly chosen by Brian. He had his band play safe, non-rocker songs like "Sheik of Araby" and "September in the Rain." Only three original Beatles songs were allowed to be played. After the audition the Beatles felt they could have done a lot better. John, Paul, and George sounded anxious during some of their renditions. In the end, Mike Smith decided not to sign the Beatles. Instead, he chose a local band called Brian Poole and the Tremeloes. It was a decision Decca would later deeply regret.

In February 1962, Stu Sutcliffe's health deteriorated rapidly. He experienced excruciating headaches and temporary blindness. One day during art class, he collapsed and never returned to school. There were times when he tried to take his own life by jumping out of a window. Shortly thereafter, Stu died while being rushed by ambulance to a nearby hospital. The Beatles were visibly shaken by the news of Stu's passing. George and Pete took Stu's death the hardest. John showed practically no emotion whatsoever. John told Astrid, Stu's closest friend, "Make up your mind. You either live or die. You can't be in the middle."

While the Beatles were back performing in Hamburg, Brian decided once again to try and find a record label that would sign a recording contract with them. Someone suggested to Brian that the band's music should be put on a demonstration disc instead of tape. The disc would look more professional and it would be easier for an A & R representative to quickly locate a song rather than having to plod through a tape in order to find a particular selection. The audio engineer, after having cut the disc, recommended to Brian that he present the songs to EMI's publishing company. The engineer arranged for Brian to meet with Syd Coleman, the chief representative of the publishing company, Ardmore and Beechwood.

Coleman listened to all the songs and offered to publish two of them. He also arranged a meeting between Brian and the head of Parlophone Records' A&R department, George Martin. Martin listened to Brian rave about the Beatles and how they would soon be bigger than Elvis Presley. Martin politely listened to the entire demonstration disc and remarked that he liked Paul's singing and some of the guitar work. He was not overly enthused about most of the music he heard, however. But he did admit "There was an unusual quality-a certain roughness. There might just be something there."

On June 6, 1962, the Beatles played mostly covers for George Martin like "Besame Mucho." After listening to their audition, Martin tried to determine if Paul or John should be the lead singer of the band. He decided, however, against that formula because it could disrupt the band's unique chemistry. He thought many of the cover songs the Beatles chose to sing were "too corny" and he wasn't thrilled with the songs they had written. The Beatles played "Love Me Do" for him, but Martin was unmoved. Martin also warned Brian that Pete Best's drumming did not meet his standards and that he would be replaced by a session drummer during recordings.

Pete Best was unceremoniously fired and replaced by Ringo Starr. Pete Best fans were outraged and hundreds of girls signed petitions demanding that Pete be brought back into the band. When the Beatles returned to the Cavern to perform, they were heckled by screaming Pete Best fans. Fights broke out inside the Cavern and George ended up with a black eye during a scuffle. Brian demanded that the club's owner provide protection for the Beatles or they would not return.

After a great deal of hesitation, Martin finally agreed that the Beatles' first single would be comprised of originals. He chose "Love Me Do" for the A-side and "P.S. I Love You" for the B-side. Martin was not keen on Ringo's drumming. For this reason, two versions of "Love Me Do" were recorded, one version with Ringo playing the drums and another with session drummer Andy White. On "P.S, I Love You," Ringo played the maracas while White played the drums. Ringo recalled later that he thought the other band members were "doing a 'Pete Best'" on him.

After the release of "Love Me Do" on October 4, 1962, almost nothing was done by EMI to promote the single. Brian jumped into action and purchased 10,000 copies of the record for himself. He had been informed that the sale of 10,000 records was the minimum required to obtain a Top Twenty hit. After hundreds of loyal fans called into the EMI sponsored Luxembourg radio station, Radio Luxembourg finally played "Love Me Do." An excited George yelled up to his mother later that night shouting, "We're on! We're on!" The single made it all the way to number seventeen on December 13. George Martin was not particularly surprised by the moderate success of the single. He thought that all the band needed was a really strong song to finally make the big time.

The Beatles began performing on popular shows like *Thank Your Lucky Stars* to rave reviews. They recorded their next single, "Please, Please Me" and it was released in January 1963. The single was received favorably by the music trade press. One music journal wrote that the Beatles had "every chance of becoming the big star attraction of 1963." An influential commentator on the music scene in England referred to the Beatles as "musically and visually the most accomplished group to emerge since the Shadows."

George Martin decided that now was the time to produce an LP filled with covers and original songs by the Beatles and that the album would be called *Please, Please Me*. The album's name was chosen in order to take full advantage of the success of the single by the same name. In a session totaling thirteen hours, the Beatles recorded such songs as "I Saw Her Standing There," "Chains," and "Misery." "Twist and Shout" had to be right on the first take because it took such a hard toll on John's throat as he shouted out the lyrics. *Please, Please Me* was released on March 22, 1963, to enthusiastic reviews by the music trade press. The Beatles were signed to do more nationally broadcast television shows.

The band continued to release hit after hit in unprecedented fashion. "From Me To You" was released on April 12, and in just fifteen days, the song became the number one hit in England. The music critics this time were a bit harsh toward the single and some thought the Beatles had lost something since their previous release. In any event, the single went on to sell half a million records in a very short time. The Beatles fourth single was "She Loves You." George Martin hated the end of the song because it sounded old-fashioned. Martin warned the group that they were ending the song the way Glenn Miller ended many of his songs, with a major sixth. The Beatles vehemently disagreed with Martin and they kept the ending just the way they envisioned it.

The Beatles fifth single, "I Want To Hold Your Hand," was released in November and it would become by far their biggest hit to date. The single had an advance order of a staggering one million copies and it instantly debuted at number one. A second Beatles LP, *With the Beatles*, was released on November 22, 1963. Advance orders totaled an amazing quarter of a million copies. This total surpassed the number of advance orders for Elvis Presley's biggest hit album, *Blue Hawaii*. The originals on the album included future hits such as "All My Loving" and "It Won't Be Long."

CHAPTER 2

BEATLEMANIA

THE BEATLES were terrified about coming to America. They had conquered Sweden, France, Italy, and of course, England. But America was a different matter entirely. Ringo confessed that, "Things used to fall right for us as a band. We couldn't stop it. The gods were on our side...but we were worried about America." George offered his opinion by stating in a column that, "Tonight we conquered Versailles....How New York will view our visit, we can only guess."

Surprisingly, several of the Beatles' singles that did well in Europe, flopped in America. "From Me To You," "She Loves You," and "Please, Please Me" were just a few songs that America's youth ignored. Of course, Capitol Records was largely to blame because they refused to release the band's music. The much smaller independent labels that did release the band's singles simply did not have the resources to spend on advertising. It was not until EMI's British chairman, Joseph Lockwood, demanded that the label in America give the Beatles a fair shake. It wasn't until "I Want To Hold Your Hand" was released that America finally took notice of this strange new band from a distant land.

John was as nervous as the rest of the band. "The thing is, in America, it just seemed ridiculous – I mean the idea of having a hit record over there. It was just something you could never do. That's what I thought, anyhow. But then I realized that kids everywhere all go for the same stuff and seeing we'd done it in England, there's no reason why we couldn't do it in America too. But the American disc jockeys didn't know about British records, they didn't play them, nobody promoted them so you didn't have hits. It wasn't until *Time* and *Newsweek* came over and wrote articles and created an interest in us that disc jockeys started playing our records. And Capitol said, 'Well, can we have their records?' They had been offered our records years ago, and they didn't want them – but when they heard we were big over here they said, 'Can we have them now?' We said, 'As long as you promote them.'"

George had traveled to America in 1963, primarily to visit his sister. He had visited several record shops and not one of them carried Beatles records. Worse than that, nobody had ever heard of them. He came back and told the rest of the band, "They don't know us. It's going to be hard. We were used to being famous by then, so we were worried about that." Paul was very reluctant about trying to win over American teenagers. "Why should we be over there making money," he asked Phil Spector. "They've got their own groups. What are we going to give them that they don't have already?"

Ed Sullivan first heard about the Beatles when he arrived in London in October 1963. Sullivan was scouting for fresh new talent for his show in New York. As it so happened, the Beatles had just arrived at Heathrow Airport the same time as Sullivan. He noticed hundreds of young people cheering and shouting. When he was told that the fans were there to greet the Beatles, Sullivan instructed his producer to find information about the band.

Sullivan, realizing the importance of booking an emerging act before anyone else, contacted Brian Epstein and negotiated a deal. Sullivan decided to sign the band immediately. Brian Epstein signed a deal with Sullivan's people that would allow the Beatles a three-show package and several concerts in the Northeast to boot. At the same time, the Beatles, particularly John, were concerned about America and how they would be received. They did not want to bomb as Cliff Richard and other British acts had during their American tours. "When we came over the first time," John recalled, "we were only coming over to buy LPs. I know our manager had plans for Ed Sullivan shows, but we thought at least we could hear the sounds when we came over. It was just out of the dark. That's the truth, it was so out of the dark, we were knocked out."

Around this time Epstein negotiated a feature film deal with United Artists which would capitalize on the band's music. No one was certain about what kind of movie it should be. There was concern that the film might end up being similar to many nonsensical pop movies like *The Girl Can't Help It*. The producer, Walter Shenson, was intrigued by the band's sense of humor and playfulness. Richard

Lester was chosen to be the film's director. He even volunteered to do the project for nothing. He was tired of making commercials and wanted to start directing feature films.

Initially, no one had any idea of a plot line. The only aspect of the film everyone agreed on was that music would be performed by the band. Later, someone suggested that Alun Owen, a playwright, should be contacted. Shenson was taken aback by this suggestion because he considered Owen's work to be dark and gritty. Shensen finally determined that the film should portray a day in the life of the Beatles. There should be realism and some comedy mixed in.

As the Pan Am Flight 101 lowered onto the tarmac of recently named John F. Kennedy Airport in Queens, New York, the band noticed what appeared to be workers signaling. John began to have second thoughts about achieving any kind of success in America. Ringo admitted later that the very thought of attempting to win over America made him "a bit sick." The pilot announced to all on board that there was a "big crowd waiting for them." Suddenly, everyone on board noticed thousands of people standing together. Everyone thought the throng of people was waiting for perhaps the president to arrive. As it turned out, this would be the largest crowd ever to appear for anyone at John F. Kennedy Airport.

As the passengers walked out onto the steps of the plane, the crowd below shouted and screamed hysterically. Moments later, the Beatles stepped up onto a platform and fielded questions from the press. The band sparred easily with the press and uttered witticisms effortlessly.

"Will you sing something for us?"

John quickly replied, " We need money first."

A reporter asked, "What about you, Ringo? What do you think of Beethoven?"

"I love him...especially his poems," Ringo replied.

"Was your family ever in show business?" one reporter asked.

John shot back, "Well, me Dad used to say me Mother was a great performer."

"What do you think of the campaign in Detroit to stamp out the Beatles?"

Paul responded, "We've got a campaign of our own... to stamp out Detroit."

The twelfth floor of the Plaza Hotel was reserved for the Beatles. Detectives constantly searched other floors for stalkers and crazed fans. The band sat around listening to their songs on transistor radios. The evening news showed the arrival of the Beatles at Kennedy Airport. Not all the newscasters approved of what they had witnessed. Chet Huntley from *NBC News* refused to show the film because he thought it was pointless.

George Harrison complained of a sore throat and went to bed early. His older sister, Louise, stayed with him in his suite so she could care for him. George was diagnosed with tonsillitis and missed the rehearsals for the show. He also missed the publicity shots in Central Park. The Beatles were driven to the Ed Sullivan Theater on West 53 Street for rehearsal. Brian Epstein walked up to Sullivan and asked, "I would like to know the exact wording of your introduction." Sullivan responded, "I would like you to get lost."

On February 9, 1964, seventy three million viewers tuned in to watch the *Ed Sullivan Show*. The number of television viewers represented about sixty percent of all

American viewers. Billy Graham even broke his rule of abstaining from watching television during Sabbath to see what all the fuss was about. The next day the major New York papers panned the group, one calling them "asexual and homely." Notably, the crime rate in America was lower than at any other time during the past fifty years.

Sullivan walked onto the stage and spoke to the audience. "Now, yesterday and today, our theater's been jammed with newsmen and press from all over the world, and these veterans agree with me that the city's never witnessed the excitement stirred by these youngsters from Liverpool who call themselves the Beatles. Now, tonight, you're gonna twice be entertained by them, right now and later. Ladies and gentlemen-the Beatles!"

The Beatles opened with "All My Loving." Each time one of the Beatles shook his head, the girls in the audience screamed hysterically. They rolled right into the next song, "Please, Please Me," and subsequently with the current number one hit, "I want to Hold Your Hand." Up until this moment, many Americans were unsure how well the band would come off. Many young people had already listened to Beatles records, but this was the first chance they had to actually see the band perform some of their biggest hits on television. Paul in particular was the true showman of the band that night. He would occasionally stare into the camera and project a certain boyish charm. John portrayed himself as all business, standing with feet planted firmly in place and bending his knees slightly in rhythm to the music.

It had appeared from the start that Paul was the leader of the band because he sang lead for most of the songs. Even during the third song, "She Loves You" with John now doing leads, the camera focused more on Paul than on John. Things would balance out a bit during their second Sullivan appearance in Miami when John would get most of the spotlight.

The Beatles had several issues to contend with when they performed on live television that night. For one thing, there were not many successful bands during that era. Many of the top musical acts of the day comprised of pop singers such as Paul Anka, Fabian, Bobby Rydal, and Bobby Darin. And when they had performed, they were normally accompanied not by their backup band, but by a studio orchestra. There was also the crucial matter of audio. Many small guitar playing combos elicited a tinny sound while performing on television. They sounded fine in the concert hall, but television had the effect of minimizing bass. And finally, most acts lip-synched while performing on television, whereas the Beatles did not, which increased the possibility that mistakes might occur during their live performance.

After the show, Paul complained about the technical aspect of their performance. CBS had not set up the equipment properly. Evidently, John's microphone sounded awful, sometimes even losing sound. During rehearsals, the Beatles made a point of working closely with the sound technicians and those running the sound booth. But a mishap occurred when the cleaners mistakenly wiped off the markings on the controls. The markings were there to help the sound engineers balance the vocals with the instruments.

Paul recounted the importance of the band's performance that night as well. "We came out of nowhere with funny hair, looking like marionettes or something. That was very influential. I think that was really one of the big things that broke us – the hairdo more than the music, originally. A lot of people's fathers had wanted to turn us off. They told their kids, 'Don't be fooled, they're wearing wigs.'" Paul recalled that American movie stars like Janet Leigh wore Beatles wigs and were being photographed wearing them. "Once a film star did that, it could get syndicated all across America. Look at this funny picture, Janet Leigh in this wacko wig-the 'mop top' wig. And so the whole mop top thing started there. And it got us noticed."

TV critic Jack Gould, from the prestigious *New York Times*, ripped into the Beatles by simply writing them off as a fad. He claimed the Beatles' performance did not stand up to all the hype the press accorded them. *The Washington Post* was similar in their criticism. *Newsweek* magazine referred to their musicianship as "a near disaster" and their lyrics "are a catastrophe." "BEATLES BOMB ON TV" was the headline blaring across the front page of the *Herald Tribune*. The paper's critic called the Beatles performance "a magic act that owed less to Britain than to Barnum." The columnist went on further to rate the band "75 percent publicity, 20 percent haircut, and 5 percent lilting lament."

John responded to the scathing media reports by stating, "If everybody really liked us, it would be a bore. It doesn't give any edge to it if everybody just falls flat on their face saying, 'You're great.'" Brian Epstein apparently took the reviews a lot harder than the Beatles, referring to them as a "vicious attack." He seriously even considered cancelling any remaining scheduled interviews. He was somehow talked out of this scheme, but his temper continued to simmer nonetheless.

A press conference was held the next morning in the

Plaza's Baroque Room. The purpose of the press conference was to announce the band's deal with United Artists to make three feature films. A woman asked the Beatles who exactly chose their clothes. John replied, "We choose our own. Who chooses yours?" "My husband," she shot back. "Now tell me, are there any subjects you prefer not to discuss?" John immediately responded with, "Yes, your husband." This elicited a huge uproar of laughter.

The Beatles handled themselves beautifully. For three hours they answered questions thrown at them with wit and charm. Not once did they seem irritated or unhinged by being the sole focus of the press' onslaught of sometimes trivial questions. At the end of the press conference, the Beatles were presented with two gold records.

The band had been booked to perform in Washington, D.C. right after the Sullivan show. On the train down the Beatles were bombarded with questions by the New York press. Sometimes the press would yell at the band members, but they would just yell back at the reporters. After the press got to know the band, they confided to them that they had wanted to bury the Beatles. Evidently, the press was accustomed to entertainers acting polite and sometimes subservient to them. The Beatles continued to smoke and drink in front of the reporters unlike many other pop stars. As Ringo explained, "And here we were, smoking and drinking and shouting at them. That's what endeared us to them." George and Ringo were fired up on board the train while Paul sat almost glumly in his seat. He looked into the camera and said "I'm not in a laughing mood, even." Apparently, he had come down from the high he experienced the day before.

In Washington, D.C., thousands of screaming fans waited for the Beatles as they pulled into Union Station. Bravely, the Beatles somehow managed to get inside two limos without being mauled. The Beatles were booked to perform at the Washington Coliseum. It was an 18,000 seat arena utilized mainly for hockey and boxing events. The Beatles were not aware that they would be playing on a round platform and that equipment would need to be moved throughout their performance.

The Beatles rushed on stage amidst wild hysteria. In fact, after the show, Paul commented that it was "the most tremendous reception I have ever heard in my life." Ringo sat perilously atop his seat while the floor shook beneath him. The other members of the band somehow found a spot to stand on amidst tons of cables and sound equipment. Finally, Paul shouted, "Good evening, Washington!" to screaming fans. The band broke out with "Roll Over Beethoven" and the audience went absolutely berserk. Several hysterical fans had to be pulled away from the stage by the police. Unfortunately, the Beatles were constantly being pelted with jelly beans throughout the concert. George later complained that sometimes the missiles would "hit a string on my guitar and plonk off a bad note as I was trying to play." The Beatles played for only twenty-eight minutes. After the show they were utterly exhausted from their high octane performance. They were totally amazed at the audience's reaction to them. "They could have ripped me apart," Ringo recalled, "and I wouldn't have cared!"

The Beatles' next booked appearance was, of all places, Carnegie Hall, in New York City. No other rock and roll act had ever performed there. Not even the King himself, Elvis

Presley, was permitted to grace the halls of this prestigious cathedral. A deal allowing George Martin to participate in recording a live album that night was shot down. Many in the business considered this a blessing in disguise because the screaming and hysterical antics emanating from the audience would easily have drowned out the band's music. As soon as the Beatles hit the stage, the crowd drowned out every word sung by the band. In fact, at one point, John stepped forward on the stage and shouted to the audience, "Shut up!" The entire performance lasted only thirty-four minutes before the Beatles decided that they had had enough and walked off.

The daily newspapers focused more on the audience's behavior toward the band than on their stellar performance. *The New Yorker* gave the band its most favorable review, saying that they were worth listening to, "even if they aren't as good as the Everly Brothers, which they really aren't." The Beatles took all the negative criticism in stride. Not even their music peers came out to greet them at any of their performances. Perhaps they believed, if only to themselves, that the Beatles represented a real threat to their careers.

The Beatles' next live television performance would be on the *Ed Sullivan Show*, this time in Miami. On February 15, the Beatles' debut album, *Meet the Beatles*, topped Billboard's album chart. In the Hot 100 singles chart, "I Want to Hold Your Hand" was number one and "She Loves You" was number two. The Beatles were enthralled with Miami. People lent the band their yachts, speedboats, and houses. The Beatles were introduced to the Miami nightclub scene as well. One night they took in a Don Rickles show at the Deauville Hotel where the band was staying. At one point,

Rickles walked up to the band and asked Ringo where he was from. Ringo replied, "Liverpool" to dead silence. Rickles responded with, "Oh, hear the applause."

There were many celebrities in the audience the night of the *Ed Sullivan Show*, including a couple of big names from the boxing world. Sitting close to the stage was none other than Joe Louis and Sonny Liston. It just so happened that Liston was in Miami training for his fight against Cassius Clay for the heavyweight title. Louis was in Miami because he was slated to provide live closed-circuit commentary of the Liston-Clay heavyweight championship fight. Paul had predicted that Clay would become the new heavyweight champion

Eying an opportunity for some unexpected publicity, a publicist arranged for the band to meet Clay at the Fifth Street Gym where he was training for the big fight. The Beatles were mocked as they entered the gym. Some of the hangers on looked at their long hair and scoffed in disgust. The Beatles grew impatient waiting for Clay and his entourage to arrive. Just as the band was about to leave, Clay arrived. "Hello there, Beatles!" Clay shouted to the band. In the meantime, photographers were busy taking pictures of the new superstars as they mugged for the cameras. Clay talked the band into getting in the ring with him. Once they were in the ring, Clay shouted, "Get down, you little worms!" At Clay's command the band flung themselves onto the canvas and lay on their backs. Then Clay picked Ringo up, held him above his head and twirled him around much to his amusement. Clay teased the Beatles some more and told them they were not as dumb as they look. To which John replied, "I know, but you are."

What America took away from the initial performances of the Beatles was that this was a band with a fresh, new sound. The band seemed to enjoy every minute they performed. It didn't hurt that their harmonies were dead on. Perhaps more importantly, they looked so different with their long shaggy hair, tight Edwardian suits, and pointy black boots. They also helped many Americans get away, at least for a short time, from grieving over their fallen leader. The band may have represented to some degree the kind of youthful enthusiasm and promise President Kennedy evoked.

When the Beatles arrived back in England they were hailed as pop heroes. They were the first British pop act to take America by storm. They were instrumental in paving the way for more British talent to follow. Soon, American airwaves were filled with the sounds of the Dave Clark Five, the Yardbirds, and Eric Burdon and the Animals. No longer would British rock music be ignored. To many, the new music represented an alternative to the more sentimental, predictable sounds emanating from both sides of the pond.

The Beatles immediately started recording songs that had been written over the past several months. "Can't Buy Me Love" was updated to include a revised lyric. The Beatles had just finished playing three shows a day for 18 days at the Olympia Theatre in Paris. The basic track took only four takes. The lyrics reflected a warm and personal feeling about accentuating love and romance over materialism. A draft of "You Can't Do That" was completed in one day. John wrote most of the song and Paul included a spirited B7 chord to the bridge. John's vocals were forceful and commanding, giving the song a hard, no-nonsense edge to it. The song would be on the B-side of "Can't Buy Me Love."

Paul composed the beautiful ballad, "And I Love Her." As lovely as the song was, it was decided that it needed something to break up the lushness of the melody. John and Paul banged out a middle eight, but even this effort did not significantly improve the song. The two decided to come back to the ballad later. When Paul eventually did finish the song, he confessed it was "the first ballad I impressed myself with." Paul pointed out that the "title comes in the second verse and it doesn't repeat."

After several takes, "I Should Have Known Better" was shoved aside as well. Clearly, the Beatles were exhausted from their tour in America. George complained of being "tired and depressed" from all the traveling and performing. After the song was recorded, Lennon stated that he did not like it very much. "Just a song," he confessed. "It doesn't mean a damn thing." The song would be on the B-side of "A Hard Day's Night."

A few days later, the Beatles recorded "Tell Me Why," a thoroughly upbeat tune John had written. John and Paul sang vocals together in another Lennon composition, "If I Fell." This song proved to be John's first attempt at writing a ballad. The song required many chord changes and it took fifteen takes to finally nail it. Lennon mentioned later that the song was the precursor to "In My Life." The two songs shared similar chord progressions as well. In each song, D and B minor are followed by E minor.

"I'm Happy Just To Dance With You," a kind of sequel to "I Want To Hold Your Hand," was hammered out by John and Paul at the piano. It was a song written specifically for George. The Beatles experimented with different sounds, such as cowbells and bongos, and George had thrown in the twelve-string Rickenbacker for good measure. The Beatles quickly learned from George Martin the technique of overdubbing and double-tracking. Suddenly, their world opened up to the possibilities of different sounds and effects.

In the meantime, the Beatles jumped right into the film project. Initially, the Beatles were offered a project called *The Yellow Teddy Bears*. The band was interested in the project but later turned it down when it was discovered the writer wanted to compose all the songs. They decided to work on another project that would eventually be called *A Hard Day's Night*. Their lines were deliberately kept short and to the point. They were not expected to act, so the script needed to be as interesting as possible. Basically, the Beatles were expected to simply play themselves. The film managed to reflect each band member's unique personality. On display, for example, is John's sarcastic wit, and Paul's boyish charm. John explained later that the pressure from all the fans and the press was far more intrusive than represented in the film.

The Beatles woke up each morning at five in order to be ready for makeup. The director, Richard Lester, had learned that the boys were not learning their lines as well as they should have. He decided to just film the boys while they talked to each other between scenes. This method allowed Lester to capture each band member's true personality.

John and Paul were asked to write an up-tempo song called "A Hard Day's Night." The song had to be exceptional since it would be heard during the opening credits of the film by the same name. Irritated by this latest request, John nonetheless banged out a song with Paul's assistance and within ten hours they delivered their masterpiece. Paul remembered that "it seemed a bit ridiculous writing a song called "A Hard Day's Night" – it sounded funny at the time, but after a bit we got the idea of saying it had been a hard day's night and we'd been working all the days, and get back to a girl and everything's fine."

The Beatles recorded "A Hard Day's Night" the very next day. The song famously opens with a solar plexus punch, namely a G7 chord with an additional ninth and suspended fourth for good measure. It has never been clearly established how George invented this opening, which further adds to its mystique. Paul wrote the bridge and sang it as well because John could not reach the high notes. This may have been Paul's design, but no one complained.

The filming of *A Hard Day's Night* was a different matter entirely. None of the Beatles could act and so the director, Richard Lester, tried to catch the boys off guard while filming in order to capture them as naturally as possible. John recalled that he felt embarrassed suddenly going right into a song just after having a conversation with another character. "The best bits are when you don't have to speak," John explained, "and you just run about. All of us liked the bit in the field where we jump about like lunatics because that's pure film."

During a photo shoot with the *Saturday Evening Post*, Ringo fell ill and collapsed. A friend rushed him to a hospital where he was diagnosed with laryngitis and pharyngitis. After much bickering, a drummer was chosen to replace Ringo. Against the band's wishes, Brian Epstein and George Martin chose Jimmy Nichol, a session drummer, to fill in while Ringo recuperated. George later stated that the Beatles should never have toured without Ringo. "I really despised the way we couldn't make a decision for ourselves then. As we grew older, I suppose we would have turned around and said we wouldn't go, but in those days it was the blind leading the blind."

Ringo was a bit put off by the bad turn of events as well. "It was very strange, them going off without me, They'd taken Jimmy Nichol and I thought they didn't love me any more-all that stuff went through my head." Perhaps Ringo had been thinking about Pete Best and feared he might suffer the same treatment Best had received by his band mates. The Beatles toured the Netherlands and Australia to masses of frenzied, screaming fans.

The premier of *A Hard Day's Night* was held in the London Pavilion. Twelve thousand onlookers jammed Piccadilly Circus in order to get near the Beatles. Earlier that day the band had a chance to watch a private sneak preview of the film. They all laughed and carried on like kids as they watched themselves. Almost all the British dailies gave the film a thumbs up. It was variously called "offbeat" and "delightfully loony." John liked the film initially, but later admitted that he thought the ending was a bit ambivalent and confusing. The film opened to the public on July 8. The movie was well received. It went over so well, the following morning, fans stood in long lines outside the theater, waiting to see what all the fuss was about. Seeing that they had a huge hit on their hands, United Artists developed dozens of more prints for distribution.

The movie critics in America gave the film mixed reviews. Highly respected critic Bosley Crowther of the *New York Times* seemed amused by the fanatics portrayed by the Fab Four, but he hated the music. He claimed that "the frequent and brazen 'yah, yah, yahing of these fellows....has moronic monotony." More hip critics were able to plug into what the Beatles were all about. One either got their music or one did not.

By the time the Beatles returned to America on August 18, their music was playing practically non-stop on radio, records, and jukeboxes throughout the nation. Their popularity was unprecedented, particularly for a British act. There were massive crowds awaiting them wherever they appeared. Not even Frank Sinatra or Elvis Presley in their heyday came close to drawing this many star-crazed fans.

The Beatles also came to America at a time when the nation was still mourning the loss of their youthful and beloved leader, President John Fitzgerald Kennedy. It seemed the country at that exact time needed something to cheer about. The conflict in Vietnam was also weighing heavily on Americans as well as the possibility of becoming involved in a war with China and Russia over the conflict in Southeast Asia. Moreover, the civil rights movement, led by Martin Luther King, Jr, was in full gear.

The Beatles certainly had their detractors as well. Spokesmen for certain religious sects accused them of immorality and many parents found their appearance and music shocking and disgusting. Many hardcore fans who attended the band's concerts complained that the high-pitched screaming and mass hysteria drowned out the music. The decibel level from this tsunami of sound had never been experienced by any audience before or since. John, on the other hand, enjoyed the raucous response from the fans. "We don't want them quiet," he claimed. "I like a riot." Not only did their music cause pandemonium, but a simple head shake or a glance directed out into the audience was enough to stir the crowd into a frenzy.

On August 23, the Beatles performed to an audience of nearly nineteen thousand at the Hollywood Bowl in Los Angeles. Another huge crowd of endearing fans listened to them near the back of the open-air amphitheater as well. Capitol Records was on hand to record the music that that evening. As soon as the band began their set, however, the sheer volume of the fan's screams drowned out the band's music. George Martin complained that "It was like putting a microphone at the tail of a 747 jet."

The Beatles continued touring in Denver, Cincinnati, New York, Philadelphia, Chicago and other major cities. Beatlemania in America had finally taken hold. Record sales for *A Hard Day's Night* soared into the stratosphere. Their songs played non-stop on the radio and jukeboxes throughout America and the rest of the world. The Beatles had earned over a million dollars from their American tour, unheard of for its time.

By August, the Beatles were the biggest buzz in showbiz. More and more demands for their time got out of control. As John explained, "It just really built up: the bigger that we got, the more unreality we had to face, the more we were expected to do – until when you didn't shake hands with a mayor's wife she starts abusing you and screaming, 'How dare they!' They were always threatening what they would tell the press, to make bad publicity about us if we didn't see their bloody daughter with braces on her teeth. We had these people thrust on us and were forced to see them all the time. Those were the most humiliating experiences."

A member of the Beatles entourage thought it would be a good idea for the band to meet the King himself. Paul was ecstatic when he heard about the possible arrangement. "Without Elvis there'd be no Beatles!" he chirped. Elvis Presley was reportedly so distraught over the Beatles success that he refused to see them. When Presley's manager was asked to set up a meeting between the two super acts, Parker informed them that Elvis had just left Los Angeles and was headed to Memphis. John took this as a slap in the face and vowed never to call Presley. Paul called Presley instead and told the King how he had all his records and had been a true fan.

Paul and John responded to all the adulation in entirely different ways. John was getting sick of it all and Paul appeared to be reveling in it. John was not amused that the audience cared more for their fame and not their music during live performances. The Beatles and the audience could not hear the band's music so what was the point of it all? John frequently stumbled across the stage between songs and pretended to talk with the audience with unkind gibberish. Such was John's state of mind. Paul, on the other hand, was kind to everyone around him.

Nat Weiss, a close associate of Brian Epstein, remembered how Paul was always kind to members of local Beatles fan clubs. "It was like his career depended on it, it was amazing how overboard he would go." Lennon was the exact opposite. He didn't want to see reporters, didn't want to see fans, and used to go nose to nose with Brian arguing about it. He'd refer to them as 'fascists' and be very tough. When people used to give them Beatles presents-dolls and things-he'd actually throw it right back in the person's face.

Didn't want to be bothered. But he felt he was being honest." As time went on, John became crazy and wild, whereas Paul appeared very conscious of his demeanor at all times. Part of his job was to keep reeling John in from acting too crazy with the fans.

"There were all kinds of trouble in the States," George recalled. "There was everyone trying to sue us. There were girls trying to get into our rooms so they could sue us for totally made-up things. There was always this very peculiar suing consciousness. I'd never heard about suing people until we went to America."

In October of 1964, the Beatles went on another tour in Britain. The shows had been booked for months and the band fulfilled all their obligations. They performed in small drafty clubs for the amount agreed to, even though in America, they had earned much more money and played in huge stadiums. The Beatles were very proud about honoring all their contracts.

The Beatles were asked to produce one more album before the end of the year. So shortly after they arrived in England, John and Paul continued writing more songs. Fortunately, they had found the time to write while on tour, and there was plenty of good material. According to John, however, the new songs sounded repetitious . They wanted to write about something other than holding hands and dancing with their sweetheart. They deliberately abstained from writing simple love songs and, instead, composed tunes with deeper emotions.

Recording *Beatles for Sale* was a relatively easy project for the band. Typically, Paul visited John at his home and the two would sit together strumming their guitars until a verse or chorus was rendered good enough to build off of. It might be that one of them would come up with a title to a song and that would be enough to inspire the pair to write a song. It took about two or three hours for the duo to write a song. There were no audio cassettes back then, so John and Paul had to remember the melody until they were able to work on the song again.

John recalled that "Eight Days A Week" was a song Paul had started to compose, and then John helped Paul complete it. Paul wanted the song to be in the movie *Help!* The band worked hard on that song, but John never seemed satisfied with it. John wrote "Help" around this time, and so it was decided that this new song, which sounded a lot more commercial, would replace "Eight Days A Week."

Attempting to come up with something heavier, the pair wrote "Baby's in Black," and "I'm a Loser." In the process of writing darker material, John and Paul realized the danger of losing favor with fans who had grown accustomed to their "yeah, yeah" material. "No Reply" reflected on rejection. John was inspired by the "image of walking down the street and seeing a girl silhouetted on the window and not answering the phone." With these songs the Beatles attempted to break new ground without alienating their base. It was a chance the band was willing to take.

As Neil Aspinall pointed out, "No band today would come off a long U.S. tour at the end of September, go into a studio and start a new album, still writing songs, and then go on a UK tour, finish the album in five weeks, still touring, and have the album out in time for Christmas. But that's what the Beatles did at the end of 1964. A lot of it was down to naivety, thinking that this was the way things were done: if the record company needs another album, you go out and make one. Nowadays, if a band had as much success as the Beatles had by the end of 1964, they'd start making a few demands."

Unlike *A Hard Day's Night*, *Help!*, their second movie, was not groundbreaking. The dialog was not as witty and sharp as it was in their first film and the plot had much to be desired. The story was about a gang of thugs attempting to retrieve an all-powerful, mystical ring. The script had originally been written with Peter Sellers in mind. Sellers, thinking seriously about his career, eventually rejected it.

Richard Lester, who had directed *A Hard Day's Night*, directed the band's second film as well. Reportedly, the Beatles had difficulty remembering their lines because they were stoned much of the time. They were so incapacitated, that after lunch, they were incapable of doing anything related to the film. John admitted that "Nobody could communicate with us: it was all glazed eyes and giggling all the time. In our own world."

The band started filming in February in the Bahamas, Austria and England. Amazingly, the Beatles were told they had to ski in several scenes, even though they had never skied before. Paradise Island in the Bahamas is where George was introduced to yoga. He met a swami who gave him a book entitled, *The Illustrated Book of Yoga*. This encounter later led to George's interest in playing the sitar.

Paul recalled that the songs that went into the *Help!* album were written primarily at John's place. The songs for *A Hard Day's Night* were mainly written by John with some involvement by Paul. Paul was also beginning to sense that John was "feeling a bit constricted by the Beatles thing."

John began feeling very anxious about being a Beatle. He recalled later that "the whole Beatle thing was just beyond comprehension. I was eating and drinking like a pig, and I was as fat as a pig, dissatisfied with myself, and subconsciously I was crying for help. It was my fat Elvis period. Happiness is just how you feel when you're not miserable. There's nothing guaranteed to make me happy. There's no one thing I can think of that would go 'click' and I'd be happy."

George later revealed that around this period John felt plump and he absolutely needed to wear glasses. "He just didn't feel right," George remembered. "He looked like Michael Caine with horn-rimmed glasses. He was paranoid about being short-sighted and we'd have to take him into a club and lead him to his seat, so that he could go in without his glasses on and look cool."

John and Paul got busy writing material for *Help!* in December. The song writing team knocked out most of "Ticket to Ride" in three hours, according to Paul. John claimed most of the credit for the song, but Paul recalled they both wrote the words and most of the music together. "Help" and "You're Going to Lose That Girl" were both collaborated on by the pair. Paul wrote "Another Girl" and "The Night Before" while John contributed "You've Got to Hide Your Love Away" and "It's Only Love." Paul had written "I've Just Seen a Face" for the film, but it did not make the cut.

It became obvious that Bob Dylan influenced the way John wrote lyrics. They were moody, whereas Paul's lyrics were more upbeat and optimistic. Around this time, John and Paul began to see themselves as serious competitors.

John particularly resented Paul being described as "the cute Beatle." Furthermore, he did not always agree with Paul's opinions to the press.

On August 14, 1965, the Beatles made their third and final appearance on *The Ed Sullivan Show*. Before the show, the Beatles rehearsed for four hours and ran through six songs. The highlight of the show occurred when Paul sang "Yesterday," accompanied only by an acoustic guitar. Next, the Beatles performed at Shea Stadium in Flushing, New York. The stadium seated 56,000 and no act had ever performed there. As the Beatles jumped onto the stage the audience let out a loud, sustained shrill that was clearly not of this earth. Mick Jagger, who was sitting with Keith Richards behind one of the dugouts, said to a friend, "It's frightening." The Beatles were stunned by the fan reaction. They couldn't hear themselves sing and they were never sure what key they were in at any given moment. John related later, "You can see it in the film, George and I aren't even bothering playing half the chords, and we were just messing around."

During their 1965 tour, it was decided once again that the Beatles should meet Elvis Presley. Brian Epstein and Colonel Tom Parker negotiated a deal at the Beverly Hills Hotel, whereby the Beatles would visit Elvis at his home in Los Angeles. John didn't want to meet the King, but eventually he gave in to the others.

The Beatles finally reached Elvis' home in Bel Air and were ushered into the living room where Elvis was sitting on a sofa waiting for his guests. John greeted the King with, "So ziss is zee famous Elvizzz!" Elvis did not appear amused by this Dr. Strangelove like impression. John noticed a lamp shaped like a covered wagon with the inscription, "All the Way with LBJ" inscribed along the side. Apparently it was a gift Elvis had received from President Johnson. John asked Elvis how he could support a man who ordered the killing of people in Vietnam. Pricilla, Elvis's wife, entered the room and apparently John began flirting with her. Elvis did not appear amused by John's impertinence and so the meeting almost ended abruptly.

Paul finally changed the subject by asking Presley if they could play music together. Elvis arranged for some guitars to be brought into the room so he and the band could jam. He apologized to Ringo for not having a drum set handy and so Ringo agreed to bang out some rhythm on the coffee table. The Beatles and Elvis sang "I Feel Fine." They all sang R&B hits along with some rock and country songs. Sometimes Elvis sang lead while the Beatles sang background vocals. Colonel Tom Parker advised some-one on the Beatles team to "tell the world they had a great time!" Chris Hutchins, the person responsible for setting up the Summit, claimed Elvis later tried to get John thrown out of the country. "Him and Edgar Hoover," Hutchins claimed. "And that famous meeting with Nixon? He was trashing the Beatles there, too."

The Beatles took a long break after a string of sold out American concerts. The film, *Help!*, was enjoyed by packed audiences in theaters throughout the world, while singles from the album were heard on every pop station. The single, "Yesterday," Paul's latest solo achievement, was released in America, but surprisingly nowhere else. It held onto the top spot on Billboard's Hot 100 for several weeks.

EMI wanted the band to record and release another

album by the end of 1965, just in time for the holidays. The song "Wait" was the only record ready to be released. It had actually been written for the album *Help!* while the Beatles were on location in the Bahamas. During the next two weeks, John and Paul had to compose and record enough songs to fill an entire album. The pressure on them was absolutely enormous.

The Beatles felt they had to break away from all the old "yeh, yeh" songs. The music world was changing rapidly, with or without the Beatles. The band realized that they needed to write lyrics relevant to their age and not to a teenager's. As Paul explained, "You can't be singing 15-year old songs at 20 because you don't think 15-year old thoughts at 20." The Beatles' influences were also changing. They were becoming more receptive to Stax and Motown performers versus Rock 'n Roll artists. Bands like the Rolling Stones, The Animals, the Bryds, and the Who dominated the airwaves in 1965. The Beatles realized they were up against some solid competition and needed to produce a deeper, heavier sound. So in October, the pair composed songs so different and varied that one would think they were from another band.

"Norwegian Wood" was reportedly written by John. He claimed to have written the entire song himself, but years later, Paul took issue with that account. Paul recalled that John wrote the first stanza, but that was all. Basically, according to Paul, the two wrote the song together in one afternoon. John and Paul almost gave up writing "Drive My Car" because they were keenly dissatisfied with the original lyrics. John thought the line "Baby, you can buy me golden rings," was "crap." John wrote "Nowhere Man," according to Paul, in response to the bad state of his marriage with Cynthia. He was put off by his wife's unwillingness to experiment with drugs. "Run for Your Life" was a good old fashion straight ahead pop song. George contributed some very effective guitar work to help guide it along.

John and Paul worked together on "The Word" and "You Won't See Me." "I'm Looking Through You" was written by Paul and may have been about his faltering relationship with Jane Asher. Paul wrote most of "Michelle" before he played it for John. It was missing a middle eight and so John suggested he add, "I love, I love you, I love you," emphasizing the word "love" each time. He had recently heard Nina Simone sing "I Put a Spell on You" with the same lyrics except "you" was emphasized. George Martin, who had been having a rough time re-negotiating a new contract with EMI, had become very influential in creating new tones and styles with the Beatles. When John suggested that a bridge had to sound like Bach, Martin wrote an instrumental bridge between the verses. Ringo proclaimed that their new album "was the departure record."

The name of the new album was called *Rubber Soul.* It was derived from a comment made by an American blues artist about the Rolling Stones. When asked what he thought about the band, he responded by saying, "Well, you know they're good, but it's plastic soul." *Rubber Soul* was received exceedingly well by the public and music critics. *Newsweek*, totally reversing themselves in their criticism of the Beatles only after a few short years, called them the "Bards of Pop." Their songs were referred to "as brilliantly original as any written today."

On December 17, 1965, music giants like Ella Fitzgerald,

Henry Mancini, Cilla Black, and Esther Phillips, paid tribute to the band in a television special called *The Music of Lennon and McCartney.* The Beatles also performed their latest songs, "Day Tripper" and "We Can Work It Out." Surprisingly, the two songs were marketed as A-sides. The show was such a hit that many established artists such as Count Basie and Ray Charles began searching through the Beatles' song catalog for material to record. By the following year, over 2,900 versions of dozens of Beatles songs were covered.

John and Paul went on to write "Paperback Writer," "Rain," and "Here, There and Everywhere." The latter song had been roughly sketched out while filming *Help!* in Austria. Paul turned his attention to a new song. Donovan remembered hearing Paul singing odd lyrics like "Ola Na Tungee/Blowing his mind in the dark/With a pipeful of clay." These lyrics would change dramatically for Paul's solo effort, "Eleanor Rigby." The first name was taken from the female lead in *Help!,* Eleanor Bron. Meanwhile, John was working on "She Said, She Said," "And Your Bird Can Sing," and "Doctor Robert."

The Beatles were becoming increasingly frustrated with the recording equipment at Abbey Road. The four-track machines were laughable anywhere else in the world. Naturally, they demanded better recording equipment in order to produce better sounding records. Surprisingly, EMI just provided the band with better studio lighting, according to George Martin. The band was impressed with records originating from Memphis. They enjoyed the blaring horn sections and driving rhythms. The Beatles sent Brian Epstein to Memphis to work out a deal so that they could use recording studios there. Memphis responded by offering the use of the studios, but at a price that was much too high. As Paul explained it, "They wanted a fantastic amount of money to use the facilities there. They were obviously trying to take us for a ride." Disheartened, the Beatles reluctantly decided to continue recording at Abbey Road.

Capitol Records released their next album, *Yesterday... and Today.* There were songs on the album that were omitted from the American versions of *Help!* and *Rubber Soul.* Capitol utilized this approach in order to produce more albums than the British versions. The American versions normally consisted of no more than 10, whereas the British albums normally consisted of 14 songs. The Beatles wanted a cover for their new album that would be extraordinary. Brian arranged for a meeting to be held with the band and Bob Whitaker. John had referred to Whitaker as, "a bit of a surrealist." Whitaker had the band sit on a couch while he placed pieces of raw meat, sausage links, and a pig's head on their bodies. As if that was not "far out" enough, he laid pieces of dismembered dolls all over them as well. Eventually, the Beatles got into the sicko mood of the Australian photographer.

The Beatles decided this was the cover for their new album. Capitol initially refused to allow the photographer to adorn their latest project, but the Beatles held their ground. Capitol blinked and promptly shipped several hundred advanced copies to Capitol's nationwide sales force. The record dealers, however, refused to stock the albums in their stores and so the albums were pulled. Capitol ended up replacing the sleeve for about a half million albums, a very costly project. John was insistent about breaking the image of the Beatles as altar boys. "I especially pushed for it to be an album cover, just to break the image," he explained. Paul later added, "We weren't against a little shock now and then, it was part of our make-up."

The Beatles' last British concert was held on May 1, 1966. The band appeared on the annual NME poll-winner's show. The band saw no point in constantly performing when they knew the studio was where they really belonged. The excuse the band used not to perform was that they could not hear themselves sing or hear their own instruments. The real reason they didn't want to do any more concerts was that their latest material was hard to duplicate in front of an audience. For example, a song like "Got To Get You Into My Life" required a full horn section. And a more intimate song like "Eleanor Rigby" required sounds only a studio could produce.

"BEATLES MORE POPULAR THAN JESUS" was the headline blaring across the front cover of an American teen magazine. The repercussions caused by John Lennon's remark in an interview touched off a storm of discontent. Many church leaders demanded burnings and boycotts of all Beatles records. Disc jockeys refused to play the band's records and ordered their listeners to do the same.

The Beatles, at least publicly, took the bad news in stride at first. They figured that before you could burn an album you would have to buy one. Beatles albums were nailed to crosses and then burned by members of the Ku Klux Klan. Word was out that John Lennon would be assassinated if he ever showed his face in Memphis. John was adamant about not retracting one word of what he had said in the infamous interview. He didn't mind if their scheduled American tour was cancelled, even though the cost of cancelling was estimated to be about a million dollars. He explained, "I'd rather that than have to get up and lie. What I said stands."

Brian persuaded John to issue a statement of apology. After several days of discussing how best to handle the crisis, John agreed that a statement of clarification would be issued. At New York's Americana Hotel, John sat in a suite surrounded by the press as Brian read a formal statement explaining what John had meant during an interview three months earlier. The statement explained that John's infamous quote was taken out of context and that, due to a declining interest in the Church of England, and therefore Christ, the Beatles' "effect appeared to be, to him, a more immediate one upon certain of the younger generation."

On August 5, *Revolver* was released. Coincidentally, "Yellow Submarine" and "Eleanor Rigby" hit the airwaves on thousands of radio stations. Critics were surprised by some of the sound effects and complexities. "Tomorrow Never Knows" was a song many listeners couldn't connect with. At that time, no critic could have predicted the album's enormous power and inventiveness. In fact, the readers of *Mojo* later ranked *Revolver* as the best album ever made.

The competition was fierce in 1966. New groups and groundbreaking sounds were taking over the music industry. The Troggs, the Beach Boys, the Mamas and the Pappas, Simon and Garfunkel, the Mothers of Invention, Bob Dylan, and the Lovin' Spoonful were just some of the artists breaking new ground and topping the charts. The Beatles knew they had to constantly progress if they wanted to stay on top of the pop music world.

Many Beatles fans were unprepared to accept this

deeper, moodier, side of the band. As John explained, "We're not trying to pass off as kids. We have been Beatles as best we ever will be – those four jolly lads. But we're not those people anymore." What should have been a time of celebration with the success of their new album was tempered by the backlash toward John's Jesus comment. Brian pleaded with John to make a formal apology to the world, but John would have none of it. John threatened not to talk to the press about anything going forward. Brian explained to John that his decision was affecting the band's financial future. He warned John that the rest of the band would continue to suffer as well, not just him. John finally agreed to go public with an apology.

On August 11, Brian set up a press conference in Chicago. Before the press arrived, Brian warned John not to act like a wise guy cracking one-liners. He told him that if the press came down hard on them, the tour would be cancelled. He even went so far as to claim that he "feared the Beatles might be assassinated during the tour." Seconds later, John broke down in tears. He asked for help. "I'll do anything," he cried. "Anything. Whatever you say I should do, I'll have to say...I didn't mean to cause all of this." He composed himself and then Brian and the Beatles entered a suite where members of the media were waiting. John sat behind a table while the other band members stood behind him in silence. Paul had "never seen John so nervous."

"If I'd have said, 'Television is more popular than Jesus,' I might have got away with it," John began. "I'm sorry I opened my mouth, I just happened to be talking to a friend and I used the word 'Beatles' as a remote thing – 'Beatles,' like other people see us. I said they are having more influence on kids and things than anything else, including Jesus. I said it in that way, which was the wrong way. I'm not anti-God, anti-Christ, or antireligious. I was not knocking it. I was not saying we are greater or better, I think it's a bit silly. If they don't like us, why don't they just not buy our records?"

A reporter stepped forward and said, "Some teenagers have repeated your statement – 'I like the Beatles more than Jesus Christ.' What do you think about this?" John thought carefully for a moment. He looked up and said, "Well, originally I pointed out that fact in reference to England. That we meant more to kids than Jesus did, or religion at that time. I wasn't knocking it or putting it down....I just said what I said and it was wrong. Or it was taken wrong. And now it's all this." A member of the press asked John if he was prepared to apologize. He tried to clarify his position once again. "I wasn't saying what they're saying I was saying," John went on. "I'm sorry I said it-really. I never meant it to be a lousy antireligious thing. I apologize if that will make you happy. I still don't know quite what I've done. I've tried to tell you what I did do, but if you want me to apologize, if that will make you happy, then okay, I'm sorry." There was silence for a moment and then someone shouted out from the back, "Okay, can you just actually say to the camera how sorry you are?"

The Beatles went on tour and appeared before the usual screaming teenage fans, just like the days of old. With much apprehension, the band travelled to Memphis and the mood on the plane became very somber. Brian felt sure John's days might be numbered. In fact, there was even talk about canceling the Memphis show. The Beatles decided to go on with the show anyhow. As Paul explained, "If we cancel one, you might as well cancel all of them."

As the plane made its descent, John quipped, "So this is where all the Christians come from." "You're a very controversial person," is all Paul could respond with, still troubled by the Jesus comment and its unforeseen backlash. George, wishing to break the somber mood with some gallows humor blurted out, "Send John out first. He's the one they want."

After the Beatles exited the plane they were ushered into an armored minivan. The Beatles were told to stay down in case of snipers. Luckily for the Beatles, the show went off without a hitch. During the second show a shot rang out while they were singing "If I Needed Someone." The band members looked at each other to see if anyone had been hit. Realizing everything was okay, they just kept singing as if nothing happened. Apparently, kids had tossed a cherry bomb from a balcony.

George was beginning to show his disdain for touring as a Beatle. He was tired of the day to day grind and the mobs of fans pressing in on them from all corners. Ringo complained that "nobody was listening to the shows." It was nearly impossible for Ringo to hear the others playing, so he had to rely on reading their body language. Many times he was reduced to playing on top of shaky platforms which negatively affected his drumming. John felt drained, emotionally and creatively. The constant pressure of touring and carefully monitoring everything he said was more than he could stand. He felt the music had died some time ago.

The next two gigs were a disaster. In Cincinnati, the Beatles played right after a rain storm and the stage was soaking wet. There was a chance the band might be electrocuted if they appeared on stage. Paul was so upset he threw up in the dressing room. Finally, Brian canceled the show, the only show they ever called off. They arranged for a makeup show to be held the next day.

At another show in St. Louis, there was a heavy drizzle that caused sparks to fly every time Paul bumped his microphone stand. After the show, the Beatles slid around inside a truck that rushed them to their sanctuary away from all the confusion and crazed fans. Around this time, the Beatles decided that they had had enough of touring. Paul, who probably enjoyed touring more than the others, admitted he was fed up with it as well. Surprisingly, attendance at the shows had been continuously dropping. Even several promoters lost money on the shows. There was no formal announcement that the Beatles had decided to stop touring forever. On August 29, the concert at Candlestick Park in San Francisco would be their last live performance. Ongoing, they would concentrate all their efforts on making records in the studio. The rumor mills turned out all kinds of speculation about their future. *Time* magazine asked the question, "Is Beatlemania Dead?"

CHAPTER 3

POST BEATLEMANIA AND THE BREAKUP

W HILE JOHN was filming *How I Won the War*, he began writing "Strawberry Fields Forever." George Martin thought the song conjured up "a hazy impressionistic dream world." John later confessed that the song was "psychoanalysis set to music." Paul was the first to come up with a new concept for their next album. He thought the album should be about another band playing all their songs. He explained to the others that the Beatles would pretend to be the Sergeant Pepper band.

Paul wrote "Penny Lane" by himself. George Martin raved about the two new songs. Brian wanted a single to be released in early 1967. Martin suggested that the two songs be linked together for their next single. He believed the single would become a smash hit. The single was released on February 17, 1967, and sold around 2.5 million copies.

It failed, however, to top the charts in England. Prior to this latest release, the Beatles had enjoyed twelve straight number one singles.

The Beatles hunkered down for several months at Abbey Road studios to work on their next album. This was the first time in four years that the Beatles had ample time to record music without a deadline looming over them. EMI had always demanded that they release four singles and two albums each year. "A Day in the Life" would be the first single completed for their new album. On January 19, the band laid out a two-track version first, comprised only of basic rhythm. Most of the lyrics were borrowed from two separate newspaper articles. One was about a Guinness heir who killed himself in a car. Another article was about four thousand potholes that needed to be filled. John later claimed that Paul's contribution to the song was the line, "I'd love to turn you on."

Paul recalled, however, that the two of them wrote the part about a man blowing his mind out in a car. The drug reference was obvious. Paul contributed the "woke up, fell out of bed" verse. He had actually written this earlier about what he called a "little piece of mine." There were still twenty-four bars left that needed to be completed. Paul came up with the idea of filling the section with an avant-garde symphonic sound that would build to a loud crescendo. George Martin liked the concept, but it was too impractical. The cost of booking a full symphony would be staggering. Then Martin had a change of heart and decided to book half of the London Philharmonic for just twenty four bars of music.

The song, "Sgt. Pepper's Lonely Hearts Club Band," was written almost entirely by Paul, as he recalled. John contributed "Good Morning, Good Morning," which was inspired by a Kellogg's Corn Flakes commercial. The two worked together and separately on, "With a Little Help from My Friends," and "Lovely Rita." John and Paul traded psychedelic sounding words with each other to come up with the lyrics for "Lucy in the Sky With Diamonds."

The recording of their latest album was not something George relished. He thought the recording process at Abbey Road "a bit tiring and a bit boring." He was not being utilized as much as the other three band members. Quite often, Paul played the piano while Ringo played the drums as they worked out the rough outline of a new song. Many of George's musical suggestions for the new album were given the thumbs down by the main songwriters.

John was dealing with his own issues during the making of *Pepper*. He was deeply depressed and his dark mood became worse, partly due to Paul's boundless enthusiasm and creativity. The contrast between the two was almost more than he could stand. As John recalled later, "I was going through murder." Amazingly, in just three weeks, the basic tracks for several new songs were completed, including, 'Fixing a Hole," "Lovely Rita," and "Getter Better." Creativity was at an all-time high for the band. Sequences were played backwards, notes distorted, and songs speeded up. At Paul's suggestion, "When I'm Sixty-four" was sped up in order for him to sound younger..."to be a teenager again."

On August 27, 1967, Brian Epstein was found dead at his home in London. No suicide note was discovered. Reportedly, some of Brian's friends claimed that he had attempted suicide on a couple of occasions. An inquest determined that the cause of death was an overdose of prescription pills he had been taking. The Beatles were shocked when they heard the news. They also became concerned about their future as a band. John was heard to say, "I knew that we were in trouble then."

It wasn't long before Paul was thinking about the Beatles' next project. He came up with the idea of the band touring the English countryside in a coach. They could write an original soundtrack for the film as well. John did not receive Paul's suggestion for this latest project very well. He thought Paul might be trying to replace Brian as the band's manager. John was only too aware that Paul oversaw most of the *Pepper's* recording sessions and it made him feel uneasy. Was Paul perhaps taking over the band?

Ever since the Beatles finished filming *Help!* a couple years earlier, they were unable to find a script suitable enough to satisfy them creatively. They did not want to make another film about a day in the life of a band semi-documentary, or anything involving a silly, pointless plot. In time, Paul's idea about a spontaneous adventure involving the band and some oddball characters caught on with the rest of the band.

Almost immediately after the *Pepper* sessions ended, the band was back in the studios working on new material for their latest album, *Magical Mystery Tour*. Paul arrived at the studio with just the first line of the song, "Roll up! Roll up! – For the *Magical Mystery Tour*," and some basic chords. Initially, the song was supposed to have been included in the *Sergeant Pepper* album, but Paul decided that it did not really fit the concept of the *Pepper* album, so it was discarded. To some, the lyrics may have meant a circus tour of sorts, and to others, the rolling of a joint. It may have sounded a bit contrived, even somewhat trivial and gimmicky. The band found it difficult to finish the song. Perhaps they had run out of energy.

Paul appeared to be the main source of inspiration for the Beatles. He kept suggesting ideas to the others who, it appeared, seemed less motivated. Paul had been thinking for quite some time about a story involving buses traveling on little "Mystery tours" along the English countryside He was influenced by a story about a group of American hippies called the "Merry Pranksters." The group took trips through the backgrounds of California. The founder of the group was Ken Kesey, the author of *One Flew Over the Cuckoo's Nest*. Tom Wolfe wrote a book about their adventures and called it the *Electric Kool-Aid Acid Test*. In the book, the Pranksters experience LSD induced mirages while attending a Beatles concert in Los Angeles. Paul envisioned the Beatles taking a similar "magical" journey in their next film. Interestingly, Paul insisted that a midget and a fat lady be included in the story line.

The completed film was provided to NEMS Enterprises so that it could be distributed, and the British rights were sold to BBC-Television. It was announced that the film would be broadcast on Boxing Day, 1967. The film was watched by fifteen million British viewers. What they probably expected to see was yet another great professionally produced film showcasing the Beatles talent. What they witnessed was a strange bus trip filmed with hand-held cameras wandering aimlessly. In one scene, the band portrayed wizards in a chemistry lab, while in another, Paul is shown hopping about the hillside singing "Fool on a Hill." The next morning, the British newspapers had a field day expressing their disgust toward the film. One *Daily Express* TV critic referred to the *Magical Mystery Tour* as "blatant rubbish."

American newspapers parroted the British papers with similar, unflattering comments on the Beatles odd little film. So bad were the outcries against the band that an American TV deal was tabled. At no time in their career had they experienced such a firestorm of criticism from all corners of the globe. Unfortunately for the Beatles, Brian Epstein was no longer around to bail his band out. Indeed, Neil Aspinall commented that, "If Brian had been alive the film would never have gone out. Brian would have said 'Okay, we blew 40,000 pounds-so what?' Brian would never have let it all happen."

John had read an article about hippies being referred to as "beautiful people." He derived from that phrase the lyric, "One of the Beautiful People." After that one line, basically, the song stalled. Paul suggested adding "baby, you're a rich man." The pair hashed out a song which they later named "Baby, You're a Rich Man." John later dismissed the song as "a combination of two separate pieces... put together and forced into one song."

The Beatles were worried about the release of *Sgt. Pepper's Lonely Hearts Club Band*. The disappointment of "Penny Lane" and "Strawberry Fields Forever" not reaching number one in the UK was still very much on their minds. After the album was released on June 1, the critics raved incessantly about how progressive and groundbreaking the songs were. The Beatles were now considered not simply an outstanding pop group, but creative geniuses as well. "She's Leaving Home" was compared to any song Schubert had ever composed.

The album was a massive commercial success, selling more than 2,500,000 copies in just three weeks after its release. In a way, the album was the beginning of a second Beatlemania phase, without all the "yeh, yeh, yeh." Music critics wrote ad nauseam about the cultural significance of the Beatles' latest effort. Timothy Leary, a famous Harvard professor and outspoken proponent of the drug culture, called the Beatles "evolutionary agents sent by God, endowed with mysterious powers to create a new human species." Remarkably, no singles were released from the album.

A month before the TV showing of *Magical Mystery Tour*, the soundtrack album was released as an EP. It was a six song album enclosed within a small book depicting the story of the mystery tour. Most critics agreed that "Fool on a Hill" and "I Am the Walrus" were by far the best of a poor lot. Although the critics panned the album as being way below Beatles standards, the album sold extremely well. To be fair, any album released right after *Sergeant Pepper* was fair game for sniping by the critics.

Paul had been working on a new song about John and Cynthia's son, Julian. The song was actually conceived while Paul was driving to see Cynthia and Julian. He wanted to cheer them up. It began, "Hey Jools – don't make it bad, take a sad song, and make it better." George Martin recalled that he thought the song was too long to be commercially successful. John asked Martin, "Why not?" Martin responded that he thought the disc jockeys wouldn't play it simply because of its length. John replied, "They will if it's us." The song ended up being seven minutes long, unheard of in the music business for a pop song. The record would go on to become the band's biggest selling single.

On the B-side of "Hey, Jude" was "Revolution." George Harrison did not care for the distortion on the record, but Paul liked it. John wanted to put out a protest song against war. For years the Beatles were told not to offer their opinions about the Vietnam War. This song may have been John's way of offering his personal opinion about Vietnam, and war in general. Around this time, John began to sense that the other band members were feeling resentful toward him. "But because they were so upset over the Yoko thing," John claimed, "and the fact that I was again becoming as creative and dominating as I was in the early days, it upset the apple cart. I was awake again and they weren't used to it."

According to John, all the songs on their next album were written in India, thirty in all. The band decided that their new effort should be a double album. The album was released on November 22, 1968. The sleeve was pure white and the title of the work was simply called *The Beatles*. The first two million copies pressed bore a serial number which gave them the distinction of a limited edition. Enclosed were four separate portraits of the band members. Unlike *Sergeant Pepper*, the *White Album*, as it would be referred to by the public, was a compilation of rock, pop, and blues tracks. Unlike *Pepper*, the songs in the album appeared disorganized to many listeners. The individual songs, however, garnered rave reviews by the same critics who abhorred the *Magical Mystery Tour* soundtrack album. *The Beatles* became their fastest selling album by far. Record stores had difficulty keeping enough of the albums in stock. The Beatles were once again clearly on top of the world.

Paul believed that when the Beatles stopped touring,

they had broken a special bond between them and their loyal fans. He wanted the band to stage another live concert tour and he was determined to have his way. "Let's get back to square one and remember what we're all about." Amazingly, a major consideration he contemplated was stage fright. After all, the Beatles had not performed in front of a live audience in two years. John and Ringo appeared receptive to Paul's pleadings, but George was another matter entirely. George did not want to endure Beatlemania all over again. Paul assured George that perhaps one live stage performance is all the band would agree upon with their producers.

The road was totally out the question for the Beatles. So a compromise was agreed to by all the band members. The Beatles would allow themselves to be filmed as they rehearsed songs for a new album. There would be no over-dubbing. The film would capture the essence of the Beatles as they meticulously worked out new songs and sounds. The Beatles wanted to go back to the basics of good old fashioned rock and roll. The film would end with the Beatles performing live on stage. It was undecided exactly where the performance would be held. Possible locations for a Beatles concert included a Tunisian amphitheater, and a venue in Los Angeles. George thought those suggestions were insane and overblown. John suggested that perhaps they could perform live in an asylum.

Filming began on January 2, 1969, at Twickenham film studios. The project's working title was *Get Back*. The title suggested that the band wanted to get back to their roots, where it all began. From the beginning, Paul took on the role as leader of the band. Everyone seemed to just listen as he described how he wanted his songs to sound. Even

John appeared utterly passive in the presence of Paul's commandeering manner. At one point, Paul sat next to George and described how he wanted part of a song to sound. "You see, it's got to come down like that," he suggested. "There shouldn't be any recognizable jumps. It helps if you sing it. Like this."

In order to complete the album, John and Paul reached deep down into their bag of older songs. They chose an old Quarry Men song, "The One After 909," to include on the soundtrack. Paul recalled later that the band didn't like the words to the song back in the day, but now the lyrics sounded fine. It was a different matter entirely when it came time for the band to rehearse the old tunes. The Beatles had difficulty playing songs they had written prior to Beatlemania. After about an hour of rehearsing, Paul decided it was time to get serious or pack it up for the day.

The tension between Paul and George in particular manifested itself when Paul remarked to George, "I always hear myself annoying you. Look. I'm not trying to get you. I'm just saying, Look, lads, the band. Shall we do it like this?" George shot back by proclaiming to Paul, "Look, I'll play whatever you want me to play. Or I won't play at all. Whatever it is that'll please you, I'll do it."

George had been growing frustrated for quite some time. He was infuriated by the way John and Paul dismissed songs he thought were good enough for their albums. He was more sensitive to Paul's instructions on exactly how to play his instrument than John or Ringo were. John stood up to Paul, but George did not have enough confidence to defend himself and promote his ideas.

On January 10, George decided he had had enough

of Paul's domineering manner and said he was quitting the Beatles. As he headed toward the exit to leave, he turned around and said, "I'm not doing this anymore. I'm out of here. That's it....see you around at the clubs." He was tired of Paul badgering him and so he drove home, presumably becoming the first ex-Beatle. Shortly afterwards, George came back to work and Paul promised not to teach George how he should play the guitar. Little did George know that John was ready to replace him with Eric Clapton if he did not return to the band.

The Beatles finally completed recording all the tracks for *Let It Be*. The band was dissatisfied with how the songs sounded and so they handed all the session tapes over to Phil Spector. Spector applied his patented '"wall of sound" to several of the tracks like, "The Long and Winding Road" and "Let It Be." Paul was extremely disheartened when he heard the finished product. Some of the tracks sounded overproduced and pretentious. Paul demanded that some of the tracks be revised, but it was too late. The damage, at least in Paul's eyes, had been done.

Paul wanted the band to sit in for some more sessions because he was extremely dissatisfied with the *Let It Be* session tapes. Amazingly, the band seemed more energetic this time. George's two contributions to the sessions were far and away better than what John and Paul had to offer. The two songs, "Something," and "Here Comes The Sun," were, to many fans and critics alike, the best cuts on *Abbey Road*. The album was released on September 26, 1969, to luke-warm praise. The *New York Times* considered it "rather dull." Advance sales for the album, however, broke all records for an LP. The album even went gold before its release date.

On October 10, a disc jockey from Detroit shocked his listeners by claiming that Paul McCartney was dead. He claimed Paul had died in a fiery car crash in 1966. Other radio stations climbed on the rumor bandwagon and soon fans frantically searched their albums for clues "proving" Paul's death. "Paul is dead" was seen in headlines throughout the world. Previously released Beatles albums reappeared in the American charts. Paul finally ended the hoax by coming forward to proclaim that he was very much alive. But he also admitted a shocking truth in that, "the Beatle thing is over."

John announced to Allen Klein, the band's manager, that he was leaving the Beatles. He was warned not to make a formal announcement because it would be detrimental to ongoing business deals involving the band. In October John told Paul he wanted to leave the Beatles. When Paul asked John what he meant, John replied angrily, "I mean the group is over. I'm leaving." George took the news in stride. He could now be his own man. As George recalled, "I wanted out myself. I could see a much better time ahead being by myself away from the band. It had ceased to be fun, and it was time to get out of it."

And so the greatest rock and roll band of all time had come to an end. Fans throughout the world could not believe that the Beatles, a band that towered over all others, had ceased to exist. Over the next several years, the music world and its fans came to realize just how influential and inspiring a band they really were. During the seventies, there were indications that John, Paul, George, and Ringo might rejoin once again as the Beatles. Sadly, it was not to be. On December 8, 1980, John was gunned down by a madman outside his home near Central Park. The pain and anguish Beatles fans experienced because of John's murder would in time be replaced by a deeper appreciation of the excitement and joy the Beatles brought to a world still very grateful to have experienced their music.

Part Two

LISTON
vs
CLAY

CHAPTER 4

KING OF THE WORLD!

MUHAMMAD ALI, then known as Cassius Clay, was born on January 17, 1942, in Louisville, Kentucky. His father painted murals for a living and his mother kept busy raising her two boys, Cassius and Rudy. She also cleaned and cooked for wealthy families. Young Cassius was introduced to boxing after someone had stolen his bicycle. He desperately wanted to punish the thief for stealing his bike. A man named Joe Martin talked Cassius into taking boxing lessons instead. If he wanted to beat up the thief, he should first learn how to fight. Cassius immediately exhibited a natural talent for boxing. He demonstrated the ability to avoid punches rather than stopping them with his arms and shoulders.

Clay fought his first amateur fight when he weighed a mere 89 lbs. He won a split decision in a contest that was featured on a local Louisville television show called *Champions of Tomorrow*. Clay would go on to win 100 out of a total 108 amateur bouts. He beat most of his opponents quite handily. In 1959 he went on to win the national Golden Gloves and Amateur Athletic Union light-heavyweight title. In Rome, in 1960, he won the Olympic gold medal in the light-heavyweight category.

Clay was constantly criticized by many of the older boxing experts after his triumph in Rome. They did not like his style of boxing. For a big man, in their view, he wasn't aggressive enough, didn't stalk his opponents the way Dempsey or Marciano did. He was interesting to watch, but he lacked the ferociousness and savagery many heavyweights were supposed to exhibit. Opponents were supposed to be punished unmercifully, not merely defeated.

Clay proudly walked the streets of the Olympic Village wearing his gold medal. He even slept with it on. After the Olympic ceremonies, Clay was asked by a Soviet Union reporter how he felt about winning the gold medal for a country that refused to allow him to dine at Woolworth's in his own hometown of Louisville, Kentucky. Clay replied to the reporter saying, "Tell your readers we've got qualified people working on that problem, and I'm not worried about the outcome. To me, the U.S.A is still the best country in the world, counting yours. It may be hard to get something to eat sometimes, but anyhow I'm not fighting alligators and living in a mud hut."

The Louisville Group, a syndicate from Kentucky, was impressed with Clay's boxing ability. They decided to provide financial backing for the young fighter. On October 29, 1960, in Louisville, Kentucky, Clay won a six-round decision in his first professional fight over the police chief of Fayetteville, West Virginia, Tunney Hunsaker. Clay had prepared for the fight by sparring with his brother, Rudy. His trainer for the fight was a local man named Fred Stoner. Because it was believed by the syndicate that Clay should have knocked his opponent out, Stoner's days were numbered. The syndicate wanted knockouts and lots of them. More decisions over questionable adversaries were not acceptable by the syndicate if Clay was to advance in the heavyweight division.

Clay wanted his idol, Sugar Ray Robinson, to train him, but the great one rejected the idea. In search of a trainer, Clay traveled to Ramona, California, where Archie Moore owned a training camp. He was intrigued with what he saw there. The training structure was a big barn named the Bucket of Blood. Scattered throughout the grounds were massive boulders with the names Jack Johnson, Joe Louis, and Ray Robinson prominently painted on them.

Unfortunately, the two men could not agree on a fighting style for Clay. Clay thought Moore was trying to get him to fight like an aggressive big man, swarming and stalking and landing big blows. Clay wanted to fight more like a big Sugar Ray Robinson. To make matters worse, Moore demanded that all the fighters help with the chores, such as cleaning, washing dishes, and chopping wood. Clay complained to Moore, saying, "Archie, I didn't come here to be a dishwasher. I ain't gonna wash dishes like a woman." Moore had had enough of Clay's resistance to anything he had to teach him. He called the Louisville Group and told them it wasn't working out between him and their fighter and that they could take him back.

Angelo Dundee was asked to take on the up and coming heavyweight contender. Dundee had been in the navy during WWII. In 1948 he decided to go into partnership with his brother, Chris, as a trainer. By this time his brother was well known and respected in the boxing community. The Dundee brothers left New York and set up their training center in Miami Beach. Many of Angelo's prospects were hungry fighters from Cuba and Latin America. The gym was at the corner of Washington Avenue and Fifth Street. The place was a dive, but it was the home of many a champion, such as Sugar Ramos and Luis Rodriguez. The hangers on at the gym claimed that Clay was a lousy puncher, kept his hands too low, and rarely attacked an opponent's body.

Clay lived at a hotel called the Mary Elizabeth. It was a hangout for pimps and two-bit hustlers. Reportedly, Clay never strayed from his strict upbringing. He never drank or dated women. When he did take in a night club, he drank nothing stronger than orange juice and never stayed out late. Clay typically began his day at 5:00 a.m. He would run along Biscayne Boulevard, and then later run from the hotel where he lived to the Fifth Street gym for training.

At first Ali was criticized for holding his hands down by his waist while boxing. It was thought that he could not lean back quick enough in order to avoid a punch to the head. Angelo learned that this was a style Ali felt comfortable with, and so he decided not to change it. His strategy was to improve the fighter's natural tendencies instead of changing them. Clay appreciated the fact that Dundee was not trying to change his style. He realized his trainer was only trying to improve or add to his boxing technique.

Furthermore, Dundee did not try to curtail any of Clay's showmanship and flair for the dramatic. He thought Clay's antics might draw large crowds to his fights.

Clay's first battle against a famous fighter was on November 15, 1962. His opponent was none other than his former trainer, Archie Moore, the "Old Mongoose." Moore had one of the highest percentages of knockouts in the history of boxing. He knocked out 141 victims out of the 229 fighters he faced. Moore, who was way past his prime, was knocked out in the fourth round. Moore retired after just two more fights.

Clay agreed to fight Henry Cooper, the British heavyweight champion. He was ranked fifth best by the World Boxing Association. Clay was overly confident with his upcoming fight with Cooper and stopped training completely one month before the bout. He complained that he was "tired of training to fight stiffs. All I want is a crack at Liston." At the time, Sonny Liston was the heavyweight champion of the world. Instead of training seriously for the upcoming bout, Clay stayed up late writing poems and playing card games with friends in Louisville.

In June 1963, Clay arrived in England for his fight against Cooper. Clay announced to the British press that he was "the uncrowned heavyweight champion of the world." "Henry Cooper will go in five," he boasted. The English did not appreciate Clay's insults toward their hero, Henry Cooper. They did not like Clay calling Cooper, "a tramp, a bum, and a cripple not worth training for." Cooper himself took the name calling in stride, perhaps realizing that all the commotion could be good for the gate.

The fight took place at Wembley Stadium in front of

55,000 boxing fans. Liz Taylor and Richard Burton were among the many dignitaries who had come to witness the spectacle. Trumpeters played as the two fighters entered the ring to do battle. It was, coincidentally, the 148th anniversary of the Battle of Waterloo. Perhaps the British would score another victory against another kind of adversary that night. Clay would be fighting at 207 lbs., his heaviest weight in any fight to date.

Cooper came out swinging in the first round. Clay appeared startled by the aggressiveness of his opponent. Clay reacted to the onslaught by hanging on to the aggressor. Throughout the round, Clay looked over to the referee each time he was hit by Cooper after the end of a break. For the first time in his career, Clay was bleeding from the nose.

In the second round, Cooper, "The Bleeder," sported an open cut near his left eye. In the third round, he attacked his opponent while Clay toyed and teased him by dancing around Cooper and keeping his hands down. One of the boxing officials ordered Dundee to warn his fighter against poor sportsmanship. In the fourth round, Cooper knocked Clay to the canvas with a powerful left hook. The knockdown was only the second in Clay's professional career. Cooper was not able to follow-up with a knockout before the round ended.

In the fifth round, Clay appeared determined to end the fight. He attacked Cooper with combinations of punches coming from all angles. Clay unmercifully battered Cooper about the head and shoulders. Blood flowed from Cooper's cuts at an alarming rate. Many fans, unable to witness more bloodshed, shouted, "Stop it!" to the referee. The referee finally stopped the fight at one minute and fifteen seconds in the fifth round. Cooper was heard to say, "We didn't do so bad for a bum and a cripple, did we?" Before long, Ali started predicting the round his opponent would fall. He even wrote poetry to describe the terrible thrashing he had in store for each of his adversaries.

Clay earnestly began his campaign of baiting Charles "Sonny" Liston into a championship fight. He flew to Las Vegas where Liston was training for the second Patterson fight. One day, Clay spotted Liston shooting craps at one of the casinos. The champ was experiencing a long streak of bad luck and Clay reminded him of it. "Look at that big ugly bear, he can't even shoot craps," Clay shouted. Liston glared at Clay and continued to throw craps.

"Look at that big ugly bear! He can't do anything right," Clay yelled.

Liston had had enough of Clay's jeering and so he walked up to Clay and threatened to rearrange his anatomy if he didn't shut up. Clay later admitted to a friend that he was scared of Liston.

The fight between Liston and Patterson turned out to be a duplicate of their first bout. The champ hammered Patterson with a pulverizing uppercut to the jaw, followed by a vicious straight right. The challenger dropped to the canvas like a dead weight. Patterson barely got to his feet at the count of nine. Had he not made it to his feet in time, the fight would have become the shortest heavyweight championship fight ever. A minute later, Liston pounded away at Patterson's body and this time the challenger dropped to the canvas and stayed there.

After Liston was declared the winner, Clay jumped

into the ring to do some showboating. He shouted into Howard Cosell's microphone, "the fight was a disgrace! Liston is a tramp! I'm the champ. I want that big ugly bear." Liston stared at Clay in disbelief. He had taken the bait. Liston turned to his trainer, Willie Reddish, and said, "Can you believe this guy? He's next." He told reporters he would destroy Clay in two rounds. He needed a little time to catch the dancer before putting his lights out.

Not long after, Liston moved to Denver, Colorado, for no apparent reason. This did not deter Clay from continuing his strategy of annoying and harassing Liston. Clay drove all the way to Denver, Colorado, for the sole purpose of irritating Liston into fighting him. As soon as Clay and his entourage arrived in Denver, Clay called the local media and told them to gather at Liston's house for "a good show." When Clay arrived at Liston's house, he had a friend knock at the champ's door. Liston opened the door and heard Clay and his buddies shouting, "Come on out of there. I'm gonna whip you right now. If you don't come out of that door I'm gonna break it down!"

Liston was angry and embarrassed about being threatened by someone he knew he could knock out easily. The champ thought Clay was all mouth and no punch. Most of the boxing experts agreed with Liston. They were convinced that Clay was a terrific showman and a sub-par boxer who could dance a little because he lacked a good, solid punch. Liston also had to be careful how he reacted to Clay because he had an arrest record and did not want any more trouble with the law. Liston agreed to fight Clay as soon as possible.

When Clay and Liston agreed to fight for the title, no

boxing expert declared publicly that Clay had any chance of beating Liston. Most experts predicted an easy knockout for the champ. This was the only practical way the champ had of ending Clay's taunts and jeers. Even after the fight contract was signed by both fighters, Clay continued his barrage of taunts against Liston. He told reporters, "I'm not afraid of Liston. He's an old man. I'll give him talking lessons and boxing lessons. What he needs most is falling down lessons."

Liston had a left jab that could easily knock out any opponent. He consistently knocked out opponents in the first round. Liston was 6'1" tall and had fists that were 15 inches in circumference. Two other giant heavyweight champions before him, Primo Carnera and Jess Willard, had smaller fists. His reach was 84" long. In comparison, undefeated former heavyweight champion Rocky Marciano's reach was only 68".

Angelo Dundee observed that Liston never proved he had great stamina. In fact, in his previous thirty some bouts, he rarely fought past the tenth round. Liston could conceivably lose to a great boxer. Dundee and Clay closely studied films of Liston's fights and looked for weaknesses. What stuck out the most was the fact that Liston was easily frustrated with opponents who slipped punches and who refused to be boxed into a corner so that Liston could pound them into oblivion. Dundee had noted that one of Liston's opponents, Mart Marshall, had actually beaten Liston by constantly moving to Liston's side, thereby never giving Sonny a stationary target. In their rubber match, Marshall was able to last the full ten rounds against the destroyer. Dundee developed a plan whereby he wanted

Clay to constantly move to his left. He called this technique, "surrounding the jab." The purpose of this tactic was to make Liston reach farther for his target, thereby causing him to tire easily. And a tired slugger, no matter how dangerous, has a chance of being beaten and even knocked out by a smart boxer. Clay trained for months for his upcoming bout with Liston by dancing to his left and snapping out lightning fast jabs.

Amazingly, the fight was nearly canceled due to Clay's affiliation with a group called the Nation of Islam. Cassius Clay, Sr. reported to the *Miami Herald* that his son had recently converted to the Nation of Islam. The leader of this religious sect, Elijah Muhammad, frequently delivered speeches condemning the white race and the civil rights movement. The announcement of Clay's conversion was supposed to have been made after the fight. The fight promoter confronted Clay and asked him if this story was true, because if it was, it would cost him a chance for the title. Clay knew he had a lot to lose, but he decided to admit to his conversion. Clay and Malcolm X had become very close friends. Malcolm X was considered by many in the white community to be an extremist. He was constantly at Clay's side throughout his training in Miami, and this did not bode well for the fight promoters. In order for the fight to go on, Malcolm X would have to leave Miami Beach immediately, but he would be allowed to return just in time to witness the fight in person. Malcolm X agreed to the terms and left town. Waiting for him on fight night, however, would be a ringside seat near Clay's corner.

The weigh-in was held in a room in the Miami Beach Convention Hall. Clay appeared smarting a denim jacket with the words, "Bear Huntin" brazenly stitched on the back of his jacket. Clay also carried a large African walking stick. The challenger shouted, "I'm the champ! I'm ready to rumble! Tell Sonny I'm here! He ain't no champ! Round eight to prove I'm great! Bring that big ugly bear on!"

Just before the official weigh-in, Sugar Ray Robinson advised Clay not to clown around. Dundee also warned Clay to behave himself because this fight was for the championship belt. Clay promised not to turn the proceedings into a self-serving circus. Minutes later, Clay and Bundini Brown, a close friend of the challenger's, entered the weigh-in room and chanted in unison, "Float like a butterfly, sting like a bee, rumble, young man, rumble!" Unfortunately for Clay, no one was at the weigh-in. Clay and his entourage arrived too early, and so they went back to their dressing room and waited for about an hour.

A little after 11:00 a.m., Clay and Bundini entered the weigh-in area and rehashed their previous chants. Clay shouted to Liston, "I'm ready to rumble now! I can beat you any time, chump! Somebody's gonna die at ringside tonight! You're scared, chump! You ain't no giant I'm gonna eat you alive!" Those who were present in the room went wild with enthusiasm. Liston sat in his chair trying not to look moved by the challenger's antics. Clay turned to Liston and yelled, "I got you now, you big ugly bear!" Once again, Liston refused to show any outward emotion in response to Clay's threats. Suddenly, Clay lunged at Liston, but Sugar Ray Robinson and Bundini grabbed Clay and pulled him away from the champ.

Standing next to the glaring Liston, Clay stood straight up as if to capitalize on his 6 foot, 3 inch height. It became clear to everyone in the room that Liston was about two inches shorter than the challenger. Liston grinned at Clay while the brash challenger shouted at the champion, "I got you now, ol' ugly bear. I got your title now. I'm gonna put a whuppin' on your butt tonight, you big ugly bear!" Liston stood there in amazement, perhaps wondering if Clay was insane. Clay was warned by representatives of the Miami Beach Boxing Commission that he would be fined if he did not stop his disruptive antics. Clay refused to stop and so Morris Klein, chairman of the boxing commission, fined him $2,500.

Clay was immediately whisked away to see Dr. Alexander Robbins, the boxing commission's physician. Robbins measured Clay's blood pressure and determined it to be 210/180, obviously much higher than normal, at least for humans. Clay's pulse rate was 110 beats per minute, far above the normal rate of 54. Robbins reported to the press that this reading could be interpreted to mean that the challenger was scared to death. He further pronounced that if Clay's blood pressure did not improve, the fight would be canceled.

According to Clay's doctor, Clay later confessed that he got himself all riled up in order to make Liston think that he was crazy. Clay explained that Liston was a bully, and bullies are afraid of crazy people. The day of the fight, the champ was the overwhelming favorite, about 7 to 1. Rocky Marciano reportedly remarked that he thought Clay was not being smart by agreeing to fight Liston. One comedian even quipped, "I'm betting on Clay....to live!"

Before the start of the fight, popular boxing dignitaries were introduced to the crowd. Jake LaMotta, former middleweight champion of the world, was introduced first to a chorus of boos. The Bronx Bull had admitted to taking a dive in his fight against Billy Fox in 1947. The boxing world turned against him ever since his admission to the Kefauver Committee. Sugar Ray Robinson entered the ring next. Regarded by many boxing experts to be the greatest fighter pound for pound, he had lost his title to LaMotta in 1943. They met five more times after that, and Robinson won four of the contests.

Clay entered the ring first. Liston did not make his appearance for another eight minutes. The long wait might have been deliberate in order to make Clay nervous. Perhaps it was Liston's way of getting back at Clay for his vicious taunts against the champion. Clay and Angelo Dundee agreed that the challenger should dance in circles around Liston, popping lightning fast jabs in Liston's face. Clay would do this while quickly moving away from the champion's vicious, pulverizing jabs. Clay later admitted that during the referee's instructions, Liston's stares scared him. The thought of getting hit by Sonny's punches frightened Clay.

When the two fighters met in the middle of the ring to hear the prefight instructions from referee, Barney Felix, Liston realized that Clay was taller than him. In fact, Liston was about to do battle with the tallest opponent he had ever faced. Even so, Liston glared right into Clay's eyes, trying to put the fear of God into him as he had done with so many other fighters. Clay stared right back at the champion. While the referee was wrapping up his instructions, Clay looked intensely at the champion and warned, "Chump! Now I gotcha, chump!" Just before the bell sounded signaling the beginning of the first round, Clay noticed Liston glaring at him as the champ shuffled his feet back and forth. So menacing was the sight, that Clay remarked later, "Man, he meant to kill me." Clay danced in his corner while waiting for the bell to ring. Liston stood quietly in his corner, staring at his prey, and visualizing the onslaught that was about to occur.

The round started and Liston began savagely attacking the challenger with blistering left jabs and long looping rights, trying quickly to end the fight. Liston, in fact, had bet on himself to knock Clay out in the first round. Throughout the round, Liston expended a lot of energy trying to put the challenger away. Clay just kept dancing around like a lightweight, dodging Liston's ferocious rights and lefts. Clay seemingly floated, moving back and side-to-side. Suddenly, without warning, Clay let loose a barrage of combinations about the head and body of the champion. Liston appeared dazed with disbelief. He covered up as best he could, but the damage had been done. Clay had proven to everyone watching and listening to the fight that he could dish it out without practically being hit.

At the end of the first round, Liston walked back to his corner and refused to sit down to rest. Clay related later that he thought to himself, "Man, you're gonna wish you had rested all you could when we pass this next round." In the second round, Liston again tried to corner Clay, but to no avail. The challenger skillfully slid away from the champ and glided back to the center of the ring where he was less vulnerable. Clay continued shooting out left jabs to the champ's face with great effect. He blasted Liston with combinations of punches that seemed to come out of nowhere. Liston looked stunned after each barrage.

A small cut appeared under Liston's left eye. This was the first time the champ had ever been cut in his entire professional career. Liston lashed out at the challenger with a long, looping left hook that caught Clay and hurt him. Liston, however, failed to capitalize on his assault, and this allowed Clay to escape further punishment.

In the third round, Liston chased Clay around the ring, trying desperately to end the fight with a knockout. Clay responded by simply dancing away from Liston's punches. As soon as the champ set himself up to deliver an attack, Clay was no longer in front of Liston. Clay was a moving target. Halfway through the round, Clay threw blistering combinations at Liston, eventually causing a mouse underneath Liston's right eye. The challenger opened up the gash that was under the other eye. At the end of the round, Liston walked back to his corner and, for the first time in the fight, sat down to rest.

At the beginning of the fourth round, it was evident that Liston's face was swollen. He continued swinging wildly at the challenger without any effect. Clay just danced out of the way of the bombs being thrown at him. Almost at will, Clay shot lightning fast jabs and straight rights in the champ's face. It was becoming apparent to many in the audience that Liston was now in serious trouble.

At the end of round four, Clay returned to his corner and complained to Angelo Dundee that both of his eyes burned. In fact, he was practically blind. Clay shouted, "Cut 'em off! Cut my gloves off!" as tears streamed down from both eyes. Dundee kept his cool while frantically washing his fighter's eyes and face with water. He kept reassuring Clay that he could still win the fight. All he had to do was run in circles around Liston until his eyes cleared. This fight was for the title, and now was not the time to cave. Realizing something was amiss, the referee started walking toward Clay's corner. Dundee noticed Felix approaching and immediately motioned to his fighter to stand up and start dancing in place for the beginning of round five. The referee related later that he had almost stopped the fight due to all the commotion coming out of Clay's corner. He was on the verge of awarding Liston with a technical-knockout victory.

The fifth round started and Clay began dancing in wide circles, trying to stay away from Liston's thunderous rights and left hooks. As the round progressed, Liston sensed something was wrong with his opponent. Clay was blinking uncontrollably and rubbing his eyes and he was not dancing like before. He was running and trying to stay away from Liston. Encouraged, Liston went on the attack. He threw powerful left hooks and killer rights at his prey. Had any of them landed, it could very well have been the end of Clay. While in a clinch, Liston let loose a barrage of body blows that made the challenger wince in pain. Most of Liston's rights and lefts missed Clay, however, and he appeared to be tiring from his desperate attempt to knock out the challenger.

At the beginning of round six, Clay went on the offensive. He threw a blistering combination of punches at Liston's head, stunning the champion. Encouraged by a lack of response, Clay threw a maddening barrage of punches, all unanswered by Liston. Clay continued to snap quick jabs at Liston's head. Almost at will, Clay dished out more punishment to the champ, who, by this time, appeared thoroughly exhausted and out-classed.

At the beginning of the seventh round, Liston was still sitting in his corner. He looked exhausted, but worse than that, he looked beaten. Clay noticed Liston spit out his mouthpiece. It was over! Clay held both arms high above his head and danced triumphantly. He was no longer a challenger to the heavyweight championship crown. He was now its king. Clay danced around the ring and performed what would later be called his Ali shuffle. It was pure mayhem inside the ring as fans congratulated the new champ. Clay lunged toward the crowd of spectators who were watching this spectacle in disbelief. He shouted, "I told you! I shocked and amazed the world! I am the greatest! I'm the king of the world! I've upset the world! Give me justice!" Howard Cosell attempted to interview him, but the new champ continued to shout well-deserved praise to himself. "I shook up the world! I'm the greatest thing that ever lived! I don't have a mark on my face, and I upset Sonny Liston, and I just turned twenty-two years old. I must be the greatest! I showed the world. I talk to God every day. I'm pretty. I'm a bad man."

Liston, now the dethroned champion, sat in his corner looking utterly dejected and dismayed. He had become the first heavyweight champion since 1919 to relinquish his title while sitting on his stool and refusing to come out for the next round. Jess Willard had lost to the incomparable Jack Dempsey in just the same way in Toledo, Ohio. After only three rounds, Willard had had enough of Dempsey's savage beatings before surrendering to the much smaller and younger challenger.

Angelo Dundee had to persuade Clay to grant an

interview with the sports writers. "Hypocrites!" Clay shouted at the reporters. "I shouldn't be talking to you." He was angry with the boxing writers. According to one source, only about four writers out of four hundred gave Clay any kind of chance to win. Clay spoke to reporters after the fight, chiding them for writing him off. He was annoyed at them for giving him practically no chance to win the title. He made fun of the criticisms they had toward his fighting style, such as holding his hands too low and quickly sliding away from punches. He warned them never to perceive him as an underdog again. He reminded the press that Liston had to go to the hospital while he didn't have a mark on his face. "I came, I saw, I conquered," he yelled out to the reporters.

Immediately after the fight, Liston was taken to the St. Francis Hospital to have his shoulder examined. He had complained to his corner about shoulder pain and how it stopped him from throwing left hooks. After examining the patient, eight doctors, including the chief physician of the Miami Beach Boxing Commission, agreed that Liston had suffered an injury to the biceps tendon of the left shoulder. This condition would be sufficient to incapacitate him and prevent him from defending himself. Dr. Alexander Robbins also released a statement saying that, "There is no doubt in my mind that the fight should have been stopped."

After six rounds of fighting, the officials had scored the contest even. The judges scored Clay as the clear winner in rounds one and six. Liston was the clear winner in round five. Liston took round two and four while Clay won round three. Many boxing fans were convinced that the fight had been fixed. There was no way a champion of

Liston's stature could have lost to this young upstart. Many regarded Clay as a bigmouth entertainer with some boxing ability. Certainly, he did not have enough talent and drive to technically knock out a ferocious fighter like Sonny Liston.

Clay attended a press conference on the morning after the fight to answer questions from the press. After discussing his take on the fight, Clay was asked if he was a card-carrying member of the Black Muslims. Clay was unsure in what context card-carrying meant. He responded by stating that he was not planning on moving into a white neighborhood or marrying a white woman. He further went on to explain that he did not have to be what society wanted him to be. He was his own man. Period. The champ explained further that, "Everything with common sense wants to be with his own. Bluebirds with bluebirds, redbirds with redbirds, pigeons with pigeons, eagles with eagles, tigers with tigers, monkeys with monkeys. As small as an ant's brain is, red ants want to be with red ants, black ants with black ants."

"I believe in the religion of Islam, which means I believe there is no God but Allah, and Elijah Muhammad is His Apostle. This is the same religion that is believed in by over seven hundred million dark-skinned peoples throughout Africa and Asia. I don't have to be what you want me to be. I am free to be who I want."

His next announcement was a real shocker. He proudly renounced what he referred to as his slave name, Cassius Marcellus Clay. His new name would be "Cassius X." About a month later he would announce that his new name would be "Muhammad Ali."

Many of the nation's newspapers had a field day regarding the new champion's name. "Black Muslims take over," were typical of many headlines across the country. Jimmy Cannon, a highly respected sports writer, wrote that, "Black Muslimism was a more pernicious hate symbol than Schmeling and Nazism." Many writers went so far as to refuse to call the champion by his chosen name. The next morning, Clay clarified his beliefs a little more. "Islam," Clay explained, "means peace and there are 750 million Islams throughout the world, him being one of them."

A rematch between the two fighters was scheduled for November 16, 1964, in Boston. Liston was the favorite to win in this "rubber" match, due to the consensus that the first fight had been fixed. Many boxing fans thought that Liston had either under trained for the fight, or he had badly injured his left shoulder while throwing a left hook in the first round.

After Ali won the world heavyweight championship, he visited Africa, where he received a tremendous welcome by adoring fans. When he returned from Africa, however, he was bloated from overeating. On the night of November 13, Ali suddenly felt ill and began vomiting. His abdomen became painful and he asked to be taken to a hospital. He was diagnosed as having an incarcerated inguinal hernia. The defect was repaired after a seventy minute operation.

The rematch between Ali and Liston had to be postponed. Unfortunately, when the fight promoters tried to reschedule the bout in Boston, veterans of foreign wars protested the fight because of Ali's draft deferment. The Massachusetts Athletic Commission jumped on the bandwagon and withdrew their permission for a fight because they claimed Liston had "mob connections."

The little town of Lewiston, Maine offered to host

the fight. The offer was quickly accepted by the promoters and the fight was set for May 25, 1965. Not since the Dempsey-Gibbons fight in Shelby, Montana, in 1923, had a championship heavyweight fight been held in as small a town as Lewiston.

A couple of days before the fight, Ali's sparring partner, Jimmy Ellis, hammered the champ's rib cage, causing severe bruises. Angelo Dundee theorized that the injury may have been a blessing in disguise. He figured Ali might want to end the fight quickly before Liston had a chance to punish Ali's body with a barrage of heavy blows.

Rumors began circulating that there might be assassination attempts on the champion's life. Malcolm X had recently been murdered and so the rumors were taken seriously by Ali and his entourage. The sheriff of the town Ali's training camp was located in told Ali and his camp that, "people were headed our way in a pink Cadillac to do harm to Ali." The training camp was promptly relocated to Lewistown, Maine.

The fight was scheduled to take place inside St. Dominick's high school hockey arena. Floorboards were placed over the ice. Dundee inspected the ring before fight time and discovered that it was actually a wrestling ring. Covering the floor of the ring was a mat resembling a trampoline and the ropes were loose. Dundee quickly ordered that the wrestling ring be replaced with a regulation boxing ring.

Fight time was 10:30 p.m. The referee for the fight was none other than former heavyweight champion Jersey Joe Walcott. Liston did not look like the Liston of old. He looked menacing, but he also appeared concerned. Ali, on the other hand, looked confident. Liston was a nine-to-five favorite just before the start of the rematch. This fight would become even more controversial than their first fight.

Ali immediately went on the offensive and slammed Liston with two hard punches. Liston forged forward and chased Ali, throwing his murderous left jab while stalking the champ. Ali simply floated away from Liston's punches and danced around the challenger. The champ started taunting Liston unmercifully, hoping Liston would blow his cool and thus make mistakes. Ali threw a straight right cross to Liston's jaw. The impact of the blow caused the challenger to fall down hard on his back. Ali refused to go to a neutral corner. Instead, he stood over Liston with both of his fists held high and shouted, "Get up and fight sucker!" Jersey Joe Walcott tried to push Ali toward a neutral corner where he belonged. Liston, totally bewildered, finally made it to his feet. Ali rushed toward Liston and started throwing lightning fast combinations. At this point, Nat Fleisher, a highly respected boxing authority, shouted to Walcott that the fight was officially over. Walcott stopped the fight.

Ali thought the punch that dropped Liston was not so hard that Liston could not have gotten up. Ali claimed he had forgotten the rules about going to a neutral corner. He also admitted he wanted to give the people their money's worth. Liston later explained to Jose Torres, newly crowned light-heavyweight champion, that he did not see the punch coming because it was so fast. Liston thought that he could have gotten up, but Ali was standing over him and the referee lost control of the fight. He stayed down until after Ali went to a neutral corner. He also claimed that he "over trained for that fight."

There was a great deal of controversy regarding the "Phantom Punch" as it was called by skeptics. Dundee explained later that, "Ali hit Liston so quick the cameras couldn't take it." The people who claimed they did see the punch land said it wasn't hard enough to cause a fighter like Liston to drop to the canvas. In reality, however, the film plainly shows Liston's head snap back just as the punch landed on Liston's left temple.

Immediately after the bout, many boxing fans charged that the fight had to have been "fixed." Liston was criticized for not having gotten up quicker. He explained that he was afraid to get up and get hit again while "crazy" Ali stood over him with his arms raised high above his head. Ali added even more mystery to the fight by claiming that he had learned the "Anchor Punch" from someone who had learned it from the great former heavyweight champion, Jack Johnson. As Ali explained the punch, "It was faster than the blink of an eye," Ali explained, " and everyone at ringside missed because they all blinked at the same time."

Ali's next battle was against former heavyweight champion, Floyd Patterson. Patterson had won five consecutive bouts and thus deserved a shot at the title. Ali mocked Patterson, calling him, "the rabbit" because he was scared. The challenger retaliated by announcing that he wanted to "reclaim the title for America." Patterson claimed that the Black Muslims were haters of white people and their religion was bad for America. Patterson went so far as to say, "I am willing to fight for nothing if necessary, just so I can bring the championship back to America." Ali answered by claiming, "The only reason Patterson's decided to come out of his shell is to try to make himself a big hero to the white man by saving the heavyweight title from being held by a Muslim." Ali responded further by calling Patterson an "Uncle Tom." The champ warned Patterson that he was going to cause him pain, and that he needed a spanking.

Ali taunted Patterson, and the challenger reciprocated by referring to Ali as Cassius Clay. Ali was deadly serious about being referred to by his Muslim name. Typically, Ali would yell to Patterson, "That ain't my name. You know my name. C'mon Rabbit, what's my name?" Even Ali's close friend and idol, Sugar Ray Robinson, received stern warnings from Ali whenever Robinson referred to Ali as Cassius Clay. While in exile years later, Ali went to Madison Square Garden to watch the Joe Frazier-Jimmy Ellis fight. Prior to the bout, the Garden's Vice President wanted to introduce Ali to the audience as Cassius Clay. Rather than stay and be humiliated, Ali walked out.

The match between Ali and Patterson was held on November 22, 1965, in Las Vegas. In the first round, Ali did not bother to throw a punch. "What's my name?" he shouted at the challenger. Apparently, he wanted to have a good time humiliating Patterson. As the fight progressed, Patterson began to tire. Patterson's trainer, Al Silvani, had to start helping him back to his stool after each round. It was apparent to everyone at the fight that the challenger was in a great deal of pain. The crowd began shouting at the referee to stop the slaughter. Suddenly, midway through the fight, Ali let loose a hard left jab, dropping the challenger to the canvas. The referee ended the bout in the twelfth round. The press came down hard on the champion, likening him to a child torturing a butterfly. Even Dundee claimed, "It was an ugly fight to watch, and one that did little to help Muhammad's popularity."

Weighing heavily on Ali's mind throughout this period was the strong possibility that he might be drafted into the military. Back on April 18, 1960, the eighteen year Clay registered for the draft in Louisville, Kentucky. On March 9, 1962, he was classified as being available for the draft. One month before his first fight with Liston, he scored badly on an aptitude test. After re-taking the test he was classified as 1-Y, which disqualified him from being drafted. This decision was highly controversial. Clay was embarrassed by the thought that people might think he was stupid. "I said I was the greatest," Ali explained, "not the smartest." With the conflict in Vietnam growing more intense, the military lowered its standard for aptitude tests. This action made Ali eligible to be drafted into the armed forces.

Ali's next fight was with George Chuvalo, a Canadian, whom the champ defeated in fifteen brutal, hard fought rounds. After the fight, Ali claimed Chuvalo was, "one of the toughest men I ever faced." Next, Ali fought Henry "the Bleeder" Cooper in May, 1966. The fight was stopped in the sixth round because the challenger suffered from a horrible cut over his left eye. Ali returned to England a few months later and knocked out Brian London in the third round. Later in the year the champion beat Karl Mildenberger from Germany.

Ali's next opponent was Cleveland Williams. The fight was held in the Houston Astrodome and drew over 35,000 boxing fans. Ali was a strong favorite at five-to-one odds. Reportedly, Williams began to have second thoughts about entering the ring against Ali. He was eventually coerced into fighting the champ. As expected, Ali totally dominated the fight from beginning to end. He knocked out Williams in the third round.

Three months after his fight with Williams, Ali was scheduled to go up against what many boxing experts considered to be his most dangerous opponent, Ernie Terrell. Terrell had gone undefeated for several years and had beaten top contenders. There was bad blood between the two fighters. Ali referred to Terrell as an "Uncle Tom" and Terrell refused to call the champion by his chosen name. At a prefight meeting between the two fighters, Ali asked Terrell what was Ali's name. Terrell answered, "Cassius Clay." Ali responded by saying Terrell was using his slave name which was totally disrespectful. "That made it a personal thing," Ali declared, "so I'm gonna whup him until he addresses me by my proper name. I'm gonna give him a whupping and a spanking, and a humiliation. I'll keep on hitting him and I'll keep talking. Here's what I'll say. 'Don't you fall Ernie. 'Wham! What's my name?' Wham! I'll just keep doing that until he calls me Muhammad Ali. I want to torture him. A clean knockout is too good for him."

Throughout the fight Ali attacked Terrell unmercifully with lightning fast left jabs and rights about the head and body. Terrell's left eye became badly damaged. Later, he claimed the champion had thumbed his eye repeatedly, but no proof of that claim ever surfaced. Ali kept shouting to Terrell, "What's my name?" followed quickly by a vicious barrage of punches from every direction. Ali won the contest by unanimous decision after fifteen rounds.

The press blasted Ali for being, according to them, disgustingly cruel in the ring that night against Terrell. One reporter claimed that Ali was becoming meaner as he "gets deeper into the Black Muslim movement." Even politicians began piling on. Congressman Robert Michael of Illinois stated that he could not understand how Americans could pay to see this man fight. According to Michael, Ali had come to symbolize draft evasion. He went on further to say, "While thousands of our finest young men are fighting and dying in the jungles of Vietnam, this healthy specimen is profiteering from a series of shabby bouts. Apparently, Cassius will fight anyone but the Vietcong."

In response to his critics, Ali repeated what he had been saying for some time now. He was a Muslim and a conscientious objector. In spite of his objections to the draft on religious grounds, Ali's 1-A status was upheld by the National Selective Service Presidential Appeal Board on March 6, 1967. A few days later, Ali was formally instructed to appear in Louisville for induction. The date was subsequently changed to April 28.

On March 22, Ali fought Zora Folley in Madison Square Garden. Folley was eventually knocked out in the seventh round. The badly beaten challenger later remarked that he thought the champ could have beaten all the top rated heavyweight champions from the past. He claimed Louis would have been too slow against the champ. Dempsey, Tunney, and Marciano would also have been beaten by Ali. The challenger praised Ali's ability to throw punches from any direction and to change styles during a fight. Unknown to many boxing fans at that time, Ali would not fight professionally for the next three years.

CHAPTER 5

THE U.S. VS ALI

A LI BECAME more and more outspoken regarding the government's attempt to draft him. "Why should they ask me to put on a uniform and go ten thousand miles from home and drop bombs and bullets on brown people in Vietnam while so-called Negro people in Louisville are treated like dogs? If I thought going to war would bring freedom and equality to twenty-two million of my people, they wouldn't have to draft me; I'd join tomorrow. But I either have to obey the laws of the land or the laws of Allah. I have nothing to lose by standing up and following my beliefs. So I'll go to jail. We've been in jail for four hundred years."

Ali upset many friends and acquaintances with his decision not to allow himself to be inducted into the Unites States military. He appeared particularly concerned about his mother's opinion toward his decision. Odessa Clay did not agree with her son's stance on not serving his country. Ali tried to explain to her how his religious beliefs prevented him from serving in the United States military, but she would have none of it. Still shaken by his mother's attitude toward his decision, Ali booked a flight to Houston, Texas, on April 27, 1967, to appear at a hearing at the Federal District Court. Ali's lawyers had scheduled the hearing in an attempt to obtain a restraining order that would prevent the Selective Service board from declaring their client delinquent if he chose not to attend the induction center in Houston. The induction center would be held at the United States Armed Forces Examining and Entrance Station. It is there where Ali would have to state whether or not he agreed to be inducted into the armed forces.

At O'Hare Airport, Ali was bombarded with questions from reporters about his controversial decision not to enlist. Possibly advised by his attorney, Chauncey Eskridge, he decided not to respond to any of their questions regarding his position on the draft. Sometime during the flight to Houston, the captain informed the passengers that one of their fellow passengers was none other than the "Heavyweight Champion of the World." One by one, Ali's fans approached the champ and asked him for his autograph. After exchanging pleasantries with some of the passengers, Ali sat back and talked to his attorney about what might transpire at the hearing and possibly the induction center. After about an hour into the flight, the plane experienced some very heavy turbulence. Several passengers, including one lady clutching a Bible, grew frightful. The woman holding the Scriptures accused Ali of causing the plane to rock violently. "God is punishing us because he's on the plane!

Cassius Clay, you turned against the true Christian God! God wants you off this plane. O forgive us, O Lord!"

At the hearing a Justice Department lawyer voiced his concern about the high-profile case and how the judgment of the court in favor of Ali might allow all Muslims to refuse induction into the armed forces. Ali was requested to stand in front of Judge Allan Hannay and state his case. Ali explained to the judge his reasons for not wanting to serve in the armed forces. He claimed that in 1961 he became convinced that becoming a Muslim would be the right religion for him. Shortly before his title fight with Liston in 1964, he had indeed become a Muslim. He told the court that he had refused to give up his new religion after the fight promoter threatened to cancel the bout due to the negative controversy brought on by Ali's religious beliefs. Ali informed the court that he was ready to leave Miami before the scheduled bout, but the promoter suddenly decided the title fight would have to go on as planned.

Ali explained to the judge that the name, Muhammad Ali, meant, "one who is worthy of praise." He had become a minister of his new religion and had spoken as a minister in eighteen of the seventy-five mosques located in the United States. He further claimed he spent an average of about 160 hours per month as a Muslim minister. Attempting to emphasize the seriousness of his devotion to his religion, Ali stated that, "My sideline is being the heavyweight champion of the world." Several of those present in the courtroom found this statement to be particularly amusing.

The heavyweight champion of the world finalized his plea to the judge by explaining his sole reason for refusing to serve in the military. He pleaded, "It's against the teachings of the Holy Koran. I'm not trying to dodge the draft. We are not supposed to take part in no wars unless declared by Allah or by a Messenger. Muhammad was a warrior fourteen hundred years ago, but he was a holy warrior fighting in the name of Allah. We don't take part in Christian wars or wars of any unbelievers. We aren't Christian or Communist." In the end, Ali was denied his motion for obtaining the restraining order. He would now have to appear at the induction center the next day or face criminal charges and arrest within the next 30 days.

Ali was very concerned about the induction ceremony scheduled the next day. He was worried about how history would judge his decision not to serve his country in time of war. "I want to know what is right, what'll look good in history. I'm being tested by Allah. I'm giving up my title, I'm giving up my wealth, maybe my future. Many great men have been tested for their religious belief. If I pass this test, I'll come out stronger than ever. I've got no jails, no power, no government, but six hundred million Muslims are giving me strength. Am I a fool to give up all this and go to prison. All I want is justice. Will I have to get that from history?"

Stokely Carmichael, a well-known black activist, had led a student riot a few days earlier at Texas Southern University. Ali asked to be driven to the university to meet with the students there. What he received was an earful about how Carmichael wanted to "burn Whitey." Ali responded by advising them that violence was not the answer to their problems. "Don't do nothing violent. We're not violent," Ali warned the crowd. A student replied that, "This is rebellion, man. They take you in the Army, they see a rebellion." Disturbed by what he had heard, Ali jumped back in the car and drove off. "They're a bunch of young fools," he declared to his attorneys.

Ali and his entourage arrived back at the hotel where they were staying. He decided to have dinner at the hotel coffee shop. When he sat down to eat, reporters hounded him with questions about the draft. One reporter informed the champ that he would not be safe in the military or prison. Ali responded by declaring, "Every day they die in Vietnam for nothing, I might as well die right here for something."

Another reporter asked why the champ didn't just play the game like other athletes. He probably would not have to actually fight the enemy in battle. He could fulfill his obligation to the military by boxing in exhibitions or teaching the troops how to stay in shape. Ali was reminded that Joe Louis served his country by entertaining the troops with exhibition bouts. The champ was also reminded that Louis had been highly critical of Ali for not serving in the military. Ali responded angrily by declaring, "Louis is the one without courage. Louis, he doesn't know what the words mean. He's a sucker."

At this point, Ali was fit to be tied and he let it all hang out. "What can you give me, America, for turning down my religion? You want me to do what the white man says and go fight a war against some people I know nothing about, get some freedom for some other people when my own people can't get theirs here?"

The champ hammered his point across some more. "You want me to be so scared of the white man, I'll go and get two arms shot off and ten medals so you can give me a small salary and pat my head and say, "Good boy, he fought for his country?"

The next morning, Ali reacted with disgust at a column he read in the *New York Times*. The columnist, Arthur Daley, wrote a scathing article about the champ. Daley blasted Ali for allowing him to be a puppet for the Muslim leaders. "The Muslims, who direct his every move," the columnist contended, "have gained a meal ticket and lost a martyr. The shrewd men at the head of the movement must think that sacrificing him is worth the price."

Daley represented how many people in the media felt about Ali's refusal to serve in the military. In 1967 the war in Vietnam was still viewed by many Americans as worth fighting. When one columnist publicly defended Ali's opinion on the draft, the backlash against him was harsh and swift. He received death threats and half of the newspapers that carried his column dropped him.

On the morning of April 28, 1967, Ali arrived at the United States Armed Forces Examining and Entrance Station in Houston. Twenty six young inductees arrived that morning to be inducted into the military. All but one would comply with the order. When the name, "Cassius Marcellus Clay" was called, Ali did not step forward as required by the proceedings. Lieutenant Clarence Hartman asked Ali to follow him to a room nearby. The Lieutenant explained to Ali that his refusal to be inducted was in direct violation of the Universal Military Training and Service Act. His refusal to be inducted could land him in prison for up to five years and a five thousand dollar fine. Hartman asked Ali to return to the inductee area and Ali complied. Once again, Ali refused to step forward and acknowledge his name. Ali was asked to state in writing his reason for not complying with the induction order. Ali agreed to this requirement and wrote, "I refuse to be inducted into the armed forces of the United States because I claim to be exempt as a minister of the religion of Islam."

Several days later, Ali's attorneys filed an appeal in federal court. They claimed that Ali's call to be drafted was unconstitutional because draft boards in Kentucky did not include their fair share of blacks. They based their opinion on the percentage of blacks living in the state and the percentage of blacks serving on the draft boards. The percentages were 7.1 versus 0.16 respectively. They also claimed that Ali's Selective Service file was filled with, "reams of letters and newspaper clippings of a prejudicial nature." The champ was therefore being deprived of fair treatment under the law.

Shortly after the public was made aware of Ali's official act of refusing to be inducted into the military, the New York State Athletic Commission refused to recognize Ali as the heavyweight champion of the world. But that was not all that would happen to the champ. On May 8, 1967, a federal grand jury in Houston indicted him. Ali was later convicted and sentenced.

Ali's life did not stagnate. He attended meetings organized by the Nation of Islam and continued to further his understanding of Elijah Muhammad's teachings. In the meantime, Ali commented on his new status as dethroned champ. He complained that the "power structure seems to want to starve me out. They want to stop me from working, not only in this country but out of it. Not even a license to fight an exhibition for charity, and that's in the twentieth century. You read about these things in the dictatorship countries where a man don't go along with this or that and he is completely not allowed to work or to earn a decent living." Ali went on to explain his views on race relations in America. "We've been brainwashed. Everything good is supposed to be white. We look at Jesus and we see a white with blond hair and blue eyes. We look at all the angels; we see white with blond hair and blue eyes. Now, I'm certain there's a heaven in the sky and colored folks die and go to heaven. Where are the colored angels? They must be in the kitchen preparing milk and honey. We look at Miss America, we see white. We look at Miss World, we see white. Even Tarzan, the king of the jungle in black Africa, he's white. White Owl Cigars. White Swan soap, White Cloud tissue paper, White Rain hair rinse, White Tornado floor wax. All the good cowboys ride the white horses and wear white hats. Angel food cake is the white cake, but the devil's food cake is chocolate. When are we going to wake up as a people and end the lie that white is better than black?"

In December 1968, Ali was sentenced to ten days of imprisonment in Dade County, Florida, for driving a vehicle without a proper license. He spent about a week in jail, but was finally released for the Christmas holiday. Ali felt very uneasy about his experience of incarceration. He felt undeterred, however, about the possibility of spending five years behind bars because of his religious beliefs. Ali remained stoic, at least in public. Boxing had been by far his main source of income. Now he was relegated to earning a living some other way. He spoke at many colleges throughout the country, but the fees he earned were hardly enough to pay for legal representation.

Beginning in 1970, Ali began a quest to regain his previous stature of heavyweight champion of the world. No other heavyweight in history was able to accomplish this great feat, including two of Ali's heroes, Jack Johnson and Joe Louis. Ali vehemently believed that the only way a champion could legitimately lose the title was in the ring. Many boxing fans agreed with him. Meanwhile, heavyweight boxing continued. A new champion would be chosen via elimination bouts between the top heavyweight contenders. Among the top contenders were Joe Frazier, Jimmy Ellis, and Jerry Quarry. Frazier was finally recognized as the new heavyweight champion on February 16, 1970, after knocking out Jimmy Ellis, a former sparring partner for Ali, in the fifth round. It was a totally one-sided fight.

A groundswell of support in favor of Ali began to manifest itself. Ali was in exile, many people thought, because the government would not recognize his religious beliefs as a reason not to be drafted. He had now become an underdog. It should be emphasized that the state boxing commissions and not the federal government banned Ali from boxing. Fortunately for Ali, the state of Georgia did not have a boxing commission. One of Georgia's state senators and the mayor of Atlanta believed that Ali had been denied his right to earn a living long enough. He was therefore allowed to fight in Atlanta.

A bout was scheduled for October 26, 1970, in Atlanta, between Ali and Jerry Quarry. In the first round, Ali dominated Quarry from the start. He exhibited some of the old Ali, but he was noticeably much slower than he had been in his previous fights. In the second round, Ali appeared tired. Quarry was able to land some devastating punches. In the third round, Ali landed several punches to Quarry's head. Suddenly, Quarry was sporting a nasty cut over one eye. The referee carefully examined the cut and stopped the fight. Ali had won his first comeback bout after spending over three years in exile.

Ali's next fight was against Oscar Bonavena on December 7, 1970, in Madison Square Garden. Ali had predicted he would knock out Bonavena in the ninth round. Early in the fight, the Argentinean rushed Ali like a mad bull. Ali backed away from the onslaught with little difficulty. The next few rounds followed the same pattern as the first round. Bonavena charged Ali and Ali swiftly backed away while firing jabs to the face, followed by the right hand. Ali appeared content to just avoid Bonavena's punches and occasionally shoved the Argentinean against the ropes. In round five, Ali looked tired. Bonavena connected with several devastating punches. Instead of cutting the ring off against Ali, however, Bonavena chased Ali around the ring. In round nine, Ali went on the attack, but Bonavena survived Ali's combinations of rights and lefts.

In the fifteenth round, Ali threw a ferocious left hook at Bonavena's jaw and the Argentinean went down. Bonavena got right back up, but his legs were wobbly. Ali punished Bonavena with more punches and he fell to the canvas a second time. Bonavena got right up again. Ali tagged him with another headshot and down he went. Ali won the fight by a technical knockout. The TKO decision was based on a rule in which a fighter loses a contest if he gets knocked down three times in the same round. Ali had shown that he was nowhere near the boxer he was prior to his comeback. He no longer danced around the ring, dodging brutal left hooks and quick straight rights. Now, the only fighter standing between him and the crown was Joe Frazier.

Angelo Dundee did not think his fighter had enough time to sharpen his skills before his bout with Frazier. The fight was scheduled for March 8, 1971, in Madison Square Garden. Experts in the field of boxing felt the Ali of old was hardly present in his fights with Quarry and Bonavena. The forty-three month layoff would be very difficult to overcome for Ali in his quest to regain the belt. Similarly, the great Jack Dempsey returned to boxing after a three and a half year hiatus, only to lose his belt to Gene Tunney in a totally one sided fight. As skillful as Ali was as a supreme boxer, he would face an almost similar fate as Dempsey did.

Ali referred to Frazier as an "Uncle Tom" and a "chump." Ali wrote a poem in response to Frazier, who "always talks about he's gonna come out smoking."

Joe's gonna come out smokin'
And I ain't gonna be jokin'
I'll be pecking and a pokin'
Pouring water on his smokin'
This might shock and amaze ya,
But I'm gonna retire Joe Fraz-yah.

Ali continued to try and psyche out the champion. "The only people rooting for Joe Frazier are white people in suits, Alabama sheriffs, and members of the Ku Klux Klan. I'm fighting for the little man in the ghetto...Joe Frazier is too ugly to be champ. Joe Frazier is too dumb to be champ. The heavyweight champion should be smart and pretty like me....Anybody black who thinks Frazier can whip me is an Uncle Tom."

The fight against Joe Frazier was unique in that it would be the first time two undefeated heavyweights would meet to fight for the heavyweight championship of the world. Their styles could not have been more different. Ali was a premier boxer and Frazier was a swarmer, constantly moving his arms while relentlessly moving forward. Each fighter would earn an astounding $2.5 million, the most any athlete had ever earned in the history of sports.

Ali did not train seriously for the fight. He believed his knockout victory over Bonavena, which Frazier failed to do during his two fights with Bonavena, was a sure sign that he could easily handle Frazier. Dundee managed to get him back in the gym for some serious training. Dundee was concerned that Ali was no longer able to quickly dodge his opponent's punches. He relied, instead, on blocking them with his gloves. More disturbing was his inability to dance effortlessly around his opponent.

The early rounds in the bout were basically a draw. Frazier bored in on Ali, throwing hard lefts and rights and always stalking his prey, never letting up. Ali snapped lightning fast jabs at the menacing champion. The challenger found the champ easy to handle with his sticking and moving from side to side. Frazier's face began to swell from Ali's jabs. On the other hand, many of Frazier's body punches landed and did a lot of harm. Too often, Ali leaned against the ropes, absorbing more punishment than he had ever experienced before. Frazier landed a hard left hook to Ali's face, but the challenger rolled with the punch. Ali taunted Frazier by telling him, "God wants you to lose tonight." Frazier snapped back, "Tell your God He's in the wrong house tonight."

Both fighters appeared weary by the eighth round. Ali continued to rest on the ropes, hoping to tire Frazier out, but the champion just kept stalking and punching, building up points in the process. At the end of the round, Dundee gave an earful to Ali. He warned him to "quit fooling around. For cryin' out loud. Stop playing. Do you want to blow this fight? Do you want to blow everything? You're giving away rounds and letting him build not only a lead but also his confidence."

In round nine, Ali danced around the ring like the Ali of old. The challenger shot wicked and accurate jabs into the champion's face. It appeared that the tide had now turned in Ali's favor. In the tenth round, however, Ali rested on the ropes while Frazier threw blistering punches to Ali's body. He was following the same strategy as he had in the earlier rounds. Ali rested while Frazier tired himself out throwing bruising punches. Suddenly, with just seconds left in the round, Ali let loose a barrage of left-right combinations and jabs to Frazier's face.

In the next round, Ali once again reverted back to leaning on the ropes while Frazier punched him at will. Two tremendous left hooks hurt Ali, causing his legs to buckle. Ali wiggled his hips as if trying to appear more hurt than he actually was. Frazier continued his relentless assault. Attempting to show the crowd he was not hurt, Ali contorted his face while pretending to be injured. Ali assured the champ throughout each round that he was unscathed by teasing Frazier with, "You can't hurt me, Joe."

In the eleventh round, Frazier let loose a left hook that landed on Ali's cheek. Ali's knees buckled under him, but somehow he managed to shake off the devastation of the assault. Again, he pretended to be hurt, perhaps more than he really was by wobbling around the ring. Finally, in the fifteenth round, Frazier hit Ali squarely on the jaw, knocking him down. Amazingly, Ali immediately rose to his feet and took the mandatory eight count. The final bell rang and Frazier was declared the winner by unanimous decision.

After the fight Ali praised Frazier by claiming he was tougher than Liston. As far as leaning on the ropes was concerned, he explained that he was resting. He realized, however, that he may have lost a few rounds because of this strategy. Frazier complained about how painful his face felt. It was covered with welts, bruises, and cuts. Ali was hurting as well. His jaw was swollen and his body was limp and he needed help getting into his limo so he could be examined at a nearby hospital.

Then the piling on against Ali occurred by many in the press. The consensus among the sports community was that Ali was obviously over the hill and that he should retire with dignity. He had made a gallant effort, but was no match against the much more aggressive, tougher, Joe Frazier. Red Smith, a highly respected sports columnist, indicated that Joe Frazer could easily beat Ali anytime, any-place, anywhere. Ali was all washed up. *Sports Illustrated* emphatically declared, "Ali's time was past."

Ali took his defeat in stride, at least publicly. He pro-claimed that he threw many more punches than Frazier and therefore he should have won the decision. He jokingly confided to Howard Cosell that, "I guess I'm not pretty anymore." Privately, Ali was stunned about his defeat. Ali said later that he was too young to appreciate his win over Liston when he became the new heavyweight cham-pion. Losing to Frazier meant that, in his mind, he had lost the title to a better fighter that night. Ali was upset that Frazier's confinement in a hospital for medical evaluation of a possible broken jaw implied that Ali really won the fight. Ali thought that Frazier had sustained much more punishment than he did, and therefore the champ should have been declared the loser.

Surprisingly, Ali's next proposed opponent was not a boxer, but one of the all-time great basketball stars, Wilt Chamberlain. Chamberlain's greatest dream, in fact, was to fight for the heavyweight championship of the world. He was determined to fight Ali. A contract was signed and the stage was set for what was sure to create a tremendous amount of interest.

Chamberlain started training under Cus D'Amato, a very reputable man in the boxing world. The basketball center, however, began to realize that he was a huge underdog. Eventually, after all the publicity and hoopla, the fight was called off. At the sign in, Ali yelled "Timber!" as Chamberlain entered the room. Chamberlain looked stunned. He and his lawyers immediately went into a nearby room and shortly afterwards announced that Chamberlain was not going to fight.

Ali's next scheduled fight would be legitimate this time. On July 26, 1971, at the Astrodome in Houston, Texas, he would go up against Jimmy Ellis, a former boyhood friend. Curiously, Angelo Dundee would be in Ellis' corner this time. Ali was gracious enough to give his consent to Dundee. The reason behind this arrangement was apparently money related. Dundee could earn a far greater share of Ellis' share than Ali would have paid him. Ali defeated Ellis with a vicious right hand punch over Ellis' jab in the twelfth round, winning by a technical knockout.

Four months later at the Astrodome in Houston, Ali

was scheduled to fight Buster Mathias. This fight would prove to be a hard sell because Mathias was overweight and looked out of shape. Ali won a one-sided decision over Mathias after twelve rounds. After the bout, Mathias graciously thanked Ali for giving him the chance to fight him and make a lot of money. The press criticized Ali for not beating Mathias more decidedly. Ali responded to his critics by asking, "How do I know just how hard to hit him to knock him out and not hurt him? How am I going to sleep if I killed a man in front of his wife and son just to satisfy you writers?"

On September 20, 1972, Ali fought Floyd Patterson again and knocked him out in the seventh round. Ali was soundly criticized for even allowing the bout to be sanctioned. Patterson was a thirty-seven year old fighter who could easily have sustained permanent, severe injury in the ring. Ali responded to his critics by declaring that Patterson was experiencing financial difficulties and desperately needed a big payday. Ali's next fight was against Bob Foster, the light-heavyweight champion, on November 21, 1972, in Nevada. Ali outweighed Foster by forty-one pounds and the bout was basically one sided in favor of Ali. In the fifth round, Foster caused a cut under Ali's left eyebrow. Ali knocked Foster out in the eighth round.

Ali's dream was to win back the title by beating Joe Frazier. But this was not to be. On January 22, 1973, in Kingston, Jamaica, George Foreman knocked out Frazier in the second round. On March 31, 1973, Ali climbed into the ring against an up and coming challenger, Ken Norton, a former marine. In the second round, Norton landed a hard right to Ali's jaw, breaking it. Ali's corner decided to have their fighter continue to fight rather than have a TKO scored against him. Up until the last round, the fight was scored fairly evenly. Norton, however, dominated the final round and subsequently won the decision. It was a huge upset in the boxing world.

After the fight, Ali reportedly stated, "I took a nobody and created a monster. I put him on *The Dating Game*. I gave him glory. Now I have to punish him bad." Ali immediately planned for a rematch with Norton. He took his training seriously this time. As in the first fight between these two men, the bout was even up until the twelfth round. Ali went all out in the final round and eventually won a very close decision. Shortly thereafter, he won a decision over Rudi Lubbers in Indonesia.

A rematch between Ali and Frazier was scheduled to be fought at Madison Square Garden. Before the fight, the two fighters were asked to watch a film of their first fight together and add their own commentary as the bout progressed. At the end of the film, both fighters started shouting insults at each other and had to be pulled apart by their respective entourages. The two fighters were fined $5,000 each for "deplorable conduct." At fight time, Ali was a slight favorite at six-to-five odds. The second fight was not as brutal as their first encounter, and Ali won a unanimous decision.

CHAPTER 6

ZAIRE AND BEYOND

Ali's next match was for the heavyweight title against the current champion, George Foreman. The bout was scheduled to be fought in Zaire, Africa, on October 30, 1974. Foreman had a very formidable record of forty wins, thirty seven by knockout, and no losses. Working against Ali was the fact that the champ had demoralized Frazier and Norton, the very two fighters Ali had lost to.

Ali started needling Foreman with sharp barbs and insults, He referred to Foreman as, "the Mummy" because he moved slow, telegraphing all his punches. "George Foreman don't stand a chance," Ali went on. "When I finish going upside that sucker's head, he'll have so many nicks and cuts, it'll look like he had a bad morning shave."

A few days before the scheduled bout, Foreman received a cut above his right eye while sparring. Rumors spread like wildfire that the fight might have to be postponed. Ali was furious when he heard about the possibility of canceling the fight. He had trained especially hard for the chance to win back the heavyweight crown. The government of Zaire even warned both fighters not to leave the country. Meanwhile, Ali kept badgering the champ, belittling his chances of holding on to the title. "Tell everybody to get to their theaters and don't be late, because I might end this in one round. I never wanted to whup a man so bad in my life. I'm getting angry just thinking about it."

In round one, Ali danced around Foreman, feeling out the champ. For the next several rounds, Ali leaned on the ropes while taking sledge hammer punches from Foreman. At the start of round eight, Foreman was tired. He was arm weary from all the punches he had thrown at the challenger. Evidently, this had been Ali's strategy all along. Dundee was appalled that his fighter resorted to such a dangerous tactic. One lucky punch from the champ could have easily knocked Ali out, or at least hurt him to the point where he could lose the fight in a decision.

Ali later explained why he had chosen this strategy, or "rope a dope," as he called it. He realized that the ring was slow, and so dancing on it all night would have tired his legs. Foreman was also cutting off the ring, and this caused Ali to have to dance even more just to get out of the way of his thunderous left hooks and looping right hand punches. Ali was concerned about getting tired if he danced around Foremen for too long. He did not want to be tired in the later rounds and then get nailed by Foreman. He decided to take some shots from Foreman by leaning against the ropes and covering up the best he could. If Foreman became too aggressive, Ali would start dancing again.

By the eighth round, it was Foreman who had run out of energy. Foreman attacked Ali with everything he had left, but Ali just rolled with the punches. Foreman missed with a right hand, turned around to face Ali, and got hit on the chin by Ali. Foreman hit the canvas hard. He looked tired and stunned. He was counted out. Ali accomplished what other former heavyweight champions had failed to do. Regain the heavyweight championship title!

Ali's next fight was against a tough fighter named Chuck, "the Bayonne Bleeder," Wepner. Ali dominated almost the entire fight. In round nine, however, Wepner punched Ali in the chest and the champ went down. The referee called it a knockdown, but Ali claimed Wepner had stepped on his foot while he was off balance. In the final round, Ali knocked Wepner down. The challenger's nose was broken and he was bleeding over both eyes. The referee stopped the fight.

Sylvester Stallone watched the fight on closed-circuit television. He was intrigued by how the audience screamed when Ali got knocked down in the ninth round. Stallone explained, "Everybody wants a slice of immortality. They want that sensation that they have a shot at the impossible dream, and that solidified the whole thing for me. Rocky came out of that fight between Wepner and Ali."

Several weeks later, Ali fought Ron Lyle in Las Vegas. Ali was trailing on two of the judge's scorecards by the end of the tenth round. In the eleventh round, Ali smashed Lyle on the jaw with a hard right and the challenger fell back. Ali threw punches from all angles at Lyle's head. The referee stepped in and stopped the massacre,

Ali and Frazier fought each other for the third and final time on October 1, 1975, in a town just outside Manila. The fight would come to be known as, "The Thrilla in Manila." Ali out-boxed Frazier in the early rounds. Ali began to tire in the middle rounds and Frazier kept pounding him with left hooks and rights. Ali got his second wind in the twelfth round and battered the challenger with blows to the head and body. In the thirteenth round, Ali landed a left hook, knocking Frazier's mouthpiece out. Frazier's left eye was completely shut by the fourteenth round.

The fighters staggered back to their corners at the end of the round. Ali was exhausted almost to the point of throwing in the towel, but Frazier's trainer beat him to the punch. He explained to his brave fighter, "Joe, the fight's over. I'm stopping it. You're taking too much punishment, and I don't want to see you take it anymore."

Ali fought Kenny Norton on September 28, 1976, in New York. Norton dominated the early rounds. Ali showed how much he had slowed down. The challenger was significantly ahead on the judge's scorecards by the end of the eighth round. Ali rebounded and won five of the next six rounds. The contest was dead even when the fighters came out for the final round. Unfortunately for Norton, his corner told him he was ahead and that he should not take chances. Norton came out and played it safe for the first two and a half minutes and then he decided to start swinging the remainder of the round. But it was too little too late, and Ali won the last round and the fight.

It was apparent to the boxing world that Ali was not the Ali of old. His speed and coordination had long been on the decline. He was a lot wiser in the ring, but his body could not take advantage of all that he had learned. Ali did not fight for several more months. He was finally matched against Alfredo Evangelista of Spain. The challenger had turned professional a scant nineteen months earlier. Even so, the fight lasted fifteen rounds, more proof that Ali was just a shell of himself.

Ali's personal life was in shambles as well. On September 2, 1976, his wife, Belinda, formally charged Ali with desertion and adultery. Several weeks later, the couple divorced and his ex-spouse received $670,000 to be paid over a five year period. A trust fund of one million dollars was set up by Ali for the benefit of their four children.

An Ali autobiography was published and released, quickly followed by a film about Ali called *The Greatest*. Ali played himself in the film. One of the very few good things about the film was the song from the soundtrack, "The Greatest Love of All." Years later, the song would become one of Whitney Houston's biggest hits.

Even during his decline Ali proved that he could still draw an audience. On September 29 he fought Ernie Shavers, a very hard puncher. 70 million viewers tuned in for the fight, which was broadcast live on NBC. In round two, the challenger hurt Ali with a tremendous overhand right. Shavers failed to follow up with more devastating blows, allowing Ali to survive the round. Ali won most of the subsequent rounds until the thirteenth round when Shavers started pounding Ali unmercifully. Ali received more punishment in the fourteenth round as well. At the start of the final round, Ali was noticeably exhausted. Somehow, he found the will and the strength to out box and out punch Shavers and he went on to win the decision.

The champ's next fight was held on February 15, 1978, against a relatively unknown fighter named Leon Spinks. The general consensus held that Ali would have no trouble with Spinks. Although he was ranked as the premier contender for the heavyweight title, he was looked down upon as having too little experience in the ring. His only real selling point was that he had won the gold medal in the light-heavyweight category at the Montreal Olympics. The fact that he had only fought eight other opponents prior to his scheduled fight with Ali was frowned upon by boxing fans. At first, Ali scoffed at the idea of fighting such an unknown boxer. What may have changed his mind, however, was the fact that Spinks was an Olympic gold-medal winner. Ali had beaten three gold-medal winners and wanted to add a fourth victim.

It seemed no one was really interested in an Ali-Spinks fight. Ali himself found it difficult to sell the fight. Ali confided to a friend, "Spinks only has seven fights. What am I gonna tell people; I'm gonna destroy him? Talking that way makes me look stupid, so I just ain't gonna talk." Ali proved once again that he could still sell tickets because the fight would be broadcast live throughout the world via closed-circuit TV in movie theaters.

When Ali stepped into the ring at Caesars Palace in Las Vegas, it was immediately apparent to everyone present that the champ looked old and out of shape. He did not look sharp and alert and the fight would bear that out. In the early rounds, Ali fought defensively. He wanted Spinks to tire himself out by throwing punches. But Spinks was young and in good shape and he never tired. Ali tried to knock the challenger out in the final rounds, but it was too late. Spinks had won a split decision. It would be the only time a challenger took the title away from Ali in the ring.

Ali felt deeply embarrassed by the loss. He was humbled because he had been beaten by someone who had almost no professional experience in the ring. He realized he had no one to blame but himself. He knew he did not train right for the title event. He did not want to retire losing this way. Soon after the fight, the ex-champ began training hard. He could be heard saying to himself, "Gotta get my title back, gotta get my title back" while running and shadow boxing. Ali had something to fight for now. He had to win the title back from someone who was merely borrowing it from him.

The rematch was held at the gigantic Louisiana Superdome, in New Orleans, on September 15, 1978. Although ABC would provide a live broadcast of the title bout, 63,532 people jammed inside the stadium. It would become the largest fight attendance at an indoor venue. And the live gate receipts totaled $4,806,674, shattering records everywhere. Ali did his part in selling tickets by promising boxing fans that this would be his last fight. If he won the fight, he would make history by becoming the only black heavyweight boxer ever to have retired as the champ.

Ali appeared very optimistic. "You can't write a movie no better than this," he pronounced. "When I beat Sonny Liston, I shocked the world. When I joined the Muslims, I shocked the world. When I beat George Foreman, I shocked the world. I am the House of Shock." Ali's appearance told a different story, however. He looked old and he spoke with some difficulty, sometimes slurring his words. Howard Cosell asked Ali to elaborate on his feelings about, "what is to be your last fight, for evermore." Cosell asked him if he had debilitated himself by getting his weight down to 218 pounds. Ali declared that he was in top shape and that if he did not defeat a fighter like Spinks, then he did not deserve to call himself the greatest fighter of all time. "I will destroy Spinks," Ali announced to the world as he stared into the TV camera.

The early rounds in the bout were uneventful. The new champ kept pressing Ali with lefts and rights, but the punches were not as devastating as they were in their first fight. Ali jabbed effortlessly at Spinks, scoring points along the way. Ali threw punches at will and Spinks did not seem to know how to respond to the onslaught. Spinks was not nearly as aggressive as he was in his first fight with Ali. Perhaps his nights of partying on Bourbon Street and lack of serious training for the bout had taken a toll on him. In the later rounds, Ali dominated the fight. It appeared that he was simply trying not to get hurt while Spinks kept plodding toward him, hoping to land a haymaker. The challenger's strategy worked and he was declared the unanimous winner. Ali became the first heavyweight boxer to have ever won a championship three times!

After the fight, Ali hinted about retirement. He announced, "I'd be the biggest fool in the world to go out a loser after being a three-time champ. My people need one black man to come out on top. I've got to be the first." Ali confided to Howard Cosell about his proposed plan to retire, saying that he was going to "sit down for six or eight months and think about it." In September 1979, he made his "official" announcement to Cosell that he indeed would retire from boxing. ABC's *Wide World of Sports* held a farewell show honoring Ali. At one point in the show, Ali told Cosell that he was grateful that he was still "intelligent enough to speak," in reference to accusations that Ali's speech had deteriorated noticeably.

Ali had earned tens of millions of dollars during his career as a heavyweight fighter. Unfortunately, by the end of 1979, he had very little money left. Much of it was lost due to terrible business ventures and theft by people he had trusted. Ali had now been retired for almost two years. He continued to gain weight and his once lightning fast reflexes were almost non-existent. He had grown bored of life outside the ring. The cheers from the crowd at ringside and the adulation from all his fans were missing. The lack of attention was more than he could bear. The champ had agreed to fight the World Boxing Association heavyweight champ, John Tate. The fight was scheduled for June. Tate was knocked out, however, by an opponent in late March, and so the bout was cancelled.

Ali decided that Larry Holmes would be the best contender for the heavyweight championship belt. King approached Ali with the chance to make $8 million for fighting Larry Holmes. Ali had never made that kind of money for one fight in his entire career. If Ali won the match, he would have won the title for an unprecedented fourth time, a feat likely never to be matched for all time. Many of Ali's friends warned him not to fight again, but Ali was insistent on earning a big paycheck for about an hour's worth of work. Ali's share would also far outshine the challenger's, which would total $2.3 million. Still, his friends warned him about the dangers of taking on a formidable opponent like Larry Holmes. They reminded Ali about his age, the layoff, the steep decline of his boxing abilities, and physical condition.

Ali did not heed the pleadings of his friends, partly because he lacked respect for Holmes' skills. He looked down at Holmes because, as Ali's former sparring partner, Holmes used to get smacked around quite a bit during their sparring sessions. Furthermore, Holmes never won a gold medal as had Frazier, Foreman, and Spinks. Ali had a pet name for any challenger he went up against. He referred to Holmes as "the Peanut" because, according to the champ, Holmes' head was shaped like a peanut. Ali further explained, "And I'm going to shell him and send him back to Plains, Georgia." Ali was feeling confident and happy. He even briefly sported a mustache and called himself "the Dark Gable."

Ferdie Pacheco, Ali's former fight physician, spoke out publicly that the champ should not fight again under any circumstances. "All the organs that have been abused will have to work harder," he explained. "His heart, lungs, kidneys, liver. Even Muhammad Ali is human and subject to the laws of nature." Howard Cosell asked Ali why he had broken his promise about never returning to the ring. Ali responded by claiming to have actually meant what he said at the time he declared he had finally retired. The real reason he decided to fight again, however, is perhaps the simplest to understand. As Ali put it, "There's nothing like the sound of the crowd when you come down the aisle and they're yelling, 'Ali! Ali!' You'd give your life to hear it."

Before his fight against Larry Holmes, Ali looked impressive. He had lost more than thirty pounds. His body was slimmer than it had been in years. But his reflexes were nowhere near as sharp as they had been. Dundee was not convinced that his fighter was in the kind of shape he appeared to be in. He felt Ali lacked the required strength and reserve that would be needed in a fight against the world heavyweight champion. Dundee discovered that Ali was taking thyroid medication which was prescribed by his personal physician, Herbert Muhammad. The pills helped Ali lose weight, but they also caused him to lose strength. Dr. Ferdi Pacheco stated that the effect of the pills was "like burning the tires off a race car and telling the driver to race without wheels."

The Las Vegas Athletic Commission ordered Ali to be examined by the Mayo Clinic because they were concerned that Ali might become severely injured during the fight, given his advanced age. He was pronounced to be "in excellent general medical health" by the clinic. The detailed report, however, indicated that Ali experienced some difficulty with his speech and coordination. The report gave the green light for an Ali-Holmes bout in Las Vegas. Just before the fight Ali looked weak and dazed. Perhaps without realizing it, he was throwing himself in front of a runaway freight train.

On October 2, 1980, Ali and Holmes met to do battle in a newly constructed arena in Las Vegas. Fans paid an impressive $5,766,125 to watch these two warriors fight it out. Before the start of the fight, Ali "taunted" Holmes inside the ring. He pretended to go after Holmes, but Ali's corner "held" him back so Holmes wouldn't get hurt. Holmes just looked at Ali in amazement. Holmes may have sensed that Ali was beaten before the fight started. Ali's antics seemed forced and almost comical, as if Ali was spoofing himself.

There was to be no fight that night in Las Vegas. Ali, absent from the ring for over two years, simply had nothing that remotely resembled an offense. Ali's once lightning fast jab was now feeble and pathetic. He kept his right arm cocked to ward off blows to his head. From the opening bell, Holmes punished Ali at will. The former champ had nothing left in him. The beating Ali sustained grew worse as the "fight" progressed. He didn't even bother to utilize the old "rope-a-dope" that had worked for him in past battles. He must have realized that Holmes was too good a boxer to fall for that old trick. The crowd was eerily subdued as Ali tried to ward off the unrelenting and ferocious assault Holmes laid on him.

At the end of the ninth round, the referee walked over to Ali's corner and asked if they wanted the fight to be stopped. Ali proudly replied that he wanted to continue to fight Holmes. Dundee warned Ali, however, that if he did not start throwing punches, he would throw in the towel. Howard Cosell, who was covering the fight, sadly remarked, "It is sad to see this." When it appeared Ali was in the midst of being knocked out, Cosell pronounced, "Oh, he's ready to go. This must be stopped. It is a sad way to end."

The tenth round was more of the same, however. Ali never went on the attack. He just leaned on the ropes while Holmes hammered away at him effortlessly. Ali's face was red and swollen from all of Holmes' punches to the head. He suffered a cut under one eye and the other was swollen shut. In all of Ali's previous fights, he had never sustained so much as a small cut or a noticeable bruise. Holmes appeared to be motioning to the judge to end the fight. Even he had his fill of this meaningless carnage.

Immediately after the tenth round, the referee walked over to Ali's corner and asked if the fight should be stopped. Dundee felt someone had to save Ali from Ali, so he finally threw in the towel. Bundini became upset about Dundee's decision and argued with him. He pulled on Dundee's sweater in protest. Dundee yelled at him, shouting "Take your goddamn hands off me. He can't take any more. He's defenseless. Get the hell away from me. I'm boss here, it's over." Ali managed to mumble, "Thank you" to Dundee. Holmes walked over to his old idol and threw his arms around Ali. The victor and the vanquished quietly exchanged words with one another as Ali sat on his stool, thoroughly exhausted, but relieved. Remarkably, the bout ended the way his first fight against Liston did.

Ali, still believing he had one more fight in him, decided to fight Trevor Berbick. He explained to whoever would listen that his bad performance in the Holmes fight was due to taking thyroid medication and not old age. Ali was badly in need of money and so he accepted an offer of $1 million by a relatively unknown promoter named James Cornelius. Maybe Ali actually thought he had a chance to defeat the fighter since Holmes had recently defeated Berbick by a decision.

The proposed contest was shamelessly billed, "The Drama in the Bahamas." The fight took place on December 11, 1981, in Nassau, and Ali ended up the loser in a ten round unanimous decision. After the fight, Ali said, "I couldn't show and now I know....Father Time got me." He rationalized the result by saying to reporters, "But at least I didn't go down. No pictures of me on the floor, no pictures of me falling through the ropes, no broken teeth, no blood.

I'm happy I'm still pretty. I came out all right for an old man." Ali's manager, Herbert Muhammad, and Ali's wife, Veronica, however, assured Ali that he had done much better than what was being reported to the public. Veronica confided to her husband, "Everybody knew you won," while his manager told the ex-champ, "You done good".

"I feel tired," Ali admitted to reporters. "Berbick was too strong, more aggressive. I just had the feeling I could do this thing. My mind said do it. But I know I didn't have it out there. I did good for a thirty-nine year old, did all right considering I'll be forty in five weeks. He tagged me with a couple hard ones and they tired me a bit. There's nothing to worry about, this is not going to bother me. But I think it's too late to come back. I always say that after fights these days, but who knows how I'll feel next week."

Ali retired for good after the Berbick fight. He had won 56 fights, 37 by knockout, and he lost only five contests. Ali had been suffering from slurred speech, tremors, and a decrease in motor skills, so in September 1984, he checked himself into a hospital for treatment. It was discovered that he had Parkinson's syndrome. The syndrome is similar to Parkinson's disease except that it is caused by blows to the head instead of chemical malfunctions in the brain. In 1986 Ali and his wife, Veronica, decided to divorce. Four months later, Ali married Lonnie Williams, a woman he had known for many years. Lonnie helped lift Ali's spirits and closely monitored his health. On July 19, 1996, Ali lit the Olympic flame at the Summer Games in Atlanta, Georgia. In 1998 the United Nations presented him with the Messenger of Peace award. In 2005 Ali partook in the opening ceremony of the Muhammad Ali

Center in his hometown of Louisville, Kentucky.

The Greatest once said these words on his behalf. "I'll tell you how I'd like to be remembered: as a black man who won the heavyweight title and who was humorous and who treated everyone right. As a man who never looked down on those who looked up at him and who helped as many people as he could....As a man who tried to unite his people through the faith of Islam that he found when he listened to the honorable Elijah Muhammad. And if all that's asking too much, then I guess I'd settle for being remembered as only a great boxing champion of his people. And I wouldn't even mind if folks forgot how pretty I was."

Part Three

THE CIVIL RIGHTS ACT OF 1964

CHAPTER 7

THE EMERGENCE OF MARTIN LUTHER KING, JR.

artin Luther King, Jr. was born on January 15, 1929, in Atlanta, Georgia. King was raised by a loving and caring family. He fondly remembered how much his community supported its black citizens. King's father, Martin Luther King, Sr., was a highly respected clergyman who tried to shelter his family from the stark realities of segregation. He was also very strict and had a fiery temper and used corporal punishment on occasion. He was a good provider even during periods when other black families suffered from the harsh effects of poverty. King greatly admired his father, and attributed his father's influence when he decided to join the ministry.

King came from a family of deeply devoted religious leaders. His maternal grandfather, A.D. Williams, was the founder of Atlanta's Ebenezer Baptist Church.

King's father married Alberta Williams, the daughter of A.D. Williams. The couple lived with Alberta's parents for a while. King, Sr. graduated from high school and then he attended Morehouse College. Shortly afterwards he became Ebenezer's assistant pastor. In 1931 King's grandfather died and King Sr. became the new pastor of Ebenezer Baptist Church.

King recalled years later that he was brought up in "a very congenial home situation where love was central and where lovely relationships were ever present." The church community provided King with the opportunity to make new friends and acquaintances. One incident, however, caused young King some painful memories. At age six he had become friends with a white child at Yonge Street Elementary. His friend's father owned a store close to where King's family lived. Later, the two friends attended separate schools and thereafter the two rarely kept in contact. King's childhood friend later confessed to King that the boy's father warned him not to play with young King any more. King asked his parents what motive the father might have had for not allowing his son to associate with him. King later recalled that, "for the first time, I was made aware of the existence of a race problem. I had never been conscious of it before."

King's father was a strict disciplinarian. Howard Baugh, a close neighbor, recalled just how hard King, Sr. could be toward his children. He witnessed one particularly brutal spanking the father gave young Martin. As he was hitting his son, he warned him, "that he was going to make something out of him if he had to beat him to death." King later joked about the whippings he received from his father. "Whippings must not be bad," he recalled, "for I received them until I was fifteen."

As King matured he began to realize the limits of living comfortably while others suffered. He saw for himself how bad off some of his friends were. As he became more acquainted with the outside world, he began to notice how much social injustice existed, not just among blacks, but among whites as well. Indeed, King showed none of the interests his father had in accumulating wealth. King also began to question the church and whether it did enough for the fight against injustice toward the black community.

King experienced first-hand another example of the race problem when he was a teenager. Miss Sarah Bradley, his high school teacher, and King, traveled to a town in Georgia for an oratorical contest. King delivered an exceptionally fine speech on "The Negro and the Constitution." It was all the more impressive because he spoke without using notes. Traveling back to Atlanta, a white bus driver ordered the two to surrender their seats to white passengers who had just boarded the bus. King refused at first, but his teacher persuaded King to surrender his seat. For several hours King was forced to stand as the bus continued on to Atlanta. King recalled years later that, "It was the angriest I have ever been in my life."

The encounter on the bus was the most traumatic experience for young King up to that point. King had witnessed his father's refusal to be treated any different than a white man. He had also seen his father bravely warn white policemen not to refer to him as "boy," but as "Reverend." King suffered the humiliation of being called "nigger" inside a store by a white man. King, still deeply hurt by his friend not being allowed to see him anymore, was determined from that moment on "to hate every white person." His hatred toward whites grew as he got older. His parents advised King not to hate the white man, but, as a Christian, to love him.

At the age of fifteen, King entered Morehouse College. He made new friends quickly and even dated young women he knew from town. Sadly, King realized he was not well prepared to take on the courses offered at Morehouse due to the educational limitations of segregated schools he had attended. One professor discovered that King was an average student who appeared humble and introverted. Another teacher noticed that the young student "had a tendency to be withdrawn and not to participate." As far as being classified as introverted and shy, his fellow classmates had an entirely different take on King.

King, Sr. had always wanted his son to enter into the ministry. King did not relish the idea in the least. Instead, King contemplated studying the law or medicine. He could not see himself preaching sermons to his flock every Sunday. He did poorly in science and so in his sophomore year he chose to major in sociology. He thought these studies would be a good step toward a career in the legal profession. During his second term King began to grow skeptical toward religion. He changed his mind, however, when he took a course on the Bible. King later related that, "I came to see that behind the legends and myths of the Book were many profound truths which one could not escape."

King, despite an average grade point average, was accepted to study at Crozer Theological Seminary in Chester, Pennsylvania. The college was ranked very high in relation to all the seminaries in the country. The student body at Crozer was less than one hundred students. There were about half a dozen blacks attending the college during this period. King studied Marx with great interest. He was influenced by Marx's belief that capitalism bred injustice and that churches did not do enough to help the disenfranchised.

Crozer provided a highly integrated mix of people from many backgrounds. King made friends with several of his classmates. They were made up of blacks, whites, and foreigners. In 1951 King graduated at the top of his class. King was fortunate to meet the Reverend J. Pious Barbour, pastor of a church. The Reverend provided lessons to students on how to become an effective preacher. He strongly believed that style and content were equally important. King began to think about methods that might help eliminate social evil. King was influenced by the lectures of pacifist Abraham Johannes Muste. Muste was often referred to as "The American Gandhi." King also began to read the teachings of Gandhi and became impressed with the concept of nonviolent resistance.

At Crozer, King was exposed to the writings of Reinhold Niebuhr. Niebuhr vigorously disagreed with the notion that Christian love could in itself improve social justice for the masses. The powerful and privileged few constituted the major cause of social injustice. He argued that these few were thoroughly self-absorbed in their attempt to better their station in life at the detriment of society in general. "Disproportion of power in society is the real root of social injustice," he explained. After reading many of Niebuhr's arguments, King became convinced that optimism based on religion alone was ineffective. Perhaps

Christian love mixed with Niebuhr's realism was the proper course to follow in advancing justice.

During the three years King attended Crozer, he encountered little in the way of racial tension. One particular incident, however, disturbed King. He and a white classmate traveled to nearby Philadelphia to dine. According to his classmate, King did not get served for about thirty minutes. Humiliated, King finally demanded that he be served. The service he received angered both King and his friend. Included with the vegetables he ordered was sand. His friend remembered that King was "surprisingly subdued. He did not want to make demands that would make a scene."

In 1952 King graduated with an A average. He won scholarships and was the class valedictorian. With the $1,200 scholarship money that was awarded him, he chose to enroll in Boston University. King attended Boston University with the goal of achieving a doctorate in theology. King began to believe that God was not merely an idea but a "personal spirit who in love creates, sustains, and orders all. By doing God's work one could subjugate natural evil from within and promote the best attributes each of us has."

King was also fortunate to meet a young music student named Coretta Scott. The two continued dating quite often after their first date. King soon discovered that Coretta was born in 1927 in Perry County, Alabama. Coretta's parents, Bernice and Obdadiah, owned a large farm. Coretta attended Lincoln School in Marian, Alabama. Coretta was awarded a scholarship which gave her the opportunity to attend Antioch College in Ohio. After graduation, Coretta was accepted by Boston University.

On June 18, 1953, Martin Luther King, Jr. and Coretta Scott were married by King's father in Marion, Alabama. King and his new bride spent their honeymoon at a friend's house. The couple traveled back to Boston and rented an apartment. King continued his studies with the idea of earning a PhD in theology. Early in 1954, King completed all of his course work and began to work on completing his dissertation.

In 1957 the Southern Christian Leadership Conference was established by Southern black leaders. King became the organization's president. King wanted to empower the black community by forming protest groups throughout the South. King also sought influence and support from the White House. He firmly believed that the president's support regarding equal rights would greatly benefit blacks. While in New York, King met two influential black leaders, Roy Wilkins and Asa Philip Randolph. Wilkins was Executive Director of the NAACP and Randolph was an organizer of the Black Brotherhood of Sleeping Car Porters. Wilkins believed in activism by way of the court system. Randolph, on the other hand, was a proponent of mass action by blacks.

The three leaders planned to hold a Prayer Pilgrimage in Washington, D.C. Organizers sent letters inviting black ministers from the South to join in the prayers for freedom on the steps of the Lincoln Memorial. An estimated thirty-seven thousand pilgrims arrived at the nation's capital. King stood before the monument of Abraham Lincoln and spoke about voting rights. He pronounced, "so long as I do not firmly and irrevocably possess the right to vote, I do not possess myself." He emphasized the power of voting in America. Citizens who voted could choose leaders who would fight for their interests.

After this highly successful rally, Martin Luther King, Jr. became the most respected leader of black people in the country. Later that same year, the civil rights bill passed with the help of Lyndon Baines Johnson, the highly influential Democratic senator from Texas. This civil rights bill was the first legislation of its kind since 1875. Around this time, the Federal Civil Rights Commission was created. Its purpose was to investigate civil rights in America. The Justice Department was authorized to enforce individual civil rights.

An important issue facing the nation was school integration. Citizens were urged by Southern congressmen to resist it. Black parents received death threats when they tried to enroll their children into all white schools. The only two Southern states to allow school integration were Arkansas and Texas. Little Rock's Central High School was the first to admit black students, but on a very limited basis. Seventy-five black students attempted to enroll in the school, but only twenty-five were tentatively approved. The parents of those students were contacted by the school board in order to dissuade them from sending their children to the school. In the end, only nine black students were allowed to attend Central High.

Governor Faubus ordered the Arkansas National Guard to surround Central High so that no black student could enter. He had, in fact, declared that no black student would ever be allowed to enter Central High. He warned that if any black student entered the school, "blood would run in the streets." As Elizabeth Eckford, a fifteen year black girl, arrived near the school, she was threatened with shouts of "Lynch her! Lynch her!" by someone in the crowd. She was spat on the face by an older white woman. Elizabeth hurried away from the mob as they chased her. Grace Larch, a white woman, accompanied her on a public bus and made sure the young girl arrived home safely.

The rest of the black students approached the school and attempted to enter the building. The Guardsmen blocked their way so that they could not safely enter. The Guardsmen, were of course, taking orders from the governor. On the first day none of the nine black students were allowed to enter the school. The story made headline news, not only in America, but throughout the world. Governor Faubus received letters from everywhere complaining about his outrageous behavior toward fellow citizens.

President Eisenhower felt compelled to act and issued an emergency proclamation proclaiming that federal court orders must be adhered to by the state. Not since the reconstruction era had federal troops been sent to the South to restore order and to protect the rights of all citizens. This was truly an historic act. This action also had an unfortunate downside. It partially caused segregationists to band closer together. Their hatred would now intensify even more.

None of the parents of the nine black students wanted their children to ever attend Central High. All nine students, however, wanted to attend. On September 25, 1957, the nine black students entered the school while federal troops closely guarded them. While inside the school they were bullied by white students.

King publicly denounced the president's handling of the racially charged incident. King pronounced, "I fear that future historians will have to record that when America came to its most progressive moment of creative fulfillment in the area of human relations, it was temporarily held back by a chief executive who refused to make a strong positive statement morally condemning segregation." King thought Faubus should get credit for helping to promote integration because, "his irresponsible actions brought the issue to the forefront of the conscience of a nation."

In 1958 King began his Crusade for Citizenship. This was a movement geared toward significantly increasing the number of black voters over the next two years. King pronounced, "Let us make our intentions crystal clear. We want freedom now. We do not want freedom fed to us in teaspoons over another one hundred years." The SCLC's goal was to increase black registration by over a million registered voters by the fall elections in 1960.

In order for a massive, social movement to succeed, King realized that the president needed to get involved. After much prodding by the SCLC, Eisenhower finally agreed to meet with leaders from the SCLC in order to discuss civil rights. On June 23, 1958, the president met with King, Ralph Abernathy, Roy Wilkins, A. Philip Randolph, and Lester B. Granger in the Oval office. The leaders provided the president with a statement indicating action points that should be taken immediately. The president listened to the group's suggestions, but made no commitment concerning any of the nine points reflected in the statement. The press was given a copy of the nine point plan so that the world would realize that Eisenhower was fully aware of their demands.

On September 3, King and Coretta arrived at the Montgomery County courthouse. When they tried to enter the courtroom, the two were blocked by a white guard. King explained that he wanted to speak to his friend's attorney. Guards responded by grabbing King's arms and twisting them behind his back. They pushed him out of the court-house and took him to a nearby police station where he was frisked, kicked, and thrown into a jail cell. King was later released when the police commissioner discovered who he was. He had recognized King from his picture on the front cover of *Time* magazine.

The judge at King's trial sentenced him to fourteen days in jail, or he could pay a fine. Instead of abiding by the court's ruling, King stood up and declared, "I could not in all conscience pay a fine for an act I did not commit and above all for brutal treatment I did not deserve. Something must happen to awaken the dozing conscience of America before it is too late. The time has come when perhaps only the willing and nonviolent acts of suffering by the innocent can arouse the nation." Influenced by the public outrage toward how King was treated, the police commissioner paid the fine and King was released. King spoke at a mass meeting the night of his release. "When one of you goes to jail and suffers brutality, no one knows about it. I am happy that I suffered just a little bit," he went on. "It makes me feel a closer part of you."

King's book, *Stride Toward Freedom: The Montgomery Story*, went on sale in September 1958. The book was about the Montgomery bus boycott. At a book signing event in Blumstein's department store in Harlem, King was approached by a middle-aged black woman. She leaned over the desk King was sitting behind and asked him, "Is this Martin Luther King?" He replied, "Yes" as he was looking down while signing an autograph. Without warning, the woman drove the sharp point of a letter opener into King's chest and began beating him. Onlookers pulled the woman, Mrs. Izola Ware Curry, away from the victim and held her until security officials arrived at the scene,

King tried not to stir after the stabbing because any motion could be fatal. It was decided not to remove the letter opener even during the ambulance ride to the hospital. After the weapon was removed, doctors explained to King that if he had sneezed while the weapon was inside his chest, his aorta would have punctured and he would have drowned in his own blood. As King explained in his autobiography, Aubre Maynard, the chief surgeon, "told me that the razor tip of the instrument had been touching my aorta and that my whole chest had to be opened to extract it." King asked that the woman who had assaulted him not be prosecuted. She was examined by authorities and determined to be mentally ill. Afterwards, she was institutionalized in a state hospital.

King attributed his unusually calm state of mind during the recent murder attempt not to any special powers he may have had, but to the power of God. King wrote in his autobiography that, "Throughout this struggle for racial justice I have constantly asked God to remove all bitterness from my heart and to give me strength and courage to face any disaster that came my way. This constant prayer life and feeling of dependence on God have given me the feeling that I have divine companionship in the struggle. I know no other way to explain it. It is the fact that in the midst of external tension, God can give an inner peace."

In February 1959, King and his wife Coretta visited

India. King spoke to a large crowd of greeters in New Delhi. King pronounced to the greeters, "To other countries I may go as a tourist, but to India I come as a pilgrim. This is because India means to me Mahatma Gandhi, a truly great man of the ages." Jawaharla Nehru, India's prime minister, met with King and Coretta. The two men discussed the struggles in India and America and the need to end racial and religious injustice. Nehru spoke about his attempts to end the caste system in India. The caste was made up of the downtrodden, or as they were commonly referred to as "Untouchables." Nehru also indicated that special privileges were being provided to the Untouchables to help compensate for all the injustices done to this group of people.

When King arrived back in America, he decided to develop a world view that would include the philosophy of Gandhi, Thoreau, and his own Christian beliefs. He pronounced, "This is a daring faith, but I choose to invest my life in it." King recalled later that the trip to India had made a huge impact on him. He had become convinced more than ever that nonviolent resistance was the correct method to use against the forces of prejudice and violence. He noted that India had won her independence by simply utilizing non-violent demonstrations and protests against racial injustice. King wrote that, "the way of acquiescence leads to moral and spiritual suicide. The way of violence leads to bitterness in the survivors and brutality in the destroyers. But the way of nonviolence leads to redemption and the creation of the beloved community."

King first met Senator John Kennedy in June 1960. Kennedy was seeking the Democratic nomination for President and seemed a sure bet to win it. They met in

Kennedy's apartment in New York. They spoke for an hour about racial tension in the country and the need for strong executive leadership. King declared that Eisenhower did not support the cause of racial equality nearly enough. The time for action was now and if the new administration did not advance the cause of the civil rights movement, then this could spell disaster for years to come. Kennedy assured King that his administration would strongly support the cause of racial equality. Kennedy spoke a great deal about his progressive voting record on civil rights. King reminded Kennedy that the senator had voted against a key measure of the 1957 Civil Rights bill. Kennedy responded by indicating that if that same bill was put to a vote today, he would not hesitate to vote for the entire bill.

In September 1960, King met Senator John Kennedy again to discuss civil rights. King did not think that Kennedy was informed enough about racial tension in America at the time. Kennedy seemed more guarded about his opinion on civil rights than he had just a few short months earlier. King refused to be seen with Kennedy at any political function. According to King, the SCLC was strictly a nonpartisan organization. King reminded Kennedy that many blacks were disenchanted with the senator and that "something dramatic must be done to convince the Negroes that you are committed on civil rights." King did not even feel there was much difference between Kennedy's and Nixon's views on civil rights.

Soon after Kennedy was elected President, King tried to meet with him to discuss how best to aggressively advance the cause of the civil rights movement. King did not receive from Kennedy's people any indication that a meeting would take place in the foreseeable future so he issued another formal request. Several of Kennedy's advisors thought that the president should meet immediately with King, but in the end, this suggestion was tossed aside. The president was convinced that meeting with King during his first year in office would be counterproductive because there was no civil rights initiative planned this early in Kennedy's first term. It was decided that Bobby Kennedy would meet with King.

In April 1961, King sat with Attorney General Robert Kennedy to discuss segregation between the races on buses and trains. There were already laws on the books prohibiting forced segregation. King asked Kennedy to ensure that the federal laws be obeyed, so that black citizens would not be assaulted. Shortly afterwards, the president spoke briefly with King in the White House. Kennedy was deeply embroiled in the Bay of Pigs disaster and so civil rights was not even brought up. Moreover, Kennedy did not commit to a formal meeting with King in the near future.

King was approached by James Farmer, a minister and executive director of the Congress of Racial Equality (CORE). Farmer was one of the founders of CORE when it was implemented in 1942 in Chicago. Its goal was to implement nonviolent methods when confronting racial discrimination. Farmer talked to King about his plans to conduct what he called "The Freedom Ride." An interracial group would ride by bus and train throughout Southern states like Virginia, the Carolinas, and farther on into the deep South until ending up in New Orleans on May 17. That day would mark the seventh anniversary of the Brown decision. The project called for the group of travelers to sit in any seat that was available. King agreed to assist Farmer in any way he could. Farmer proudly declared that, "We propose to challenge every form of segregation met by the bus passenger."

Sixteen people were chosen for the journey, among them John Lewis, who had participated in the Nashville sit-ins. The volunteers met in Washington and were instructed on their legal rights and how to conduct themselves if arrested. The group was exposed to simulated acts of violence, like being punched, stomped on, or worse. This role playing was imperative because the group needed to be aware of how dangerous their mission was. Each member of the group was given the opportunity to return home. They all agreed to stay.

The first serious incident occurred when John Lewis tried to enter a restroom designated, "For Whites." He was threatened by two white youths who warned him to use the restroom reserved for blacks only. Lewis informed the pair that the Supreme Court made it constitutional for anyone to use any waiting room in interstate terminals. The two white youths threw him to the floor and kicked him repeatedly.

In May a bus full of freedom riders arrived at the terminal in Anniston, Alabama. When the bus finally rolled out of the terminal, they were followed by a gang of heavily armed whites. Members of the mob shot out the tires, trapping everyone inside. The bus was set on fire. All of the victims inside the bus forced their way out before it exploded. The mob attacked the riders with clubs. When the injured victims arrived at a nearby hospital, no one helped them.

When Reverend Fred Shuttlesworth received word about the incident, he immediately formed a rescue mission to save the freedom riders. Neither the Klan nor the police tried to stop Shuttlesworth and other black leaders from rescuing the victims. They were taken immediately to Birmingham, Alabama. The other bus was stopped by another white gang after it crossed into Alabama. The mob forced their way inside the bus and began beating the riders with chains and blackjacks. When the bus arrived at the Birmingham bus terminal on May 14, there were mobs of whites carrying bats and chains. Police arrived late at the scene. Some riders got off the bus and entered a waiting room reserved for whites only. As they walked toward the lunch counter, the men were pulled away and beaten with pipes. One victim required fifty-three stitches.

The drivers of the Greyhound and Trailways buses refused to take the freedom riders any farther. Deciding to fly into New Orleans, the riders arrived at the airport, but were greeted by more gangs. The police stepped in to protect the riders, and they managed to board a plane headed for New Orleans.

The press provided coverage of the unprovoked attacks toward the freedom riders, including pictures of the injured. The world took notice of the racial injustice in America and the White House took notice also. Realizing the movement should continue, a new Freedom Ride was planned immediately. Warned that they might be murdered, several riders had wills made out.

No incidents occurred until the riders arrived at the Birmingham bus station. The police taped sheets of newspaper over all the bus windows so no one could see out. Eugene "Bull" Connor, Birmingham's police chief, ordered the riders to be placed under arrest. The riders immediately went on a hunger strike. After a couple of days, "Bull" Connor approached the Freedom Riders and explained to them that he was going to have them transported to the college campus in Nashville. The riders responded defiantly that they were headed to New Orleans. Connors ordered his men to transfer the riders to the Alabama-Tennessee border.

Attorney General Robert Kennedy swung into action. He contacted Alabama officials in order to initiate negotiations. Meanwhile, President Kennedy strongly indicated that the protest movement must stop immediately. Kennedy was concerned about the publicity the protests were generating and how it might affect his upcoming summit conference with Nikita Khrushchev, the Soviet Premier. After much negotiating, Robert Kennedy was assured by Alabama Governor John Patterson that the Freedom Riders would be escorted into Montgomery, Alabama by state police.

The trip to Montgomery went on without incident until they reached a bus terminal just outside of Montgomery. Suddenly, the riders realized there was no protection in sight. There was supposed to be local police protecting the riders. Just as the riders stepped off the bus, a large group of white people ran from inside surrounding buildings and attacked the riders with clubs, chains, and other deadly weapons. Three riders were beaten unmercifully and John Seigenhaler, the Justice Department representative, was beaten unconscious.

Robert Kennedy was immediately contacted by an official from the Department of Justice's Civil Rights Division. He was told about the brutal onslaught and that there was no protection at all for the riders. The riders were rescued by Ralph Abernathy and members of the Montgomery Improvement Association and were given protection. Robert Kennedy firmly believed that the state and local police deliberately refused to uphold the law. He ordered federal marshals into the city to protect the riders.

King spoke out against the violence that occurred in Montgomery by declaring that Alabama Governor John Patterson was primarily responsible. According to King, Patterson was "consciously or unconsciously aiding and abetting the forces of violence." King could not see how local governments in the South could be trusted to protect all of its citizens. He pronounced that, "Among the many sobering lessons that we can learn from the events of the past week is that the Deep South will not impose limits upon itself. The limits must be imposed from without. Unless the federal government acts forthrightly in the South to assure every citizen his constitutional rights, we will be plunged into a dark abyss of chaos."

President Kennedy was concerned about how politicians in the South might react to any assistance he might provide the riders. But he was also deeply concerned about the public's reaction to the racial violence against the riders. So Attorney General Kennedy took immediate action. He ordered the Justice Department to stop any effort that would impede interstate travel for any United States citizen. Next, he sent federal marshals into Montgomery and persuaded Alabama's governor to have the National Guard ready.

As soon as King and Abernathy heard about the latest incident, they flew down to Montgomery to meet with the Freedom Riders and discuss what had transpired. A rally was scheduled to be held at the First Baptist Church

Sunday night. Around the time of the rally, hundreds of white people clutching weapons stood near the church. Just as the people inside began singing freedom songs, the mob outside started throwing rocks at the church and breaking windows. They shouted racial slurs and threatened to set fire to the church.

King urged everyone in the church to keep the faith and not be fearful of the angry mob outside. At a moment when it appeared the mob was about to tear down the front door of the church, King bravely pronounced, "Let us join hands together and sing." King called Attorney General Robert Kennedy to inform him that the situation was growing dire by the minute and that something had to be done immediately. According to those present, King was extremely upset that the church and those in it might be burned.

Worried that the people inside the church were going to get seriously hurt, Robert Kennedy contacted Alabama's governor and advised him to send the National Guard to the church as a means of supporting the marshals who were already there. When the governor resisted, saying that the leader in charge of the Guard could not guarantee King's safety, Kennedy exploded. He warned the governor again about sending down the National Guard. The governor complied with the request and declared martial law. The church was sealed off from the mob. The next morning, all the people inside the church were safely escorted to their homes.

Determined more than ever by their efforts, the riders wished for the continuation of the Freedom Ride. Soon, new volunteers joined the cause. King declined to join them because he was needed for fundraising events. The riders headed to a university in Mississippi, where they planned to integrate the facilities there. They were promptly arrested and sentenced to sixty days suspended sentence, including a two hundred dollar fine. All those arrested and sentenced refused to pay the fine. Kennedy called King and promised that he would have the jailed students released. King explained to Kennedy that the conscience of the students would not allow them to pay any fine if they believed they did not do anything unlawful or immoral.

The riders were taken to Parchman, a state prison. The Freedom Riders were thrown into cold, damp cells with dirty mattresses. The riders spent their time together singing freedom songs as a way of fighting the effect of their horrible, oppressive environment. The guards warned the riders to terminate their singing. When the riders refused to stop, the guards promptly removed the mattresses. The guards even used cattle prods on several of the students.

The Freedom Ride movement began bearing fruit when on November 1, 1961, Robert Kennedy authorized the Interstate Commerce Commission to officially negate all segregation involving interstate travel facilities such as restrooms and dining areas. King himself called this, "a remarkable victory." King wrote a letter about what he had learned from the events that had transpired. "Public relations is a very necessary part of any protest of civil disobedience. The main objective is to bring moral pressure to bear upon an unjust system or a particular unjust law. The public at large must be aware of the inequities involved in such a system. The world seldom believes the horror stories of history until they are documented via mass media. Certainly, there would not have been sufficient pressure to warrant a ruling by the ICC had not this situation been so well-publicized."

King decided to confront segregation in one particular area of the South. He chose to focus his attention on Birmingham, Alabama. He called Birmingham the "biggest, toughest, most segregated city in the South." King believed that if the nonviolent movement could achieve victory in Birmingham, success might be achieved in other major cities in the South.

The project was initiated on April 3, 1963. The first phase of the movement involved boycotting and picketing department stores that had segregated restrooms. The boycott immediately affected stores because the city's population was 40% black and so profits dropped significantly. On April 6, a group of about thirty protesters marched peaceably to City Hall. "Bull" Connor ordered the protesters to disband and leave. When they politely refused to end the march, they were arrested and thrown in jail for parading without a permit. Connor's objective was to allow as little publicity as possible regarding the protester's march.

The next day, King's brother, A.D. King, led a march in Birmingham. Supporters of the march stood on sidewalks and cheered as the protesters passed by. "Bull" Connor and his police force were on hand warning the sympathizers to disperse. The police had attack dogs ready if they needed them. The crowd ignored Connor's command. Suddenly, one of the police force's dogs attacked a black man.

Several days later, King discovered that lawyers working for the city were in the process of obtaining an injunction against demonstrations. The problem for King was that if the injunction was approved and it was appealed, it could be tied up in the courts for quite a while. In the meantime, the campaign in Birmingham could be stalled indefinitely.

King responded by making sure the media was present as he was being served with injunction papers by the sheriff. The press reported on the entire event. King followed this up by scheduling time for a press conference the next day. At the conference, King told the attendees, "We cannot in all good conscience obey such an injunction, which is unjust, undemocratic, and unconstitutional misuse of the legal process." King assured the press that the campaign would continue. When asked if he would lead the next march, King responded that he would, stating further, "I am prepared to go to jail and stay as long as necessary."

King was now faced with a new dilemma. The movement's assets could not cover all the bond money needed to allow the jailed demonstrators to be set free. Without the demonstrators, it would be difficult to hold a sizable march. Also, perspective volunteers would think twice about joining the movement if they could not be assured that they would be bailed out of jail.

King wrestled with the problem after listening to his advisors. Instead of taking time to raise funds for the campaign, he decided to lead the next march as he had promised. He reasoned that his credibility would come into question if he did not. He was later to write, "There comes a time in the atmosphere of leadership when a man surrounded by loyal friends and allies has to come face to face with himself."

The marchers started their procession the next day, Good Friday. Leading the marchers were King and Abernathy. As they headed toward City Hall the marchers sang out loud, "Freedom has come to Birmingham!" The marchers were ordered to stop by "Bull" Connor and his police force. Photographers snapped pictures as King

and Abernathy got down on their knees and began pray-
ing. Suddenly, the two men were grabbed and pushed into
a police wagon and rushed to the police station where they
were thrown into separate jail cells.

Solitary confinement was now King's new home.
There was little sunlight and no mattress or bedding. He
was not allowed to place a phone call to anyone, not even
his attorney. Two days later, King was allowed to see two
attorneys. His good friend, Harry Belafonte, provided bail
money which allowed the demonstrators to be set free.

When Coretta King found out about her husband's
incarceration, she called President Kennedy and informed
him of the situation. King's attorneys handed him a copy
of a letter written and signed by several white Birmingham
ministers. In the letter the ministers indicated how wrong
the demonstrators were and how they were influenced by
outsiders. King decided to write his response to the letter.
"I am in Birmingham because injustice is here…just as the
Apostle Paul left his village of Tarsus and carried the gospel of Jesus Christ to the far corners of the Greco-Roman
world, so am I compelled to carry the gospel of freedom
beyond my own home town…Injustice anywhere is a threat
to justice everywhere."

King went on to write, "We have waited for more
than 340 years for our constitutional God-given rights.
The nations of Asia and Africa are moving with jet like
speed toward political independence, but we creep at horse-
and-buggy pace toward gaining a cup of coffee at a lunch
counter. There is no obligation to obey unjust laws that are
out of harmony with the moral law. I had hoped that white
moderates would understand that the present tension in

the South is a necessary phase."

King's "Letter from a Birmingham Jail" was smuggled out of jail, printed and distributed to the public. He was eventually allowed to go free. More determined than ever, he continued the next phase of the campaign. King and his staff now planned to use school children as a means of gaining sympathy from the public. They were taught methods of nonviolent confrontation. King and his advisors were concerned, however, about the possibility that children might be killed.

On May 2, a group of children began marching peaceably from the church to City Hall. Connor ordered his men to arrest the marchers and place them in paddy wagons. An even larger group of children started marching from the church to City Hall. As the marchers approached Connor and the police force, Connor shouted, "Let 'em have it!" High pressured hoses were turned on the children. The force of the water knocked many of them down to the ground. Onlookers began protesting the violence. When bystanders refused to disperse, police dogs were unleashed on them.

Television viewers watched in horror and disbelief. By now, about three thousand nonviolent protesters had been jailed. The city had run out of facilities large enough to handle any more arrested protesters. Business leaders and ministers agreed that something had to be done in the form of a compromise. On May 10, it was announced that an agreement had been reached between both parties. It was called the "Birmingham Truce Agreement." The agreement called for desegregation of restrooms, lunch counters, fitting rooms and other facilities commonly used by the public.

Although the proposed "March on Washington" grabbed most of the attention of those who were following the civil rights movement, more was being done. King was supporting smaller protest movements in the South. For example, in Danville, Virginia, local demonstrators met resistance from local law enforcement. Violence erupted and so the civil rights leaders called on King to come down and support their cause. Unfortunately for the cause, Justice Department officials secretly tried to end the demonstrations.

On June 11, Governor George Wallace stood at the entrance of the University of Alabama in an attempt to prevent blacks from integrating with the white population. President Kennedy addressed the nation that same day, proclaiming, "We are confronted primarily with a moral issue. It is as old as the Scriptures and it is as clear as the American Constitution. The heart of the question is whether all Americans are to be afforded equal rights and equal opportunities, whether we are going to treat our fellow Americans as we want to be treated."

Kennedy's tone became more powerful and emotional. "One hundred years of delay have passed since President Lincoln freed the slaves, yet their heirs, their grandsons are not fully free. They are not freed from the bonds of injustice; they are not yet freed from social and economic oppression. And this nation, for all its hopes and all its boasts, will not be fully free until all its citizens are free."

"We preach freedom around the world, and we mean it. We cherish our freedom here at home. But are we to say to the world – and much more importantly to each other – that this is the land of the free, except for Negroes; that we have no second-class citizens, except for Negroes, that we have no class or caste system, no ghettoes, no master race, except with respect to Negroes? I shall ask the Congress of the United States to act, to make a commitment it has not fully made in this century to the proposition that race has no place in American life or law." Shortly after the president's address to the nation, the bill was passed down to Congress for a vote.

Hours after Kennedy addressed the nation, NAACP field secretary, Medgar Evers, was gunned down in Jackson, Mississippi. Evers was rushed to the hospital, but was pronounced dead on arrival. He became the first civil rights leader to be assassinated. An extremist, Byron de la Beckwith, was indicted for the murder, but he was never convicted. King told a crowd gathered to pay respects to their fallen hero that, "Nothing can bring Medgar back, but the cause can live on."

On June 19, Congress received a new civil rights bill to be enacted into law. A few days later, Kennedy met with King and other black leaders. He was informed that a march on Washington would occur in the near future. Kennedy told the leaders that he thought it was a bad idea because he could not guarantee the marchers safety. Kennedy was finally convinced of the necessity of the demonstration and he agreed to do all he could to support it.

President Kennedy had been concerned for months that the march might turn into a bloody spectacle. By July, however, fear that the march could turn deadly began to subside. In fact, at a press conference on July 17, President Kennedy publicly supported the rally. Kennedy was assured by King and others that there would be no civil disobedience during the march.

King made it clear that the chief purpose of the march was "to arouse the conscience of the nation over the economic plight of the Negro." Other civil rights leaders also wanted to make it clear that another purpose was to try and get the civil rights bill passed in the Congress. The bill was a hard sell for President Kennedy. The march could help get the bill passed by stirring the American people and their representatives into action.

On August 28, 1963, "The March on Washington for Jobs and Freedom" took place. People traveled from all over the country to attend the march and support the passage of the civil rights bill. At the Washington Monument supporters of the movement gathered, including such celebrities as Lena Horne, Joan Baez, Bob Dylan, Marlon Brando, and Sammy Davis Jr. People sang freedom songs, hymns, and ballads.

Kennedy was deeply concerned about the safety of the civil rights supporters. He made certain the National Guard law enforcement personnel stood guard over the gathering. The marchers also had parade marshals designated to protect them. Fortunately, no violence broke out on that momentous day. Around noon the marchers headed toward the Lincoln Memorial. It was here where speakers would address the marchers. The last speaker of the day was Dr. Martin Luther King, Jr.

King recalled months later that he had planned to speak from a prepared speech that day. Suddenly, he became inspired by the joyous response he received from the audience. King was deeply moved. He looked out into the faces of those who had traveled so many miles to come to Washington to be inspired about the movement. "I started out reading the speech," he recalled, "and then, just all of a sudden, – the audience response was wonderful that day – and all of a sudden the thing came to me that I have used – I'd used it many times before, that thing about 'I have a dream' – and I felt that I wanted to use it here. I don't know why, I hadn't thought about it before the speech."

King waited for the applause to subside and then he began to speak. "Five score years ago, a great American, in whose symbolic shadow we stand," King pronounced, "signed the Emancipation Proclamation...But one hundred years later, we must face the tragic fact that the Negro is still not free. They had come to Washington to cash a check. When the architects of our republic wrote the magnificent words of the Constitution and the Declaration of Independence, they were signing a promissory note to which every American was to fall heir. This note was a promise that all men would be guaranteed the unalienable rights of life, liberty, and the pursuit of happiness. America had not kept that promise regarding the Negro," King went on to explain. "The Negro instead had been given a check that had bounced."

"I say to you today, my friends, so even though we face the difficulties of today and tomorrow, I still have a dream. It is a dream deeply rooted in the American dream. I have a dream that one day this nation will rise up and live out the true meaning of its creed – we hold these truths to be self-evident, that all men are created equal."

"I have a dream that one day on the red hills of Georgia, the sons of former slaves and the sons of former slave owners will be able to sit down together at the table of brotherhood. I have a dream that one day, even the state of Mississippi, a state sweltering with the heat of injustice, sweltering with the heat of oppression, will be transformed into an oasis of freedom and justice."

"I have a dream that my four little children will one day live in a nation where they will not be judged by the color of their skin but by the content of their character, I have a dream today."

"I have a dream that one day, down in Alabama, with its vicious racists, with its governor having his lips dripping with the words of interposition and nullification, one day, right there in Alabama, little black boys and black girls will be able to join hands with little white boys and white girls as sisters and brothers. I have a dream today!"

"I have a dream that one day every valley shall be exalted, every hill and every mountain shall be made low, the rough places will be made plain, and the crooked places will be made straight and the glory of the Lord shall be revealed and all the flesh shall see it together."

"This is our hope. This is the faith that I go back to the South with. With this faith we will be able to hew out of the mountain of despair a stone of hope. With this faith we will be able to transform the jangling discords of our nation into a beautiful symphony of brotherhood. With this faith we will be able to work together, to pray together, to struggle together, to go to jail together, to stand up for freedom together, knowing that we will be free one day."

King's passages were met with tremendous applause and cheerful cries by tens of thousands of the faithful. "Let freedom ring from every mountainside in the East, from every peak in the West, even from those in the South. When we allow freedom to ring, when we let it ring from every village and every hamlet, from every state and every city, we will be able to speed up the day when all of God's children-black men and white men, Jews and Gentiles, Protestants and Catholics – will be able to join hands and sing in the words of the old Negro spiritual, 'Free at last, free at last: thank God Almighty, we are free at last."

The conclusion of King's speech was met with deafening applause. King, as well as many others, may not have realized it, but that speech would become one of the most memorable and emotional speeches ever uttered by an American. The speech would forever symbolize the core of the civil rights movement in America. And it would forever be remembered by all Americans who saw and listened to the speech either on television, or heard it on the radio or experienced firsthand in Washington, D.C.

At the end of the speech, Bayard Rustin stood at the podium and asked the audience for their approval of the goals intended to be achieved by the march, such as passage of the Civil Rights bill, desegregation of schools, a $2 minimum wage, a federal jobs program, and federal enforcement to end discriminatory employment practices.

The march gave the civil rights movement a new beginning. The march allowed the movement to gain the kind of momentum it needed in order to push forward civil rights legislation. There were road blocks to be sure, such as the threat of a filibuster in the Senate. It was also essential that economic legislature be passed in order for blacks to gain some kind of foothold in the American dream. As one civil rights leader explained, "the roots of discrimination are economic."

King never came to terms with his popularity. He was

always inundated with requests to speak at one function or another. Andrew Young felt that King had no personal ambition and this fact was instrumental in his extraordinary high integrity and the trust he bestowed on the people who believed deeply in him. As one friend explained, "King ain't after nothing. Most of the time you see him trying to get somewhere to sleep."

A bomb was tossed into Birmingham's Sixteenth Street Baptist Church while a Sunday school session was in progress. Four little black girls were murdered as they were preparing to sing and twenty-one children were injured. A woman voiced her concern by stating, "My God, we're not even safe in church." King proclaimed, "Never in Christian history within a Christian country have Christian churches been on the receiving end of such naked brutality and violence as we are witnessing here in America today. Not since the days of the Christians in the catacombs has God's house, as a symbol, weathered such an attack as the Negro churches."

Violence broke out immediately in Birmingham. The streets were crowded with whites and blacks beating each other. Two black teenagers were shot and killed during the mayhem. King showed his anger by proclaiming that George Wallace should take most of the blame for this incident, "for his defiant, irresponsible words and actions have created the atmosphere for violence and terror on the hands of Governor Wallace." At the eulogy for the murdered little girls, he took the high ground. He called the murdered children, "martyrs of a holy crusade for human dignity. They did not die in vain. God still has a way of wringing good out of evil."

King tried to explain why he was so deeply involved

with the civil rights movement. "We have," he told an audience once, "a responsibility to set out to discover what we are made for, to discover our life's work, to discover what we are called to do. And after we discover that, we should set out to do it with all of our strength and all the power that we can muster."

King was home with his wife Coretta when news came over the television that President Kennedy had been shot in Dallas. Coretta remembered later that her husband said to her, "Oh, I hope that he will live, this is just terrible. I think if he lives, if he pulls through this, it will help him to understand better what we go through." News reports informed the world that President John Kennedy had succumbed to his wounds and was pronounced dead. King sat motionless and speechless for several minutes. Then he said to Coretta, "This is what is going to happen to me. This is such a sick society. I don't think I'm going to live to reach forty."

King told reporters after the assassination, "While the question 'who killed President Kennedy?' is important, the question 'what killed him?' is more important. Our late president was assassinated by a morally inclement climate. It is a climate filled with heavy torrents of false accusation, jostling winds of hatred and raging storms of violence. It is a climate where men cannot disagree without being disagreeable, and where they express their dissent through violence and murder." King fell ill after the assassination. Only with much effort was he able to attend Kennedy's funeral. After the funeral, he pressed on with speaking engagements in New York.

CHAPTER 8

THE CIVIL RIGHTS ACT OF 1964

On January 3, *Time* magazine named King, "Man of the Year" and featured a picture of him on its cover. The only other black to have been honored in this way was the leader of Ethiopia, Heile Selassie. *Time* explained their choice by stating that, "King had been selected as a man-but also as a representative of his people for whom 1963 was perhaps the most important year in their history...Few can explain the extraordinary King mystique. Yet he has an indescribable capacity for empathy that is the touchstone of leadership. By deed and by preachment, he has stirred in his people a Christian forbearance that nourishes hope and smothers injustice."

King continued his frenzied pace of speaking engagements. The tremendous schedule he kept took its toll on his health. He constantly suffered from fatigue and exhaustion.

Finally, his wife stepped in and made her husband check into a hospital for an examination. Not only did the doctors warn that he was significantly overweight, but he was suffering from high blood pressure and a severe virus. He had nothing left in him.

Earlier in the year, King had been nominated to receive the Nobel Peace Prize. Eight members of the Swedish parliament stated that King had been selected because he "had succeeded in keeping his followers in the principle of nonviolence." The competition that year included former President Dwight D Eisenhower, and French President Charles de Gaulle.

While King was resting at St Joseph's Infirmary, his wife informed him that he had just been awarded the 1964 Nobel Peace Prize. King and his wife were not totally surprised by the announcement because he was considered a strong favorite a week earlier. King, at thirty-five, would become the youngest recipient of the prestigious prize since its inception in 1895. Coretta King suggested that a portion of the $54,000 prize money should go toward their children's college education. King thought otherwise. He strongly believed that the money was not an award for him personally, but for the civil rights movement.

King said, "This is an extremely moving moment in my life." Many leaders from across the world congratulated King for winning this prestigious award. "Bull" Connor, on the other hand, failed to agree. "They're scraping the bottom of the barrel when they picked him," he complained. J. Edgar Hoover was equally irritated. "He was the last person in the world who should ever have received it." Hoover blasted King further by calling him the "most notorious liar in the country."

Barry Goldwater won the Republication nomination for President in 1964. Goldwater was seen by many as an extremist. It may have been a sign that the party was moving away from moderate Republicanism. The nominee hated the Civil Rights Bill of 1964 and even called it socialistic. In fact, he was one of only a handful of Republicans who voted against the bill when it reached the Senate. King was worried that the country was headed in the wrong direction and that something needed to be done quickly.

King's next project was a "get out the vote" campaign. The tour would cover fifteen cities in the North before the 1964 elections. King first visited Chicago, Cleveland and Los Angeles, and asked black church leaders to encourage their members to vote on November 3. He told audiences that he believed Lyndon Johnson's opponent, Barry Goldwater, "is a threat to freedom." He warned that if Goldwater won the presidential election, it would cause "violence and riots...on a scale we have never seen before." The day before the election, he was forced to make a public appearance in response to what appeared to be a dirty trick. Reportedly, anonymous leaflets had been circulating in several large cities urging voters to send in write-in votes for King. Apparently, this was an attempt to take votes away from Johnson.

Goldwater was soundly defeated by Johnson in November. The nation was still grieving over its fallen leader. Johnson took full advantage of the country's conciliatory mood and placed his full weight and influence behind the bill. It helped that Johnson was from the South and that he was a genius at getting things done. Also helpful was the fact that right wingers were battling each other over the bill. Right wing moderates and extremists vehemently disagreed about civil rights.

King and several other black leaders were invited to the White House to witness the signing of the Civil Rights Bill of 1964. It was signed into law on July 2. Johnson spoke to the nation that day and proclaimed, "The new law does not give special treatment to any citizen. The new law does, however, say that those who are equal before God shall now be equal in the polling booths, in the classrooms, in the factories, and in hotels, restaurants, movie theaters, and other places that provide service to the public." King and other civil rights leaders called the bill an act of "good faith," but for too many black Americans, freedom was being provided much too slowly.

The Civil Rights Bill of 1964 was the most comprehensive bill of its kind in the history of our nation. It was now against the law to deprive all citizens of the right to use public accommodations. Equal employment opportunities would now be enforced by a federal commission. Everett Dirksen, a moderate Republican, was asked why he had supported the bill. He replied by quoting Victor Hugo, the famous French novelist. "No army can withstand the strength of an idea whose time has come." But Southerners were quick to inform the White House that Johnson would be "damned sorry" come election time in November. Despite the threat and possible damage to the Democratic ticket, Johnson and Humphrey went on to defeat Barry Goldwater in a crushing landslide.

In December 1964, King met with President Johnson to discuss the voting rights bill. Johnson advised King that

he could never get the bill through Congress at the present time due to the Southern bloc. He explained that there
were many more bills related to his Great Society program
that took precedence over the voting rights bill. Johnson
claimed these other bills would help the Negroes as much
as any voting rights act. King argued that political reform
was as essential as any Great Society program. Johnson
feared that certain members of Congress from the South
might block Johnson's proposed program if the voting
rights bill ever came up for a vote.

1965 would be the year in which King would press
for the rights of all citizens to be able to vote in America.
"I have been to the mountaintop," he would say at church
meetings. "I really wish I could stay on the mountain, but I
must go back to the valley." The valley for King meant going
back down to Mississippi and Alabama where the sweltering heat of injustice lay. King stopped in Washington, D.C.
to urge President Johnson to continue the fight for the passage of the voting rights bill. Johnson warned King that it
would not be easy to pass a voting rights bill so soon after
the passage of the landmark civil rights bill.

King compared Selma, Alabama in 1965, to the way
Birmingham was in 1963. According to King, Sheriff Jim
Clark initiated "Gestapo-like control of county and local
government. The gun, the club, and the cattle prod produced the fear that was the main barrier to voting- a barrier
erected by 345 years exposure to the psychology and brutality of slavery and legal segregation. It was a fear rooted
in feelings of inferiority." King and other black leaders
decided to campaign in Selma, Alabama, for the purpose
of registering as many voters as possible. King believed that

the ballot was the ultimate weapon against oppression and bigotry. "If you give us the ballot," he explained, "we will elect men of good will to the legislatures." Selma seemed like a good choice to hold the initial campaign because although there were 15,000 blacks living there, only 350 of them were registered.

The sheriff in Selma did not allow more than a few black people to meet as a group without arresting them. Sheriff Jim Clark went so far as to send his deputies into places of worship to see if church services were indeed being held or if civil rights issues were being discussed. Andrew Young compared Selma to South Africa in that both places did not allow public meetings and only a few people were allowed to walk down a street at any one time. King made his intentions known regarding the strategy he would implement in Selma. Speaking to hundreds of blacks at Brown's Chapel Methodist Church, he said, "We must be willing to go to jail by the thousands. We are not asking, we are demanding the ballot."

Initially the demonstrations in Selma were peaceful. Having learned the lessons of Montgomery and Birmingham, the white citizens, as directed by Mayor Joe Smitherman, basically paid no attention to the demonstrators. Blacks stood for hours at the courthouse waiting patiently to be registered to vote. They were told to come back another day because the office was closed. When applications were completed, they were unceremoniously thrown into the round file. Blacks were made to jump through hoops by being forced to locate two registered voters that could vouch for them. Since it was next to impossible to locate blacks who were allowed to be registered to vote, perspective voters were shut out of the process.

On February 2, King decided to lead protesters to the courthouse in order to demand quicker voter registration for blacks. King reminded his followers at a meeting that violence would play no part in the demonstrations. "I do come to tell you tonight that violence may win a temporary victory, but it cannot win permanent peace." King explained that out of all the Negro citizens living in Selma and adjoining counties, only fifty-seven people had been allowed access to the registrar's office. To make matters worse, none had received word of a successful registration. Many blacks had been jailed just for attempting to register. "Now we must call a halt to these injustices," he demanded.

Before marching to the courthouse, King advised his followers about the importance of not providing the law with an excuse to break up the demonstration. He warned them that, "we're all going to walk tighter today. We're going to walk together because we're not parading. We will obey every traffic law, every traffic signal we will stop for. We will not stand in the way of egress and ingress. We will not do anything to block the orderly process of the movement in the community."

The demonstrators had only walked three blocks before they were stopped by Captain Baker. He warned them that, "this is a deliberate attempt to violate this city's parade ordinance. You will have to break up into small groups." King explained to Baker that they were not disobeying any law. All the protesters were doing was exercising their constitutional right to walk toward the courthouse in an orderly fashion. Baker immediately had all the protesters arrested for marching without a proper permit to parade.

The recent winner of the Nobel Peace Prize now sat in jail, and the whole world took notice. King wrote later, "When the King of Norway participated in awarding me the Nobel Peace Prize, he surely did not think that in less than sixty days I would be in jail. By jailing hundreds of Negroes, the city of Selma, Alabama, had revealed the persisting ugliness of segregation to the nation and the world." Although most of the protesters were released, King and Abernathy refused to allow themselves to be set free because of the sensational publicity they received. The two remained in jail for the next several days. King pointed out that there were more Negroes in jail than there were on the voting rolls.

While King remained in jail, Malcolm X arrived in Selma in response to an invitation by SNCC. Malcolm X spoke at Brown's Chapel and advised the audience that it was necessary for blacks to answer violence with violence. He confided privately to Coretta King that his stance would help King's non-violence program because whites would favor King's philosophy over Malcolm X's. Malcolm X was assassinated two weeks later at the Audubon Ballroom in New York City.

On August 6, 1965, President Johnson signed the new Voting Rights Act. The Attorney General of the United States could now send federal registers into areas where discrimination had been evident. It also allowed the federal government to abolish prerequisites to voting such as literacy tests, and poll taxes. King viewed the Voting Rights Act of 1965 as "one of the most monumental laws in the history of American freedom. We had a federal law which could be used, and use it we would. Where it fell short, we had our tradition of struggle and the method of nonviolent direct action, and these too we would use."

The success of the voting rights bill became obvious after just a few short months. More than 300,000 blacks had become registered voters for the first time. Most of the Southern states now had more than 50 percent of blacks registered to vote. King appreciated the effect of the new law on newly registered black voters, but he advised Johnson to implement more effective enforcement of the law.

King began to look beyond the civil rights movement during the summer of 1966. Vietnam was probably the biggest concern to most Americans. The war had polarized most of the country. No longer was the movement and voting rights the most important moral issue of the day. King could no longer stay silent on his opinion of the war. He held a fervent anti-war position and was roundly criticized by the White House and other civil rights leaders for taking such a hardline stance. "I am not going to sit by and see the war escalate without saying something about it," he advised the nation. "It is worthless to talk about integrating if there is no world to integrate in," he reasoned. King believed that racial hatred, poverty, and the war were all "inextricably bound together."

Now that the Voting Rights Act had passed, King turned his attention to the war on poverty. King pointed out to the nation that blacks suffered much more than whites when it came to poverty, the Vietnam War, infant mortality, and unemployment. There were twice as many blacks as whites suffering from the effects of poverty, unemployment, and death in combat. King announced his decision to reach out to President Johnson, and the leaders of the

Soviet Union, China, North and South Vietnam, and others in an effort to "make an urgent plea for all sides to bring their grievances to the conference table." King explained to reporters why he publicly opposed the war. "I held back until it got to the point that I felt I had to speak out." He soon realized the implications of his stance against the war when many black citizens came forward and vigorously criticized him.

The Black Power movement was becoming more and more popular, particularly among younger blacks. The movement wanted change now, not later. The movement claimed that integration was an idea that would never work and that blacks must band together and create their own power structure. Pooling together economic resources and creating political strength among blacks was more realistic than asking for justice from the white community. Racial pride was essential. King sympathized with the movement to a certain degree, but he did not agree with its overall strategy. He believed that blacks should not try to isolate themselves from the white community, but should work with it. The road would be tougher, but he believed success would be achieved and the results would be permanent.

King came to the conclusion that the civil rights movement had been focused primarily on segregation in the South for too long. It was now time to shift the civil rights movement's resources to the North. He also wanted to create a strategy that would attack poverty head on. He chose Chicago because he believed if the movement could achieve success there the movement could achieve success anywhere in the country. He strongly believed that non-violent demonstrations would help blacks express their frustrations and could lead to real progress in the fight for equal opportunity for jobs and better housing.

He discovered, however, that the same rhetoric he used in the South did not have the same effect with blacks in Chicago. The northern blacks were tired of promises of equality and King's stirring speeches did little to inspire confidence in the American dream. Blacks in Chicago had turned cynical because, according to them, nothing of any significance had ever been accomplished for them. The turnout for King's demonstrations was much lower than expected and the marchers were not as enthusiastic as the followers in the South. When rioting broke out, King and other black leaders proved to be ineffective in stopping them. King's ambition was to prevent more riots from happening by resolving the issues that caused rioting in the black communities. King and the other leaders would focus their attention on school desegregation, housing, and jobs.

For many in the movement, one of the impediments to progress was the man in charge of Chicago, Mayor Richard Daley. Daley publicly supported the movement instead of denouncing it. Daley insisted that great strides were being made, but King was not convinced. He feared that Daley would merely claim progress was being made while in reality, nothing significant was being accomplished regarding civil rights in Chicago.

In July rioting broke out between the police and some young blacks. Some black youths had turned on a fire hydrant because of the intense heat. Police arrived at the scene and turned off the hydrant. One of the black youths and a policeman began fighting. Gangs of black teenagers began throwing rocks at police cars and looting businesses.

After several days of violence, the rioting ended. Two blacks had been killed and several hundred people were injured.

King gave a speech soon after the incident. He told his audience, "There are thousands of Negro boys and girls packed in this area. And they turned on the fire hydrant the other night because it was hot. They don't have air-conditioned houses. So often it's seven or eight people living in two rooms. They don't have the comforts and conveniences of life. So they were trying to get a little water. They didn't have a swimming pool, so they had to turn on the fire hydrant, and they were forced to turn it off. Certainly a little water wouldn't have hurt anything in that situation.....I think it's our job to work as passionately to get rid of these conditions as it is to get rid of the violence."

King and his followers marched in predominately white neighborhoods. Bricks and other lethal objects were hurled at them by angry whites. During one of their marches, the movement was confronted by the American Nazi Party headed by George Lincoln Rockwell. In a negative way King was impressed with the amount of hatred the Chicago whites had shown. The rest of the nation, he believed, could take a lesson in hate from whites living in Chicago. "I've been in many demonstrations all across the South, but I can say that I have never seen, even in Mississippi and Alabama, mobs as hostile and as hate-filled as I've seen in Chicago."

Surprisingly, several conservative blacks criticized King's peaceful demonstrations. They accused King and his followers of creating ill will between the white and black communities and they demanded that the demonstrations be canceled immediately. One black leader complained, claiming that the demonstrations had, "set back peaceful integration in these neighborhoods many years." King responded to his critics forcefully. "You want us to stop marching, make justice a reality," he replied. "I don't mind saying to Chicago-or to anybody-I'm tired of marching. I'm tired of marching for something that should have been mine at birth. If you want a moratorium on demonstrations, put a moratorium on injustice.....I don't march because I like it. I march because I must, and because I'm a man, and because I'm a child of God."

King was totally taken aback by the harsh response by whites in Chicago. He told Mayor Daley, "Our humble marches have revealed a cancer." After a march through Gage Park, whites responded harshly to the protester's presence. King stated that he had "never seen anything so hostile and hateful." His faith in the idea that whites and blacks could live and work together was being severely tested. He had hoped that he could awaken the conscience of "the great decent majority." On the other hand, King realized that without non-violent demonstrations, America could never know how deep racism really was. Before there could be a cure, the nation needed to know how bad the malady of prejudice and injustice, or as he put it, the "cancer" was.

Black organizers decided that because no significant progress was being made, a march on Cicero was next. Cicero was targeted mainly because it was all-white and had become symbolic of discrimination in the North. In 1951 a bloody riot broke out when a black family attempted to live there. As recently as 1966, two blacks had gone there looking for jobs. One of the job seekers was beaten to death. King was asked not to march in Cicero, but King refused to give in. Rather than face a bloody conflict in Cicero, black leaders met with Mayor Daley and other city officials and hammered out a housing agreement. Black militants thought that the agreement did not go far enough. King thought it was a good start. It was decided that the march would go on.

On September 4, a black leader and a couple hundred of their followers marched on Cicero. They were protected by 2,000 National Guardsmen, but that was not enough to deter whites from harming the demonstrators. They were attacked so unmercifully by rock throwing whites, they had to abandon their demonstration.

King went back to Atlanta. His cause in Chicago was heavily criticized as having been a failure. King felt depressed after his Chicago campaign of non-violence. Especially after this experience, black militants were becoming even more vocal. Nonviolence had its day and now it was time to try a more aggressive approach. "Black Power" was becoming the new battle cry. The Vietnam War was by now the number one issue in America. King's remarks against the war did not go unnoticed by the Johnson administration. John P. Roche, a top advisor to the president, told Johnson that one of King's antiwar speeches, "indicates that King-in desperate search of a constituency-had thrown in with the commies. The civil rights movement is shot-disorganized and broke. King had chosen to oppose the war so that he always would have a crowd to applaud." *The Washington Post* claimed that King's assertions about the war included, "sheer inventions of unsupported fantasy." *Life* magazine declared that, "he goes beyond his personal right to dissent when he connects progress in civil rights here with a proposal that amounts to abject surrender in Vietnam."

By the end of 1967, King had become convinced that a significant redistribution of wealth needed to be established in order for social justice to have a chance of becoming a reality. According to King, the white business establishment was not moved by pleas for morality. He realized that action and not idealistic speeches was the only means by which true change could occur. Businesses only reacted favorably to the civil rights movement when boycotts and protests negatively affected profits. King advised his advisors that, "We must recognize that we can't solve our problem now until there is a radical redistribution of economic and political power. America is deeply racist and its democracy is flawed both economically and socially. The black revolution is much more than a struggle for the rights of Negroes. It is forcing America to face all its interrelated flaws-racism, poverty, militarism, and materialism."

In early 1968, King was busy organizing his Poor People's Campaign. He had planned in late April to walk with thousands of the nation's destitute to voice their concerns in Washington, D.C. This event would include all people, no matter their religion or nationality. It would truly be a cross-section of this nation's needy. Something, however, would change King's planned march scheduled for April 22.

King became more and more outspoken against the draft. Anti-war activists like Dr. Spock and many others were being indicted by Johnson's Justice Department for their stance on the war. He publicly and vigorously denounced all charges against the activists. He agreed openly with Eugene McCarthy's anti-war campaign and he chastised Robert Kennedy for not taking a stronger stand against the war in Vietnam. He supported antiwar protesters who were brave enough to declare the war unjust and inhumane.

On January 31, sanitation workers in Memphis showed up for work, but were sent home due to rain. Later in the week it was discovered that black employees were only paid for two hours of work for the day they were sent home, but white workers were paid for the full day. The black union immediately sent a letter to Mayor Henry Loeb with a list of demands. Loeb promptly ignored those demands. The black workers marched to City Hall to protest against unfair treatment. Representatives met with Mayor Loeb to express their grievances. Loeb refused to talk any further with the strikers and complained publicly that they were, "flaunting the law." Black leaders responded by calling for a strike on March 28. King agreed to head the march.

A black-power militant group calling themselves the Invaders decided to join the peaceful, non-violent demonstrators in Memphis. King was alarmed by their presence. He was assured that the militants would in no way negatively influence the peaceful march. Shortly after the march began, trouble ensued. The militants had begun dropping out of the procession and committing violent acts. King told the organizers to call off their march.

The peaceful protesters obeyed King's order, but the militants continued looting. Fearing that King and Coretta's lives were in danger, his aides convinced King to get out of harm's way immediately. In the aftermath of the curtailed march, a black teenager was shot and killed by police. Dozens of others were beaten with clubs, and 300 were arrested. The looting and arson got so out of hand that the governor of Tennessee sent thousands of National

Guardsmen to Memphis. King was disheartened by the march's failure. He blamed himself even though most of the planning had been in the hands of other black leaders. He was also unaware that so many black militants were stationed in Memphis.

King and his aides needed to decide what their next move would be. They could either stay in Memphis and continue fighting for the sanitation workers or continue with the Poor People's March in Washington, D.C. They concluded that they would continue with their march in Washington, but first they would march a second time in Memphis on April 8. King was fearful that another march in Memphis might end with violence. King and his advisors met with the Invaders to discuss the radical organization's plans for cultural programs designed to benefit the black community. King responded favorably to their goals and indicated that he would try to obtain financial support for their programs.

Heavy rains fell on Memphis on the night of April 3. There were even warnings of possible tornadoes. Andrew Young noticed King looked despondent. "I don't know when I've seen him as discouraged and depressed," Young related. Ralph Abernathy observed that King's weary demeanor was "grim and businesslike." King was deeply upset about how badly the Memphis march went and he was extremely anxious about the upcoming march in Memphis. Fear, however, should not deter their efforts to move forward with the planned events. King proclaimed to his advisors that, "I'd rather be dead than afraid. You've got to get over being afraid of death," he went on to explain.

A rally at the Mason Temple was planned for that

evening and Ralph Abernathy was the scheduled main speaker. This break would allow King to enjoy a much needed rest. Shortly after Abernathy arrived at the Mason Temple, he became aware that the crowd wanted to hear King speak, not Abernathy. Abernathy immediately contacted King, who was resting at the Lorraine Hotel, and pleaded with him to speak at the rally. King agreed to speak at the church. After an introduction by Abernathy, King stood up and looked out at the audience. He told them that the second march would go on even if it meant ignoring a federal court injunction.

King talked about how he had to deal with crisis early in his life. He quietly told the audience that when he arrived in Memphis for the rally and the march, he had heard about threats against his life. He told the audience that this was nothing new to him. For a long time he lived in the shadow of death as if it was following him. He had always confided to his closest associates that he believed his days were numbered. And now he felt it was time to confide to the public what he had known and feared for some time now.

"Like anybody, I would like to live a long life. Longevity has its place. But I'm not concerned about that now. I just want to do God's will. And He's allowed me to go up to the mountain. And I've looked over, and I've seen the promised land. I may not get there with you, but I want you to know tonight that we as a people will get to the promised land. So I'm happy tonight. I'm not worried about anything. I'm not fearing any man. Mine eyes have seen the glory of the coming of the Lord."

After the speech King felt exuberant, almost cheerful. He had dinner at a close friend's house and then he arrived at the Lorraine Hotel early the next day. King stayed up late talking with his brother and friends until 6:30 a.m. He woke up at noon and spent the day discussing strategy. Among the many topics they talked about was how they should best deal with the Invaders. King also spoke to the group about death. At one point, he turned to Ralph Abernathy and said, "Ralph, don't ever employ anybody on the staff of SCLC that used violence to reach our goals, even on a temporary basis." Abernathy wondered why King had told him this. Those words to Abernathy would be his last words to a friend he had known for fifteen years.

King stepped outside onto the balcony right outside his room. He spoke with aides who were just below him in the parking lot. He chatted with Jesse Jackson, who was standing next to him. Jackson introduced King to a musician, Ben Branch, who happened to be the leader of the Breadbasket Band. King asked Branch if he could play, "Take My Hand, Precious Lord" at the rally scheduled for that evening.

Suddenly, the group of men heard a loud sound, perhaps a firecracker. King was hit in the neck by a gunman's bullet. He flew backwards and dropped to the concrete floor of the balcony. Blood gushed from a huge hole in his neck. Martin Luther King, Jr., proponent of nonviolence and winner of the Nobel Peace Prize, was dead.

The next day President Johnson ordered all federal flags to be flown at half-mast. He proclaimed the following Sunday to be a day of national mourning. Money donated by whites to SCLC broke all records. On April 5, in Memphis, hundreds of clergymen, both black and white citizens, somberly marched in unison to City Hall in Memphis in order to show their support to the sanitation workers. A week and a half later the black sanitation workers received the pay they rightfully deserved.

Riots broke out shortly after King's funeral.. Throughout the nation dozens of cities fell victim to the anger and disgust of many blacks. They looted and burned stores and battled the police. It took several days before order was restored. Forty six people had been killed and almost forty thousand had been injured during the riots. President Johnson later recalled how sick he felt as he saw black smoke "from burning buildings fill the sky over Washington and as I watched armed troops patrolling the streets for the first time since the Civil War."

Black educator, Charles Willie, a former Morehouse classmate of Martin Luther King, Jr. wrote that, "By idolizing those whom we honor, we do a disservice both to them and to ourselves. By exalting the accomplishments of Martin Luther King, Jr. into a legendary tale that is annually told, we fail to recognize his humanity-his personal and public struggles-that are similar to yours and mine. By idolizing those whom we honor, we fail to realize that we could go and do likewise." Christine Farris, the sister of Martin Luther King, Jr. emphasized that, "My brother was no saint, but an average and ordinary man."

The danger many of King's friends and acquaintances feared was that history would view him as the man who almost single-handedly improved the lives of blacks in America. Many others, they argue, suffered alongside King during the height of the civil rights movement in the fifties and sixties. Civil rights activist Diane Nash declared, "The movement made Martin rather than Martin making the movement. If people think that it was Martin Luther

King's movement, then today they-young people-are more likely to say, 'gosh, I wish we had a Martin Luther King here today to lead us. If people knew how that movement started, then the question they would ask themselves is, 'What can I do?' ''

Part Four

THE TONKIN GULF RESOLUTION

CHAPTER 9

THE SEEDS OF WAR

D URING WORLD WAR II, Vietnam was invaded and eventually taken over by Japan. Curiously, Japan allowed the French to continue occupying Vietnam as the war raged on. Ho Chi Minh formed the Viet Minh for the sole purpose of fighting French colonialism and the Japanese occupation. Japan withdrew in 1945, but the French educated Emperor Boa Deo stayed in order to control an independent Vietnam. Ho Chi Minh's army seized control of the city of Hanoi and shortly afterwards declared himself President. On September 2, 1945, he proudly declared Vietnam independent from French rule.

Before he died, President Roosevelt made it clear that he was in favor of decolonization of Indochina. Roosevelt, however, felt that the "brown people in the East" were not yet capable of governing for themselves. He believed it would take these people decades before they were in a position to run their own nation. He thought that a kind of trusteeship should be set up so that, after much guidance, the nations in the East could become totally independent. He turned to several nations who had been victorious in World War II. China and Great Britain decided they were not interested in Roosevelt's plan. France, on the other hand, was very receptive to the idea of neo-colonization, and gratefully accepted Roosevelt's offer. France's leader, Charles de Gaulle, was only too willing to possess the natural resources of Indochina. Roosevelt gave in to de Gaulle's ambitions in Indochina as long as the French leader promised independence to his colonies.

For the next several years after the end of World War II, Indochina was looked upon as an important strategic location. Cold War fears intensified during this period. There was a great deal of apprehension about the region ultimately falling into the hands of the Communists. The loss of Indochina to the Communists was not an option in the eyes of the free world. France was therefore given a free hand as far as their interests in colonization were concerned. Independence would have to wait until the threat of a Communist takeover was no longer a possibility.

Harry Truman knew next to nothing about the region and its people's desire for independence. He had no special reason to support the people's fight for self-government. Ho Chi Minh, leader of the anti-Japanese resistance, had pleaded with Washington to help support Vietnam's craving for independence. His pleadings essentially fell on deaf ears because the State Department thought it was much more important to be conciliatory with France, one of the chief allies in the war. It was also believed by the State Department that if Ho Chi Minh's rebels took over the region, instability in the region would most likely occur. Moreover, Ho Chi Minh's letters to Truman reminding him of the wartime promise of independence through self-government were buried deep inside a black hole. By 1946 France had imposed its will on Indochina with the idea of complete control without regard to independence in the future. In response to this usurpation of power, the Viet Minh declared that a state of war existed between France and the Vietnamese-led Viet Minh.

In March 1947, Truman addressed the nation with a major speech. He warned his fellow citizens that Communist aggression against free people anywhere in the world needed to be stopped. He warned that the Soviet Union in particular posed a great threat to free nations everywhere. He was convinced that the Soviet Union was interested in total world domination. Truman wanted France to receive support from America because it acted as an anti-Communist bloc in Western Europe and in Indochina.

When Dwight Eisenhower came into office as the new president in 1953, he basically expressed the same line of thinking as Truman. Indochina was important to America's interests and it must be defended at all costs. He warned that the world must not waver in the face of naked aggression. Eisenhower explained that, "we failed to halt Hirohito, Mussolini, and Hitler by not acting in unity and in time, that marked the beginning of many years of stark tragedy and desperate peril." Eisenhower famously coined an expression which would be repeated for many years to come in relation to Vietnam, namely "the falling domino principle."

Eisenhower agreed to continue subsidizing the cost of the war between France and the North Vietnamese. Between 1952 and 1954, it cost American taxpayers $2.6 billion to help support France's military effort. It was felt by many in the administration that supporting France in the war effort was preferable to the United States getting directly involved, particularly while fighting the North Koreans. The French people grew disgusted with the war as French casualties mounted. The French government began to seriously consider sitting down with the enemy and negotiating a peace settlement. Before that could happen, however, the French army needed a major victory which would allow them to negotiate from strength.

The real end to the war between the French and the Vietnamese occurred in March 1954 at a French garrison in Dienbienphu. The French made the mistake of luring the enemy toward the garrison so that they could fight a conventional battle instead of one fought deep in the jungle. General Henri Navarre believed that the Viet Minh would not be able to engage his forces without running out of supplies. So in effect, Navarre hoped Vo Nguyen Giap and his army would attack his troops. The French did not expect the Viet Minh to surround the garrison and hold it hostage. Eisenhower, fearing another Korea, refused to send American combat troops in order to rescue the French soldiers. Vice President Nixon, on the other hand, supported the idea of using air and naval bombardments against the Viet Minh. In the end, Eisenhower took no action against the enemy.

Two months later on May 7, 1954, the French garrison surrendered at Dienbienphu. The administration tried in vain to get the French to continue their effort in Indochina.

Both the French and the English refused to join the United States in defeating the Viet Minh. Meanwhile, an international conference sponsored by the British and the Soviets was held in Geneva for the purpose of ending the conflict. The European nations had neither the desire nor the resources to fight an enemy the French could not defeat.

On July 20, treaty negotiations at Geneva, Switzerland, divided Vietnam along the 17th parallel. It was decided that both sides of the seventeenth parallel would allow only a very limited military presence. Ho Chi Minh wanted control of the North and Bao wanted control of the South. In 1956 nationwide elections were to be held for reunification. But in 1955, Ngo Dinh Diem, a staunch anti-Communist, replaced Bao to become President of the Government of the Republic of Vietnam.

Months before the French surrendered to the Viet Minh, Eisenhower had been planning a new method of stopping Communist aggression in Indochina. He helped form a coalition of nations comprised of the United States, France, Britain, New Zealand, Thailand, Australia, Pakistan, and the Philippines. The organization was called the Southeast Asia Treaty Organization, or SEATO. The organization proved to be ineffective because the allies were not convinced that the spread of Communism was a real threat in Indochina. Undeterred, Eisenhower chose another option that would hopefully end Communist aggression in the region.

Eisenhower chose Ngo Dinh Diem to become the leader of South Vietnam. Diem came from an influential Catholic family and was a staunch anti-Communist. He had gone into exile in 1950 because he could not get

along politically with the French or the Viet Minh. After
Vietnam was partitioned in 1954, Diem became premier
of South Vietnam with Eisenhower's complete support.
In October the administration promised Diem military
training, equipment, and economic support. By 1961 the
Eisenhower administration had spent a staggering $7 bil-
lion in defense spending.

By the end of 1960, Diem had managed to keep
American combat troops out of the conflict with the Viet
Minh. It appeared Diem was the solution to the problem of
halting any Communist advance into South Vietnam. The
American Embassy perceived Diem, however, as a problem. He was not popular among most of the civilian population because of his cold persona and his pro-Catholic
beliefs, which happened to be a minority religion in that
part of the world. He did not use American funding very
effectively and his army was not properly trained to fight
an aggressive and determined enemy.

In December 1960, the National Liberation Front,
or NLF, was formed by Diem's enemies in the North. The
NLF's purpose was to organize resistance to the regime. The
administration in Washington viewed this organization as
a puppet to Hanoi. Enemies of this organization referred
to them as the Vietcong, which was short for Vietnamese
Communists. Ho Chi Minh had formed a popular entity
which attracted many Vietnamese interested in expelling
the Americans who, in their minds, had obviously replaced
the French as the new occupiers and oppressors.

The Vietcong were not just made up of guerilla factions hiding in the jungles waiting to take on the enemy.
They included professionals such as teachers, architects,

lawyers, and engineers. They administered intelligence gathering among other functions needed to support the rebels and they stayed hidden within cities throughout South Vietnam. The peasants from the South also joined the Vietcong because they distrusted Diem. Diem had promised land-reform for the peasants, but instead he decided to support major landowners.

When Kennedy took office, he explained to the nation that, "Our problems are critical. The tide is unfavorable. The news will be worse before it is better." He had expressed this same warning during his campaign for the presidency. The status quo was being tested by many people determined to be independent and not ruled by a dictator or regime. He asked his fellow citizens to be the "watchmen on the walls of freedom."

In January 1961, Soviet Premier Nikita Khrushchev pledged to support "wars of national liberation" throughout the world. He wanted to exploit the turmoil that was occurring throughout the world. Many new nations were attempting to break away from colonialism, thus causing instability. This pledge by Khrushchev was partially intended to help unify the Communist cause in North Vietnam. After Kennedy's inauguration, Eisenhower strongly suggested to Kennedy that combat troops would need to be sent to Southeast Asia. Kennedy took the suggestion under advisement, but did not act on it.

Kennedy believed that defending and supporting free institutions from the tyranny of colonialism and Communism would benefit America and the free world's interests. At his inauguration the new president promised that we will "bear any burden, fight any foe." Kennedy took a proactive approach in dealing with Communism. He believed the best way to deal with it was to "move forward to meet Communism rather than waiting for it to come to us and then reacting to it."

Kennedy viewed Vietnam as the most important region in that part of the world. He referred to it as the "cornerstone of the free world in Southeast Asia." In time, America would expend most of its energy and military might fighting Communist insurgents. Kennedy was careful, however, not to confront the opposition head-on militarily. He decided to take a middle course by expanding America's involvement, but at the same time, limiting support. This option would prove to be extremely risky, but for now this seemed to be the most reasonable course of action.

In 1961 Vice President Lyndon Johnson toured several Asian countries. During his tour he visited Diem in Saigon. Diem requested more aid and advisors in order to significantly expand the size of his army. Johnson assured Diem that he was essential to America's objectives in Vietnam. Indeed, Johnson referred to Diem as "the Churchill of Asia." Diem was promised one hundred additional military advisors and four hundred Green Berets. Moreover, the White House agreed to bolster the South's army to 200,000 in order to ensure success against the Vietcong.

Kennedy's primary strategy was to wage a very limited war and at the same time support the South Vietnamese government. Kennedy was careful not to appear bold or too aggressive in his decisions on how to deal with Hanoi. In fact, he hesitated in making any major decision to assist South Vietnam until he firmly believed Diem's government was about to go under. Ho Chi Minh's main goal, on the other hand, was to fight until Vietnam became fully independent and reunified.

Kennedy increased U.S. aid, but refused to commit combat troops for fear of getting bogged down in a major military conflict with the Vietcong. The president also authorized an increase in the number of military advisors from 685 to 16,700. The president also sent 400 American Green Beret Special Advisors to South Vietnam to help train South Vietnamese in counterinsurgency techniques. The Green Berets' role soon expanded to include establishing fortified camps in specific strategic locations in order to discourage infiltration by the North Vietnamese.

Khrushchev once again threatened his commitment to wars of liberation, including the conflict in Vietnam. Some of Kennedy's advisors warned him that now was the time for an all-out effort to fight Vietcong insurgents. They believed that the strategy of relying on containment would fail miserably. Kennedy responded to his more hawkish advisors by approving more of the same, namely limited amounts of aid. Kennedy was, after all, mainly focused on the Berlin crisis at this time.

In the fall of 1961, 26,000 Vietcong troops attacked South Vietnamese soldiers. In response to this onslaught, Maxwell Taylor and Walt Rostow visited South Vietnam in order to review the situation. They reported back to Washington and advised Kennedy to send more American advisors and 8,000 more combat troops. Additionally, McNamara strongly suggested sending 200,000 combat troops. The Joint Chiefs of Staff seriously contemplated the option of sending a significant number of combat troops to Vietnam. Kennedy, however, decided not to send any combat soldiers. He did not want to get pulled into a situation that seemed to require more and more U.S. involvement. Bobby Kennedy, the United States Attorney General, and the president's brother, was even more emphatic when he bluntly stated to Kennedy's advisors that "we are not sending combat troops." Later, Kennedy sent a letter to Diem indicating American support to help Vietnam "preserve its independence."

In December Vietcong guerillas took over much of the countryside in South Vietnam. South Vietnamese troops were frequently ambushed almost at will by the Vietcong. The cost to America now reached a staggering one million dollars a day. Kennedy sent high level administration advisors to meet secretly with North Vietnam's foreign minister in Geneva. Their mission was to negotiate a peaceful settlement to the conflict in Vietnam. "We got absolutely nowhere," one of the advisors reported back to Kennedy.

In May of 1962, Defense Secretary Robert McNamara visited South Vietnam and publicly declared, "we are winning the war." Indeed, McNamara was receiving optimistic reports from military intelligence indicating that the South was beating back the insurgents handily. He told a House committee that the situation in Vietnam would be resolved by "terminating subversion, covert aggression, and combat operations. I've seen nothing but progress and hopeful indications of further progress," he added. Kennedy was grateful to hear upbeat reports about Diem's success and thus was able to focus more on matters such as Soviet missiles in Cuba. For the time being, at least, the White House felt confident that progress was being made in Vietnam.

Bolstered by the good news, Kennedy commanded

McNamara to start planning an exit strategy concerning America's involvement in the region. McNamara conceived of a three year plan which would dramatically reduce the number of U.S. combat troops in Vietnam. All advisors would be withdrawn by 1968 at the latest. By 1968 the last remaining U.S. combat troops, probably in the neighborhood of fifteen hundred, would finally come home. It is not certain whether Kennedy agreed or disagreed with McNamara's plans for the future, but it is well documented that Kennedy valued the Secretary of Defense's assessments and opinions.

Kennedy was concerned that America's involvement in Vietnam could hurt his chances for re-election in 1964. It was important to put Vietnam on the back burner as quickly as possible so that it would not be a political liability. He ordered that there be no "unnecessary trips to Vietnam, especially by high ranking officers." It was absolutely imperative that no U.S. combat troops be sent to the region except as a last resort. Kennedy realized that any serious involvement in Vietnam would be hard to reverse. If he was to send in combat troops and then later reverse course by removing the troops, he could be accused of cutting and running from the Communist aggressors. He realized that his image as the leader of the free world could be tarnished forever.

Diem became more and more of a liability to the White House. For one thing, Diem was hostile toward the Buddhist majority in South Vietnam. His repressive style of government caused many Buddhists to demonstrate against his government. It was not unusual for Buddhist monks to perform self-immolations. Kennedy, who was Catholic, found it disheartening that another Catholic leader like

Diem was the cause of these horrid acts of self-violence. Kennedy was deeply concerned that the images provided by the media showing peaceful monks setting their bodies on fire in protest to a government his administration supported would not go over well with the American people.

Kennedy now seriously entertained the idea of a coup against Diem. His advisors informed him that the Vietnamese generals lacked the guts to pull off such a feat. Kennedy realized that such a venture had serious repercussions if it failed. He remembered only too well the humiliation he experienced with the Bay of Pigs disaster. Kennedy was primarily worried about two issues regarding a possible coup. He needed to know beforehand the chances of the coup's success, and he wanted to be able to keep the public in the dark regarding the administration's involvement in the coup.

Before fully committing to the overthrow of Diem's regime, Kennedy once again tried to exert pressure on Diem to reform his corrupt government. He insisted that Diem end his repressive policies against the Buddhist population. Bobby Kennedy wanted Henry Cabot Lodge, the ambassador to Saigon, to inform Diem that Kennedy was more than just unhappy with his leadership. He needed to be warned that if the White House demands were not met, Diem would not receive the support required to fight the Vietcong and his government would collapse.

Lodge reported to Kennedy that it now appeared a coup by Diem's own generals was in fact imminent. Kennedy had second thoughts about the coup, even calling it "silly." He cautioned, "We could lose our entire position in Southeast Asia overnight." But it was too late to halt what had already been set into motion. On November 1 at 1:45 p.m., the coup was launched. Kennedy insisted to his advisors that the United States must not be implemented in Diem's overthrow. Diem called Lodge and asked what the United States' attitude was toward the coup. All Lodge could tell Diem was that, "I am worried about your physical safety." He added that he was willing to assist in getting Diem safely out of the country. It is unclear if Diem agreed to accept Lodge's offer.

The next morning, Diem, who had been hiding somewhere outside of Saigon, agreed to surrender to the generals as long as they promised he would be escorted out of the country unscathed. The generals were unwilling to guarantee his safety and troops tried to capture Diem. Diem somehow escaped and hid inside a Catholic church. He was promptly arrested and placed in an armored carrier. Shortly after he was arrested, Diem was assassinated. When Kennedy first heard about Diem's murder, he suddenly exited from a meeting with the National Security Council. According to Maxwell Taylor, he had a "look of shock and dismay on his face." Kennedy may have convinced himself that the coup would be bloodless. A high level advisor related that he had "not seen him so depressed since the Bay of Pigs." It was reported later that Diem was in possession of a briefcase filled with a million dollars at the time of his capture.

Kennedy stated at a press conference in mid-November that his administration was working on ways "to bring Americans home, permit the South Vietnamese to maintain themselves as a free and independent country, and permit democratic forces within the country to operate."

On November 21, Kennedy told a high level advisor that beginning in 1964, he wanted an in-depth report analyzing all the options on how to best deal with the situation in Vietnam. Included in the report would need to be options on how to get out of that region. He wanted to ease the United States' relationship with Cuba as well because he felt current policies had not been very effective thus far.

On the afternoon of November 22, 1963, President Kennedy was savagely gunned down in Dallas, Texas. Vice President Lyndon Johnson was hurriedly sworn in as the new Commander-in-Chief aboard Air Force One en route to Washington, D.C. Johnson would prove to be prophetic when he warned that, "If we get involved in that bitch of a war my Great Society will be dead." From the moment Johnson was sworn in, he feared the very real possibility of escalation in Vietnam. He tried not to dwell too much on the war because he wanted to focus on the great changes he had in store with his Great Society. He wanted to be remembered as the greatest achiever of social reform America had ever known.

Johnson feared that a deeper involvement in Vietnam would hurt his chances of passing any of his domestic programs. He also feared losing an election which was fast approaching. The last thing he needed, in his view, was a major military conflict with fierce, determined Vietcong guerrillas. On the other hand, he did not want to be the president who lost Vietnam to the Chinese and Russians.

Senate Majority Leader Mike Mansfield, after arriving back from a visit to Saigon, indicated that he believed Diem had wasted the 2 billion dollars America had spent supporting South Vietnam. Mansfield, a close friend of Johnson, argued that getting bogged down in Vietnam could be disastrous for Johnson's administration and the country. He stressed that Johnson should instead devote all his time and energy to his Great Society program. Other advisors, however, argued that to give up on South Vietnam would tarnish America's image for generations to come. Nations fighting for their independence could never trust America to come to their aid. Indeed, the United States might have to send additional troops to South Korea in order to deter Communist North Korea from attacking its neighbor.

After Kennedy's assassination, McNamara paid another visit to Saigon. He wanted to see for himself how things were going. As usual, he reported publicly that the recent assassination of Diem did not negatively influence the situation in South Vietnam. In fact, he suggested the Vietcong didn't have a prayer. Privately, however, McNamara realized that the situation was terrible. He felt the administration had been misled. With Diem out of the way, many of the administration's advisors thought the situation in South Vietnam would improve. On the contrary, Diem's death created a political vacuum. Buddhists and Catholics fought for power. Many other new groups sprung up to fill the power vacuum. McNamara warned Johnson that within the next few months, he could expect a Communist take-over of South Vietnam. Johnson was stunned by the report. Johnson thought that walking away from Vietnam would certainly injure American prestige throughout the international community and embolden America's enemies.

The Vietcong and the North Vietnamese immediately became even more proactive in their insurgency. Just weeks after the coup, the Vietcong took over more of the countryside in South Vietnam. More and more soldiers and supplies were sent deeper into South Vietnam. While desertion rates climbed higher and higher among the South Vietnamese, the Vietcong had no trouble recruiting men for the war effort. Many villagers throughout the countryside could not be trusted to fight for the South, so they had to be disarmed.

By June of 1964, Vietnam had caused Johnson a lot of anxiety. Most of the public and many in Congress were unsure about how to handle the Vietnam crisis. Barry Goldwater constantly complained that the president was not doing all that he could do to meet the challenges head-on. Indeed, there was no prospect of a stable regime any time soon. Johnson wanted to deal with Vietnam after the November elections. Early in the summer the Gallup poll surveyed the public's feelings toward Vietnam and found that 58% of Americans favored a UN army to deal with Southeast Asia. Johnson, however, did not believe anything positive would ever materialize if the UN took charge of the situation. By the end of July, Johnson wanted to bolster the morale of the South Vietnamese people.

Johnson increased secret military efforts called Operation 34-A or OPLAN 34-A. This plan had been cleared by the 303 Committee, a secret arm of major clandestine operations. McGeorge Bundy headed the committee and it included Pentagon and CIA representatives. Raids were conducted by South Vietnamese commandos off the coast of North Vietnam. The program encouraged more extensive South Vietnamese intrusions into North Vietnam. Fishermen were also kidnapped and held against their will in an attempt to obtain information about North

Vietnamese activity. U.S. advisors were also involved in this operation. American destroyers gathered electronic and other kinds of military intelligence.

The Communist leadership in North Vietnam grew increasingly alarmed about America's intentions. They were not so much concerned about the United States supporting the South Vietnamese government as they were about America providing military aid and combat troops. They feared that an invasion by the U.S. and the South was fast approaching. They asked the Soviet Union for better protection from the imminent invasion. The Soviets provided anti-aircraft missiles and radar equipment, which were mounted around the largest cities in the North and along the coastal areas of the Tonkin Gulf.

It was important for the U.S. military to determine where the North Vietnamese hid their radar transmitters. Knowing their locations would benefit impending bombing raids by the U.S. military. South Vietnamese commandos infiltrated enemy territory in order to aggravate the radar transmitters. By doing this, their signal could be picked up and measured by U.S. intelligence vessels near the coastline of the Tonkin Gulf.

Together with intelligence gathering, the U.S. military trained the South Vietnamese on how to operate Norwegian-built patrol boats called Swifts and Nasties. The boats could travel very fast and were armed with light weaponry. Raids conducted by the South Vietnamese crews were postponed indefinitely until they were thoroughly trained by U.S. Navy Seals. Bad weather also held up the attacks. President Johnson agreed to extend these experimental raids to a full year. The American commander of the Seventh Fleet, Admiral Ulysses Grant Sharp, Jr., ordered the U.S. destroyer, *Maddox*, to move in the vicinity of the Gulf of Tonkin. In charge of the *Maddox* was Captain John J. Herrick, an Annapolis graduate and a veteran of two wars.

Captain Herrick was warned not to get closer than eight miles from the shores of North Vietnam. The United States was uncertain about what mile limit the North Vietnamese adhered to. It could be a three mile limit or a twelve mile limit. Some argued that the twelve mile limit was probably the correct limit because other Communist nations used it. Captain Herrick was also ordered to stay in touch with the command center in Saigon so that he could learn about any possible commando operations from the South Vietnamese. The U.S. could not afford to be suspected of being involved with any South Vietnamese commando raids.

The *Maddox* made a quick stop at the port of Keeling in Taiwan in order to obtain electronic equipment and several electronic specialists. The sonar aboard the *Maddox* was not up to standard and several members of his crew lacked experience in handling such equipment. On August 1, the *Maddox* was within nine miles from the coast of North Vietnam. The captain had sighted what he initially thought were North Vietnamese-manned patrol boats. He dutifully reported this disturbing information to the Seventh Fleet. He was informed shortly afterward that what he saw were Swifts returning from a covert operation.

CHAPTER 10

THE TONKIN GULF INCIDENTS

URING THE EVENING and early morning of July 30-31, 1964, a 34-A operation took place against two North Vietnamese islands somewhere in the Gulf of Tonkin. Four South Vietnamese high-speed gun boats bombarded the islands of Hon Me and Hon Nieu. The original aim was to knock out radar equipment with explosives. When the raiders met heavy resistance from the North Vietnamese, the commandos retaliated with cannon fire and machine gun blasts. Robert McNamara had stated that the government of South Vietnam, "saw them as a relatively low-cost means of harassing North Vietnam in retaliation for Hanoi's support of the Vietcong." The next day the *USS Maddox*, engaging in electronic espionage, began patrolling the same area. On Sunday morning, August 2, three North Vietnamese torpedo boats attacked the

Maddox in international waters. Reportedly, the North fired 37-mm shells, none of which hit the destroyer. The North Vietnamese may have assumed the *Maddox* had been part of the covert attacks. The *USS Maddox* and four F-8E *Crusader* planes from aircraft carrier *Ticonderoga* sank one and severely damaged another North Vietnamese boat. The torpedo boats tried separately to shoot down the planes, but their machine guns either jammed or were simply too unreliable to work properly. Many years later the pilot in one of the aircraft, James Stockdale, would become the vice-presidential running mate alongside Ross Perot in the 1992 presidential election. It had appeared that one of the smallest navies in the world had the audacity to take on arguably the largest and most powerful navy in the world. It was hard to believe the North Vietnamese would attempt such a suicidal exercise in futility.

An emergency meeting was held at the home of Dean Rusk early Sunday morning. Included in the meeting was General Earle G. Wheeler, the Joint Chiefs of Staff chairman, Deputy Secretary of Defense Cyrus Vance, Thomas Hughes of the Bureau of Intelligence and Research, and Undersecretary of State George Ball. After their discussion on what may have transpired based on the information presented to them, they called a meeting with Johnson.

Johnson asked the group, "What's the big emergency?" When told that an American destroyer had been attacked, Johnson asked how this information was known to be true. What was known or thought to be known about the incident was provided to Johnson. The president thought for a moment and asked, "We weren't up to any mischief out there, were we?" Ball responded by reminding the president that he had signed off on the 34-A operations late last year. Johnson responded by saying he remembered approving the operations. He asked if a 34-A operation occurred in the area where the attack took place. He was told that one of the covert operations may have taken place a couple days prior to the attack on the destroyer.

Johnson concluded the meeting with a story. "It reminds me of the movies in Texas. You're sitting next to a pretty girl and you have your hand on her ankle and nothing happens. And you move it up to her knee and nothing happens. You move it up further and you're thinking about it a bit more and all of a sudden you get slapped. I think we got slapped."

Four days after the incident, Defense Secretary McNamara and Joint Chief of Staff Chairman Wheeler met with several prominent senators to explain what had transpired. They informed the senators that the attack was totally unprovoked and that the covert attacks on Hon Me and Hon Ngu were in no way related. McNamara stated that, "Our navy played absolutely no part in, was not associated with, was not aware of, any South Vietnamese actions, if there were any. I want to make that very clear to you. The *Maddox* was operating in international waters, was carrying out a routine patrol of the type we carry out all over the world at all times. It was not informed of, was not aware of, had no evidence of, and so far as I know today has no knowledge of any possible South Vietnamese actions in connection with the two islands that Senator Morse referred to."

Johnson next met with General Maxwell Taylor, the new U.S. ambassador to South Vietnam. Taylor strongly suggested a military response against the attack by the North Vietnamese. Johnson ignored the general's suggestion and instead decided to warn Hanoi against another such attack. Johnson was under the impression that the information presented to him about the attack seemed "a bit murky and we won't have any retaliation." Via the Voice of America, Johnson alerted the North Vietnamese government to be "under no misapprehension as to the grave consequence which would inevitably result from any further unprovoked offensive military action against United States forces." Johnson also placed a call via the "hot line" to Moscow and spoke with Soviet Prime Minister Khrushchev assuring him that the United States did not wish to widen the conflict between North Vietnam and South Vietnam. He informed Khrushchev that on the other hand U.S. ships should not be attacked in international waters without provocation.

Peculiarly, on August 2 and 3, the North Vietnamese mentioned nothing publicly about the incident. Not wanting to show weakness to the aggressors, Johnson announced on the 3rd that patrols would continue in the Gulf, this time with two destroyers instead of one. The destroyer *C. Turner Joy* was sent to support the *Maddox*. Johnson insisted that no retaliation against the North Vietnamese would occur. Maxwell Taylor complained that Johnson's response was mild and could perhaps prompt Hanoi to continue with more attacks. For the time being the crisis appeared to be over.

The president was worried about appearing "soft on Vietnam," as Barry Goldwater described him. Goldwater, who was running against Johnson in the 1964 presidential election, constantly bombarded the Johnson administration with harsh criticism. He claimed the White House was not forceful enough in its response to North Vietnam's aggression against the South. Goldwater issued a statement stating, "We cannot allow the American flag to be shot at anywhere on earth if we are to retain our respect and prestige."

The Joint Chiefs of Staff began laying out plans to dispatch fighter-bombers to South Vietnam and Thailand. They poured over maps of North Vietnam and located oil and ammunition depots to destroy. Admiral Sharp ordered the carrier *Constellation* to join the *Ticonderoga*. The two destroyers were ordered to stage maneuvers along the coastline of North Vietnam and within eight miles of it. Some viewed this as egging the North Vietnamese into a naval battle. Indeed, Rear Admiral Robert B. Moore determined that the North Vietnamese had, "thrown down the gauntlet and should be treated as belligerents from first detection."

On Tuesday morning, Johnson called on McNamara and ordered him to locate possible North Vietnamese targets such as "one of their bridges or something." He was thinking in terms of a military response against any future unprovoked attacks by the North. McNamara assured the president that he would have his targets. Reportedly, Johnson shouted at some admirals, further expressing his anger and disgust at the recent turn of events. "The whole goddamn navy is out there, all those ships and planes, and you can't even sink three little PT boats," he yelled at them. Johnson wanted to know why the boats were not pursued and destroyed. He was told that naval peacetime rules allowed retaliation against aggression, but naval forces could not pursue the aggressors.

On August 4 at 7:40 a.m., the *Maddox* reported that

preparations were on the way by North Vietnamese torpedo boats to attack two U.S. Navy destroyers, the *Turner Joy* and the *Maddox*. Fighter aircraft from the *Ticonderoga* were launched to protect the two destroyers. Shortly thereafter, the *Maddox* reported that the unidentified vessels had disappeared from the radar screen. Johnson immediately met with Democratic congressional leaders. They were informed of an impending attack by the North Vietnamese. It was generally agreed that some sort of military action, including a congressional resolution supporting the president, should be forthcoming. Additionally, firm, swift retaliatory airstrikes against North Vietnamese torpedo boat bases should occur. Early that afternoon, messages from the *Maddox* began arriving in Washington.

McNamara phoned Johnson indicating that two American destroyers were under attack. The two destroyers reported that they were about 60 miles off the coast on North Vietnam, still in international waters. On the afternoon of August 4, the *Maddox's* commander raised doubts that an attack had even taken place. According to the commander, "freak weather effects" on radar may have been misinterpreted. He also indicated that there were no "unusual sightings." The *Maddox* commander further suggested that a "complete evaluation" be undertaken. Furthermore, North Vietnamese gunboats were definitely operating in the area, but no solid proof was offered to support the attack. Thus far, no U.S. casualties were reported and there were no visible signs of damage on board the *Maddox*. McNamara later claimed that a North Vietnamese shell fragment was later found and sent to the Pentagon where it was examined. The commander of the U.S. Pacific

Forces, however, assured Johnson that an attack had indeed taken place. Johnson asked McNamara for a definitive report outlining exactly what had transpired in the Gulf of Tonkin. McNamara postponed airstrikes until he was convinced there was enough evidence to suggest that an attack had taken place against the destroyers.

McNamara spoke with Admiral Sharp, Commander of Pacific Forces in Honolulu. Sharp reported that there was a possibility that the second attack never occurred. This prompted McNamara to meet with the Joint Chiefs of Staff. The Joint Chiefs indicated that an attack definitely had taken place. CIA Director John McCone thought the North Vietnamese were reacting defensively to the U.S. attack. Johnson asked for Congress to support military action and a resolution as well. He was worried about another Korea. McGeorge Bundy was later to recall, "In my time with Lyndon Johnson, I do not remember a large decision more quickly reached." Johnson determined that the incident was significant enough to help pass a resolution which would allow him to go to war with North Vietnam.

Johnson authorized limited retaliatory airstrikes against the torpedo boat bases and nearby oil storage dumps. By attacking the North Vietnamese, Johnson silenced his staunchest critics, particularly Barry Goldwater. Johnson, however, broke new ground by ordering the American military to attack North Vietnam. This was the first step in creating a possible escalation of the war and perhaps widening it. With the November elections coming up in the not too distant future, Johnson was also deeply concerned about not widening the war. In fact, he and others on his staff publicly stated that "we seek no wider war" in several discussions and speeches.

Later that night, Johnson went on television and told the country in a prepared speech about the "attack" and about "open aggression on the high seas against the U.S." The next day at a speech at Syracuse University, Johnson called the attacks "unprovoked and deliberate." That same day he sent the Tonkin Gulf Resolution to Congress for their approval. About 85 percent of those Americans polled stood behind President Johnson's handling of the conflict. Most newspapers agreed with the president as well. On August 7, after two days of hearings and debate, the resolution won almost unanimous approval in the House of Representatives and the Senate.

The U.S. Senate voted for the resolution 98 to 2. The only two dissenting votes were cast by Senator Wayne Morse of Oregon and Ernest Gruening, the first person to be elected U.S. senator from Alaska. Morse pointed out that, according to him, the newly adopted resolution granted war powers to the president, but the Constitution only granted these same powers to the United States Congress. Both Morse and Gruening's protests were essentially ignored by the press and public alike. The House vote, which took only forty minutes to conclude, was even more one-sided, 416 to 0.

Wayne Morse was a stern man who began his political career in Washington, D.C. in 1945 as a socially liberal Republican. He supported better education for the masses and sided with labor. He became a Democrat after realizing that the Republicans were not progressive enough. He was not well liked in the Senate because fellow senators found him abrasive and boring. On the morning of

August 6, Morse was informed by a Pentagon officer that the *Maddox* had been involved in raids conducted by South Vietnamese commandos. When the Senate convened later that day, no one listened to what Morse had to say about America's involvement in covert operations against the North Vietnamese.

Johnson served notice to the North Vietnamese that America was determined to help South Vietnam fight Communist aggression. Many advisors argued that even if South Vietnam fell into the hands of the Communists, it was better for America to be perceived as a true ally if it kept slugging away instead of cutting and running. The administration further believed that at the first opportunity, airstrikes must be launched against North Vietnam. On February 6, a U.S. army barracks and a helicopter base were attacked by Vietcong soldiers at Pleiku. Several Americans were killed and five aircraft were destroyed. Johnson immediately ordered airstrikes against North Vietnam. The day after the attack, McGeorge Bundy returned from a trip to South Vietnam and strongly advised the president that a program of sustained reprisals should be implemented. He warned that defeat would be inevitable without this policy. Shortly after these warnings, ROLLING THUNDER was initiated. This policy called for gradually intensified airstrikes against the North. The Joint Chiefs of Staff advised Johnson to go for a big knockout punch rather than smaller but frequent airstrikes.

Shortly after ROLLING THUNDER was initiated, it became obvious that larger and more frequent airstrikes were needed. To make matters worse, reports were arriving in Washington indicating that the situation in South

Vietnam was deteriorating rapidly. For this reason, Johnson authorized more and bigger airstrikes. The chief targets were industrial and transportation systems. The president later authorized strikes against power facilities and steel manufacturing plants. Napalm was also becoming a favorite means of destruction. The expanded war from the air easily became a pretext for sending troops to protect American air bases.

The massive bombings on the North's production and supply facilities resulted in hundreds of millions of dollars in damages. The North's agriculture was ruined as well. Many cities were thoroughly destroyed beyond recognition. Although the bombings were officially not directed toward the people of North Vietnam, McNamara estimated off the record that as many as 1,000 people per week were killed during the heaviest periods of bombing.

North Vietnam's response to the bombings was pragmatic and immediate. Those who survived the bombings were moved from the target areas and taken to the vast countryside of the North. Facilities still in operation were transported out of the damaged cities and were later hidden in caves and underground bunkers. The leadership in Hanoi was very concerned about future attacks by the U.S. They had come to realize firsthand how powerful and frightening America's military might was. The possibility of negotiating a settlement to the conflict was put on the table for discussion by the leaders.

Not everyone under Johnson agreed with this new initiative. General Westmoreland requested more Marine landing teams so that the air base in Danang could be better protected. Maxwell Taylor, however, was concerned that American combat troops were not properly trained to fight guerrilla style warfare in the dense jungles of Vietnam. Taylor's concerns were largely ignored. It seemed the current strategy was used in order to satisfy short term objectives rather than long term solutions. On March 8, Johnson approved the request for two Marine battalions, including tanks and 8-inch howitzers.

Westmoreland advised that even more combat troops and artillery were needed in order to head off any large scale invasion by the North Vietnamese. Taylor continued to express deep concern that adding more combat troops could cause America to be so entrenched in Vietnam that it would be difficult to withdraw in the near future. He believed the nation could be headed toward a much larger and longer conflict than anyone could have predicted. He foresaw a possible Dienbienphu disaster in the making. A strategy was developed by Taylor, McNamara, and the Joint Chiefs at a conference in Honolulu. The main objective was to deny the enemy any major victory while continuing to bomb North Vietnam. Hopefully, this would allow time for the South Vietnamese to build up their military.

Johnson publicly announced to the nation that the heavy bombing was in response to enemy aggression. The public was not made aware of South Vietnam's deterioration and the need to protect it from further deterioration by bombing the North. The public was also told that U.S. troops were in Vietnam to protect installations and were not there for offensive operations.

Fearing the nation was headed toward disaster, several highly respected Democratic senators suggested to the president that a settlement be negotiated. Protests against the war were held on college campuses throughout the country. Many of America's allies appealed to the president to reverse America's escalation in the conflict and to work for a permanent peace.

In reaction to his critics, Johnson called for a five-day cessation of bombing while he indicated to Hanoi that America would scale down its bombing if North Vietnam would end its attacks. The net effect of these actions did not increase the chance for a settlement both sides could agree to. In the end, Hanoi claimed that the bombing pause was a "worn-out trick of deceit and threat." The North, there-fore, refused to end its aggression.

A few months later, Westmoreland asked for an additional 179,000 combat troops. He had determined that South Vietnam desperately needed America's help in holding off enemy aggression. Even Maxwell Taylor agreed that more U.S. troops were needed in order to fight the Vietcong. In July Johnson authorized the use of B-52s to perform saturation bombing in South Vietnam. The bombing of North Vietnam intensified as well. Johnson was careful not to announce to the world that a declaration of war against North Vietnam existed. He feared a war declaration might cause China or the Soviet Union to join in the conflict against the U.S.

In a speech to the nation on July 28, Johnson announced 50,000 more troops would be sent to South Vietnam. He feared that a withdrawal now would be the death knell of South Vietnam and he did not want that to happen on his watch. Upholding policies that were in place since the late 1940s was absolute. Johnson and many members of his cabinet feared a major withdrawal would negatively affect America's standing in the world. Chaos could very well erupt in other countries.

Johnson did not want to conquer and occupy North Vietnam. His main strategy was to force the North to negotiate a settlement with the U.S. Johnson and his administration underestimated the North Vietnamese's will and determination to drive the Americans out of Vietnam and to take over the South. It was outrageous at the time to consider the Vietcong as a match against America's military might.

Mike Mansfield warned Johnson that the nation was supporting his stand on Vietnam because he was the president, not because the American people understood and welcomed his strategy. In time, Mansfield feared, the country could turn against the president on his war stand. Many senators felt Vietnam was not an important enough region to get bogged down in. They also feared that no matter how many combat troops the president sent to fight the North Vietnamese, America could not win against an entrenched, determined enemy. Johnson listened to the senators' arguments, but he could not be persuaded to change his mind about defeating the North.

Johnson was certainly not alone in his conviction that the enemy could and would be destroyed. The first combat troops to hit the ground running were convinced that the enemy could not successfully defend themselves against any major U.S. military assault. The Vietcong would soon learn the harsh reality that they were simply outgunned and outnumbered.

Johnson strongly believed that the conflict needed to remain limited at all times in order to avert a war with China or the Soviet Union. But on the same token he was convinced the war had to be won in the near future so that the public at home would not protest. Unfortunately, these two strategies conflicted with one another.

Air power was used extensively against Vietnam because it was believed that heavy and continuous bombing could annihilate an enemy's war making capacity. Without the means to manufacture war material, the enemy could not possibly win and would eventually be forced to negotiate a settlement. Moreover, the American people were more likely to support a bombing strategy because less American lives would be lost.

The air war, however, did not bring the expected results Johnson wanted. It became obvious that conventional military wisdom regarding saturation bombing could not be applied to Vietnam. Nevertheless, Johnson increased the number of strikes and targets. Beginning in 1966, Johnson ordered more and more airstrikes against industrial and transportation facilities in North Vietnam. Petroleum storage facilities, steel factories, and power plants were added to Johnson's target list.

In order to minimize the number of civilian casualties, the population living in the cities was dispersed over the more rural areas of the country. Industries were hidden in caves and concealed underground. It had been estimated that as many as 30,000 miles of tunnels existed throughout the North. Many civilians who dwelt in heavily bombed areas lived underground. Ferries and pontoon bridges replaced bombed concrete bridges. In order to avoid detection, the bridges were placed under water during the day.

The Soviet Union and China provided aid to the North, which more than compensated for the loss of their military equipment due to U.S. bombing. The Soviet Union, more than China, had the ability to provide sophisticated military equipment. Moscow saw this as an opportunity to closely ally them with North Vietnam. The Soviets were hoping to be able to deter China from developing a strong relationship with North Vietnam. Ho Chi Minh used this rivalry as a means of receiving much needed aid from both countries. He hoped that both nations would try to outdo the other in providing military equipment and supplies.

The effectiveness of the bombing was negatively impacted by several variables. Most notably was the long monsoon season, which began in September and lasted for many months. Areas farther north near Hanoi and nearby cities had in place strong air defense systems. The Soviet Union provided North Vietnam with ground to air missiles and MIG fighters. In fact, the heavy bombing may have inspired the rural population to support the war effort even more. The cost of the airstrikes was staggering. By 1968, the cost of lost aircraft over Vietnam was estimated to be $6 billion dollars. In America, the public was becoming more and more outraged at the expense and inefficiency of the bombing missions.

The effect of U.S. combat operations by 1967 was hard to accurately gauge. In open battles, the American forces typically prevailed. The real trouble existed in areas such as thick jungles and swamps where the enemy could lay booby traps and ambush U.S. combat troops. As the war progressed, the "body count" became the war statistic of choice. It was very difficult, however, to measure with any degree of accuracy the number of enemy dead. The Vietcong and noncombatants were virtually indistinguishable. One marine claimed, "If it's dead and Vietnamese, it's VC, was a rule of thumb in the bush."

By 1967 it was clear to any rational observer of the war that the conflict could easily drag on for several more years. A journalist had declared that each American blow "was like a sledgehammer on a floating cork. Somehow the cork refused to stay down." By this time there were 450,000 combat troops fighting in Vietnam. Westmoreland warned that if an additional 200,000 troops were not sent, the war could drag on for at least another five years.

Negotiations for a peaceful settlement were reportedly attempted hundreds of times between 1965 and 1967. Neither the Johnson administration nor the North Vietnamese government was willing to concede enough in order to arrive at a tolerable agreement for both sides. The North Vietnamese were also hoping that the American people would eventually demand an end to the war. Johnson was skeptical about North Vietnam's intentions to negotiate because he believed all they wanted was for the bombing to end.

It was difficult for either side to compromise because a wide gulf of differences existed between them. The North Vietnamese were outraged by America's involvement in Vietnam. To them the Geneva Accords had been violated by the U.S. In their view, America would need to withdraw all its troops, remove its bases, and end all military action against their country. Hanoi wanted South Vietnam to settle its own issues without American involvement. Hanoi was adamant that unification of the two countries could not be negotiated.

The U.S. promised to end the bombing if Hanoi would

begin a de-escalation of its attacks against South Vietnam. Vice President Hubert Humphrey indicated that allowing the Vietcong to be included in a unified government would be like "putting the fox in a chicken coop." Under no circumstances would the U.S. allow South Vietnam to become Communists.

By mid-1967 Johnson's hopes of a final victory diminished dramatically. He was unable to end the war militarily and through negotiations. The home front was becoming more difficult to deal with as the cost of the war and lives lost accumulated with no end in sight. He became increasingly worried that the war could affect his chances of being re-elected the following year.

There existed in America two groups of people as far as the war was concerned. The "hawks" were composed of conservative Democrats and right-wing Republicans. They believed North Vietnam must be defeated. If the South lost the war, America's prominence in the world would mean very little to other struggling nations trying to become independent. The "doves" represented a much smaller group but they were very loud and persistent. Martin Luther King, Jr., Norman Mailer, and Dr. Benjamin Spock were just a few of the many famous people who expressed their concern about what they believed was an immoral war.

Senator William Fulbright, an early dissenter of the war, conducted highly critical televised hearings on the war. Joan Baez, the famous folk singer, refused to support the war by not providing funds toward the defense budget by way of her income tax. Protesters stood in front of the White House and shouted "Hey, hey, LBJ, how many kids have you killed today?"

By the summer of 1967, 13,000 Americans had lost their lives in the war. Johnson called for a ten percent surtax as a way of paying for the war's escalating cost. 30,000 draft calls per month became the norm as well. Johnson's approval rating for how he was handling the war plunged to 28% by the fall.

Johnson was extremely worried that there might not be an honorable way out of this undeclared war. He became disenchanted with the Joint Chiefs of Staff recommendation of more and more bombing raids. "Bomb, bomb, bomb, that's all you know," he complained to them at several of their meetings. He shot down time and time again General Westmoreland's recommendation to mobilize the reserves and thus expand the war dramatically. Johnson feared that China might directly get involved with the conflict.

As long as Westmoreland claimed that progress was being made, Johnson refused to accept the possibility that defeat was imminent. He realized that the bombing had not destroyed the will of the North Vietnamese. But he did not want trouble with the hawks because that meant open conflict with them. He feared that an investigation of the airstrikes might be initiated by prominent hawks in Congress. He was not prepared to have an open battle with anyone over the war.

McNamara, as well as many of Johnson's trusted advisors, had been showing signs that America could not continue on its current course. Johnson was deeply wounded by his critics, but refused to listen to reasonable alternatives to end the war. Johnson responded to his critics by privately discrediting them as ill informed. To counter the critics at home, Johnson directed "truth teams" to rebut speeches and media sources that criticized the war effort. Statistics were provided to the media indicating a dramatic rise in enemy dead. Westmoreland arrived in America for the purpose of assuring the nation that the war was winnable and in the end, North Vietnam would be defeated. "We are making real progress," he assured the media. He announced to Congress that the enemy may not yet have been defeated, but they were badly hurt.

In late 1967, the North Vietnamese decided to go on the offensive instead of fighting a defensive war. The North may have been concerned about the heavy casualties they had sustained thus far and were not willing to continue the same strategy. The North Vietnamese planned a massive offense against the South in early 1968. The plan was to lure American combat troops away from heavily populated areas. The Vietnamese would then attack major cities in the South. Finally, the North hoped that the Saigon government would collapse and the people from the South would join the Vietcong. An offshoot of this plan would be for the U.S. to withdraw their support if indeed the South Vietnamese government did collapse. North Vietnamese soldiers attacked and subsequently occupied a Marine garrison near the Laotian border. Meanwhile, Vietcong guerilla fighters stole supplies from cities throughout the South.

The North Vietnamese plan worked as expected. It worked so well that General Westmoreland ordered reinforcements into Con Thien, Loc Ninh and many other towns in order to drive the Vietcong out. Johnson insisted that the strategically important garrison of Khe Sanh must be held at all costs. While the garrison was being defended, however, the North Vietnamese and Vietcong planned their next great offensive. This attack would occur at the beginning of the Vietnamese's most festive holiday, the lunar New Year known as Tet.

CHAPTER 11

THE FALL OF
VIETNAM

Prior to the Tet offensive, North Vietnam and South Vietnam had ceased all military activity and were in the midst of celebrating the Tet holiday. The North's objective was to attack the South while its people prepared for the holidays. Vietcong guerillas pretended to be regular civilians and began sneaking weapons into the cities and towns of South Vietnam.

On January 30, 1968, the Tet offensive began. The Vietcong attacked dozens of provincial capitals, major cities, and hamlets. They also attacked a major airport, the Presidential palace and the general staff's headquarters. The U.S. and South Vietnam were taken totally by surprise because the U.S. military underestimated the resolve and tenacity of the enemy. The North Vietnamese and the Vietcong were badly beaten just the year before. The U.S military concluded that the North would not mount a major assault any time soon.

Henry Kissinger was quoted as saying that Tet "brought to a head the compounded weaknesses of the American position. Tet was seen as a military victory by America, but it was a political defeat in the countryside for Saigon and the United States." McGeorge Bundy told the president that, "a great many people, even very determined and loyal people, have begun to think that Vietnam really is a bottomless pit."

The highly respected CBS news anchor, Walter Cronkite, reported on the air that, "we are mired in a stalemate. To say that we are closer to victory today is to believe, in the face of the evidence, the optimists who have been wrong in the past." Johnson was deeply affected by Cronkite's assertions and he began to believe that public opinion against the war would rise and continue to rise.

Before the Tet offensive, a Gallup Poll revealed that 50 percent of Americans thought the U.S. military had been making steady progress. After the Tet offensive, the number fell to 33 percent. Moreover, 49 percent of the American people thought that the United States should have never offered military assistance to South Vietnam. To make matters worse for the administration, a *New York Times* article reported that General Westmoreland was asking for 206,000 additional combat troops.

On March 12, 1968, the peace candidate, Eugene McCarthy, won a surprising 42.2 percent of the New Hampshire presidential primary popular vote. Johnson had decided not to enter that primary because, officially, he wanted to concentrate totally on the problems of the United States. McCarthy pronounced in many of his speeches that the administration wanted "no wider war."

"Yet," he went on to declare, "the war is getting wider every month. Only a few months ago we were told that 65 percent of the population was secure. Now we know that even the American embassy is not secure."

Johnson reacted to this latest news by publicly announcing that America would continue to fight the North Vietnamese aggressors. He declared the need to "win the peace on the battlefield by supporting our men who are doing that job there now." The big question Johnson now faced was whether he should send more than 200,000 additional troops to Vietnam. He was deeply concerned about how the American people would react to a larger U.S. military presence in Vietnam.

On January 23, a U.S. Navy intelligence ship, the *U.S.S. Pueblo*, was captured by the North Korean government. 14,000 U.S. reserve units were alerted into action. During his presidential campaign, Nixon frequently used this incident as an example of the lack of leadership in the White House.

A high level meeting between Johnson and many of his senior advisors was held. Among those in attendance was Arthur Dean, who helped end the Koran War, Cyrus Vance, Dean Acheson, General Omar Bradley, Maxwell Taylor, and Matthew Ridgeway, McGeorge Bundy, and Walt Rostow. Johnson was totally in favor of ordering more troops to Vietnam. Many of the men at this meeting had supported Johnson on his war strategy, but now they were uncertain about America's ability to beat the North Vietnamese. Johnson was appalled by all the negative criticism to the war effort thus far. "Somebody had poisoned the well," he declared.

After the meeting, Johnson was scheduled to deliver an important speech to the nation on March 31. In an earlier draft of the speech and before the meeting with his senior advisors, he called for a draft of fifty thousand men along with a tax surcharge to help raise money for the war. This portion was deleted from the draft and replaced with words of restraint and peace. In the speech, Johnson announced to the American people that he would call for a unilateral partial bombing halt. Then the real bombshell exploded.

"With America's sons in the fields far away, and with America's future under challenge here at home; with our hopes and the world's hopes for peace in the balance every day, I do not believe that I should devote an hour or a day of my time to any personal partisan causes, or to any duties other than the awesome duties of this office – the presidency of your country. Accordingly, I shall not seek, and I will not accept, the nomination of my party for another term as your President."

Militarily, the speech was extremely important. Johnson now placed a limit on the number of American combat troops in Vietnam. The number of troops fighting there would hold at 543,000. The "Vietnamization" policy would now be initiated more vigorously.

Martin Luther King Jr. had been a highly visible, outspoken opponent of the war. On March 31, he warned the administration and the nation that something had to be done to raise the hope of those living in the ghetto. He warned about how bad the riots could be during the upcoming summer if nothing was done for the poor and hopeless. Several days later, King was gunned down outside his hotel room in Memphis, Tennessee. Riots broke out in over one hundred cities throughout the country.

Then, just two months after King's assassination, Robert Kennedy was assassinated while running in the Democratic presidential primaries. He had given a celebratory speech to his campaign staff in California, when moments later, he was gunned down. Kennedy had become the most popular peace candidate running for President.

Vice President Hubert Humphrey's campaign was doing badly. He was consistently lagging behind Nixon by 8 percentage points in the polls. Democratic leaders were concerned that they would lose the national election and they demanded something major from the administration. Johnson finally called for a complete halt to the bombing. He also agreed to stop rocket attacks on South Vietnam's cities. Talks between representatives from the United States and North Vietnam were scheduled to begin on November 6, just one day after the presidential election.

The effect of these proposed talks helped Humphrey's campaign immensely. Nixon's lead now shrunk to only a two point lead. But South Vietnam's Thieu announced suddenly on November 1 that he would not become a part of the peace talks. Thieu had shown public enthusiasm for the talks for quite some time. Now he stated that he was against sitting down with the Vietcong. Johnson refused to go ahead with the talks without Thieu. The chance for a peaceful settlement to the war had evaporated. In the presidential election, Nixon won the popular vote, 43.4 to Humphrey's 42.7.

In 1969 Henry Kissinger announced that, "We will not make the same old mistakes. We will make our own." New methods were indeed tried, but the results were about the same. The mantra of the Nixon administration was, "peace with honor." But peace with honor, Nixon felt, meant widening the war dramatically. In the end, Nixon basically mimicked Johnson's attempt to make Vietnam independent without the threat of any Communist influence. He favored an all-out war short of using nuclear weapons.

Nixon won the 1968 presidential election by influencing enough voters to believe he would end the war and achieve "peace with honor." Many people who listened to his inaugural address thought he would end the war quickly. Hanoi was worried because they suspected Nixon would escalate the war. H.R. Haldeman later quoted Nixon as saying, "I call it the Madman Theory. I want the North Vietnamese to believe I've reached a point where I might do anything to stop the war. We'll just slip the word to them that, 'For God's sake, you know, Nixon is obsessed about Communism. We can't restrain him when he's angry – and he has his hand on the nuclear button.'"

Part of Nixon's thinking was that he wanted to take advantage of the rivalry that existed between the Soviet Union and China. He thought this would lead to better relations between these two countries and America. The hope was that the three countries would negotiate for arms limitations by way of détente. The two Communist nations, Nixon believed, would only negotiate with America if the U.S. military proved it could stand up to any aggressor and was willing to fight to the end.

On March 18, 1969, Nixon ordered the massive bombing of Cambodia, a neutral country. Over the next several months, 3,650 B-52 bombing raids took place. The president believed he could eventually make the North

Vietnamese drop to their knees if they sensed that the war was now expanding. He claimed that he learned the lesson from Eisenhower during the Korean War. According to Nixon, Ike sent word to North Korea and China that America would not tolerate a war of attrition. The implication was that the United States was willing to escalate the war dramatically. "And within a matter of months, they negotiated," Nixon explained. The U.S. military would, over the next several months, drop more than 100,000 tons of bombs on Cambodia. It would represent four times the total tonnage of bombs dropped on Japan during the Second World War. Alexander Haig, military advisor under Kissinger and subsequently Secretary of State under Ronald Reagan, would later say about Cambodia that, "It was enemy territory – it was not Cambodian territory, and we had every right, legally and morally, to take what action was necessary to protect our forces."

Strategically, the massive bombing of Cambodia coincided with the continued withdrawal of United States combat troops from Vietnam. This operation would become popularly known as the "Vietnamization" program. Nixon fretted over the possibility that the "Vietnamization" process might be misinterpreted by Hanoi. He was concerned that the North might think America was "cutting and running" from the Vietnam crisis. He wanted Hanoi to realize that America was withdrawing its troops honorably.

At first the bombings were met with little resistance by the enemy. Follow up bombing missions, however, were met with a much more lethal response. The American people and Congress were kept in the dark about these missions because Nixon was afraid of a public backlash against this strategy. Eventually, stories about the missions were leaked to the press and the White House responded with denials. Reporter William Beecher of the *New York Times* was one of the first to write about the secret bombings. Nixon ordered illegal wiretaps in order to determine where the leaks were coming from.

Ho Chi Minh died on September 2, 1969, at age seventy-nine. A testament he had written was immediately released. He was certain that the Americans would be defeated, but that he would probably not live long enough to see it happen. He wrote in the testament that, "We, a small nation, will have earned the unique honor of defeating, through a heroic struggle, two big imperialisms-the French and the American-and making a worthy contribution to the national liberation movement."

On April 30, 1970, Nixon gave a speech in which he warned American citizens were living in an "age of anarchy." He claimed that, "in the United States, great universities are being systematically destroyed." He warned that the country could be reduced to a "pitiful, helpless giant." He explained, in his mind, that bombing Cambodia could bring an end of the war sooner than later. "If we fail to meet this challenge, all other nations will be on notice that despite its overwhelming power the United States, when a real crisis comes, will be found wanting." Nixon also announced that he would rather be a one term president than be the leader of a country who experienced its first defeat.

The fallout after Nixon's speech was immediate. Protesters on college campuses throughout the country cried out against the bombing of Cambodia. Several campuses were closed down in order to minimize violence taking place there. Nixon, angered by the protesters, referred to them as "bums." At Kent State University, several students were killed while confronting the police. In early May, over 100,000 protesters demonstrated against the bombing of Cambodia and the Kent State killings.

Congress jumped into the fray in response to Nixon's secret bombing of Cambodia. In June, the Senate voted to terminate the Tonkin Gulf Resolution of 1964. Two U.S. senators put forth an amendment to cut off all funds slated for military operations against Cambodia after June 30. Another amendment called for the withdrawal of all U.S. military personnel by the end of 1971.

Nixon was surprised about how loud and angry the criticism had become toward his policy against Cambodia. He struck back hard by ordering more secret domestic surveillance to determine links between radical domestic organizations in America and overseas. He bluntly proclaimed to political leaders that if "Congress undertakes to restrict me, Congress will have to assume the consequences." Nixon explained to his staff, "Don't worry about divisiveness. Having drawn the sword, don't take it out – stick it in hard." "No more screwing around with political opponents," he warned his advisors.

The public outcry against the Cambodian bombardment eventually subsided to the point where Nixon was able to survive the crisis. His survival was partially due to the removal of American combat troops from Cambodia. The Senate passed the amendment to cut off all funds supporting the Cambodian operations, but the House turned it down. This allowed Nixon to order more bombings of Cambodia.

Nixon and Kissinger, after two years of trying new

methods of dealing with the North Vietnamese, had noth-ing really to show for. In fact, the situation in Vietnam had actually gotten worse. North Vietnam refused to even sit down with representatives from America and South Vietnam to discuss any possible solution that would bring about a peaceful settlement. A study in late 1970 by the National Security Council reported that North Vietnam would never agree to removing its soldiers from South Vietnam.

A poll taken in late 1971 revealed that 71 percent of Americans thought the nation was wrong in sending com-bat troops to Vietnam. Indeed, 58 percent believed that the war was downright immoral. Nixon's positive poll num-bers regarding his handling of the war plunged to 31 per-cent. More and more Americans thought the rate of troop withdrawal from Vietnam was not fast enough. The Senate once again tried to force Nixon to remove all American sol-diers from Vietnam by a certain date once North Vietnam released all its prisoners of war. The House rejected the concept of a specific deadline and nothing came of the res-olution to end the war.

On March 30, 1972, the People's Army of North Vietnam invaded the South with 120,000 troops and Soviet tanks. The American intelligence community was surprised by the timing and locations of the massive invasion. The North Vietnamese easily defeated all opposition that lay in its way. Thieu ordered most of his troops to protect the towns and villages, leaving the Mekong Delta and populations around Saigon vulnerable to attack. What the North tried to prove to Nixon was that Vietnamization was a failure and that America was doomed to fight in Vietnam indefinitely.

Nixon responded to this assault by ordering 700 B-52

strikes over the demilitarized zone. The fuel depots were hit by ferocious air attacks in and around Hanoi. Kissinger immediately met with Soviet Premier Leonid Brezhnev. Kissinger informed Brezhnev that the United States was willing to allow the North Vietnamese military to stay in the South after a cease-fire. This concession represented a major change in American policy toward the Vietnam crisis. Kissinger blamed the invasion on the Soviets and he warned the Soviet leader that if the war dragged on much longer, relations between the Soviets and America could become damaged beyond repair.

The North Vietnamese rejected Kissinger's olive branch out of hand. The North felt sure that victory would be theirs. They believed that it was just a matter of time before America lost its resolve to defeat the North Vietnamese. Nixon pondered long and hard for a response to this latest setback. "If we were to lose in Vietnam," he explained, "there would have been no respect for the American president..." On May 8, Nixon proclaimed to the American people that he had ordered the mining of Haiphong Harbor and more bombing attacks.

On August 15, 1973, the bombing over Cambodia finally ended. A month earlier, Congress began an investigation to determine if the bombing of Cambodia constituted a crime. The orders to conduct secret bombings of Cambodia eventually became public. In response to this, Nixon, as we have seen earlier, ordered illegal wiretaps of White House staff members and members of the media. The Watergate break-in and the burglary of Daniel Ellsberg's psychiatrist's office needed to be covered up for fear of reprisals by Nixon's opponents. As more and more evidence came forward implementing Nixon's cover-up of the Watergate break-in, certain members of Congress began the process of impeaching President Nixon.

Part of the impeachment hearings involved the secret bombing of Cambodia. After all, a neutral country had been bombed under the guise of secrecy by an administration that failed to alert Congress of its intentions. The charges were subsequently dropped from the indictment. A congressman later stated that, "It's kind of hard to live with yourself when you impeach a guy for tapping telephones and not for making war without authorization."

On November 6, 1973, the War Powers Act was approved by Congress. Remarkably, it was passed over Nixon's veto. Essentially, it limited the amount of time a president could send troops to a region engaged in conflict without Congress' approval. The law required that the president notify Congress within forty-eight hours of any military movement toward war. The chief executive was also required to withdraw troops in sixty days absent Congressional approval of military activity. Moreover, an amendment was passed that banned funding of American military operations in Indochina. By this time, Nixon's standing with the public was at an all-time low. He lacked the credibility and power that was required to carry out his war policy.

The negotiations in Paris continued to go badly. Neither side would budge on the issue of the future of South Vietnam. In late 1973, Thieu ordered ground and air assaults on enemy bases. The North Vietnamese reacted strongly with counterattacks and achieved major victories. They regained territory that had been taken by the South and were now capturing territory formally controlled by

Saigon. North Vietnam now seemed to be in control of the war. They were on the offense while the South Vietnamese fought a defensive war. Additionally, the North had an abundance of war material that could easily be utilized within hours by their advancing armies in the South.

South Vietnam's economy was also spiraling out of control. The United States sharply reduced its military aid from $2.3 billion in 1973 to just $1 billion a year later. The dramatic rise in global inflation helped create a yearly inflation rate of nearly 100 percent. Unemployment soared while morale in the military sunk to new levels. Thieu's political future looked very uncertain. The Buddhists cry for peace grew louder. They demanded that Thieu seek a peaceful settlement with the Communists. Even the Catholics whom Thieu counted on for support began a campaign designed to end government corruption.

President Nixon resigned in disgrace over the Watergate scandal in August of 1974. Thieu could no longer count on the kind of support Nixon had provided him. Kissinger continued to beg Congress for more and more military aid. Kissinger argued that America was morally obligated to support South Vietnam against Communist aggression. Failure to do so would have, in his words, a "corrosive effect on our interests beyond Indochina." A defiant Congress failed to heed his warnings. Many argued that by aiding Thieu's government, Thieu would be more likely to prolong the war rather than negotiate toward a peaceful settlement. Senator Edward Kennedy declared that now was the time to put a stop to America's "endless support for an endless war."

America's drastic cuts in aid took a huge toll on South

Vietnam's ability to fight an aggressive and determined enemy. The South Vietnamese armies were incapable of sustaining any kind of meaningful assault on the Vietcong. Air attacks were becoming fewer and far between because of the shortage of fuel and supplies. In 1974 the desertion rate reached an alarming 240,000, the highest to date. The will to fight on grew increasingly more difficult and thoughts of surrender began to creep into the minds of many South Vietnamese.

In December of 1974, the North Vietnamese attacked Phuoc Long. Many South Vietnamese soldiers were either killed or captured and large amounts of supplies were taken. Many viewed the easy victory as more evidence that America was no longer vigorously supporting the war effort in South Vietnam. The North Vietnamese were prepared to launch full-blown offensive strikes against its enemy through 1976. They were confident that resistance from the United States armed forces would be minimal. America had grown sick of the war and it wanted out. Hanoi's leadership firmly believed that once America made up its mind to withdraw from Vietnam, it would never return.

In early 1975, the North Vietnamese launched a massive attack against South Vietnamese forces in the Central Highlands. The North captured Ban Me Thuout and quickly seized control of the highlands while Thieu ordered his vastly outnumbered forces to retreat in the hopes of creating a formidable wall of resistance against the Vietcong. Panic ensued and hundreds of thousands of refugees fled the area while South Vietnamese soldiers were cut down by enemy fire. Civilians died by the thousands from gunfire or starvation. Within a short time, the towns of Pleiku and

Kontum were captured by the North Vietnamese. Hanoi now believed that 1975 would bring them total and complete victory against America and South Vietnam.

For the first time in over a decade, Hanoi sensed that total and complete victory was at hand. As the armies of North Vietnam infiltrated deeper into enemy territory, hundreds of thousands of villagers fled from the onslaught. The North Vietnamese armed forces attacked and captured Hue and Danang, meeting very little resistance. The defending army fled toward the city of Saigon out of desperation. The United States watched in horror as South Vietnam collapsed. American intelligence was shocked at the lack of resistance the South Vietnamese exhibited. Congress was in no mood to entertain President Ford's insistence on spending an additional $300 million to help bolster the armies of the South. Ford argued that the fall of South Vietnam would weaken America's image across the globe. Congress responded to President Ford by reminding him that it was useless to spend money on the South's armed forces if they refused to fight the enemy effectively. Congress did, however, agree to spend $300 million on the evacuation of Americans from Vietnam and humanitarian aid. American soldiers would also be allowed to rescue American citizens from the South. Beyond those specific purposes, there would be no more expenditures toward the war effort.

Even at this late hour there were those who held on to the fantasy that somehow South Vietnam could successfully defend Saigon and perhaps turn the war around. By mid-April, it was hard not to see that Saigon looked like a city under siege. One eyewitness wrote in his diary that the beggars were "out en masse now, and increasingly aggressive, tearing at your pockets or your car windows." Others more fortunate were reduced to selling everything they owned that could not be carried. Finally, Thieu was asked to resign by American Ambassador Martin. He was told it would be for the good of the country, and so he stepped down. He bitterly blamed the United States for South Vietnam's humiliating defeat. On May 1, 1975, Vietcong soldiers hoisted a flag over Ho Chi Minh City. President Ford proclaimed a few days later that the Vietnam War was "finished as far as the United States is concerned."

The end of the war left many Americans feeling frustrated and angry. Many questioned the government's real motives by getting involved in a war that seemed unwinnable from the very beginning. Others asked how a large, industrial nation such as the United States could be beaten by a much smaller, rural nation. The defeat of South Vietnam never truly became a political issue between the Democrats and the Republicans because both parties had for the most part supported the war. Sadly, Vietnam quickly became a non-issue during the 1976 presidential campaign. The media barely mentioned Vietnam on its nightly broadcast. Many Americans refused to even discuss the war. Columnist Joseph C. Harsch remarked that, "Today it is almost as though the war never happened. Americans have somehow blocked it out of their consciousness. They don't talk about it. They don't talk about its consequences."

Of the 2.15 million men and women who were sent to Vietnam, 1.6 million of them actually saw combat. Those who served were disproportionately black and poorly educated. A young man had a much greater chance of serving in Vietnam if he had never studied in college during the period of the Vietnam conflict. That changed in 1971 when student deferments no longer ensured that a college student would not be sent off to war. The homecoming many Vietnam vets received was often harsh and cruel. Many were spat upon by those who had protested the war. They were looked upon by many as cold-blooded killers who did not belong in civilized society. Many vets who came home for good found it difficult to earn a living wage due to their lack of job training. Depression and serious sleep disorders affected hundreds of thousands of veterans. The euphemism, "Post-traumatic stress disorder" replaced the shockingly cold, "shell-shock" that categorized traumatized veterans from past wars.

To many, the Vietnam War made it clear that the United States, although powerful, had limitations under certain circumstances. The military might of China and the Soviet Union deterred the United States from unleashing its full military capability. The United States, in its determination to halt Communist aggression in South Vietnam, placed itself in harm's way. The nation intervened in a local struggle between a weak and corrupt government and an aggressive, tenacious adversary. Many argue that the United States placed too much importance on saving South Vietnam from the Communists, that the area was of little significance. Others maintain that the terrain was too treacherous to do battle in and that we should have stayed out of the region for practical reasons. Others argue that America's involvement in the war was a "noble cause" and that America should never turn its back on nations willing to fight for freedom against oppression. They argue that America did not go all out militarily. One thing can be agreed upon by everyone, however. The question of whether or not America should have defended South Vietnam from North Vietnam's aggression will forever remain unsettled.

Part Five

THE WARREN COMMISSION REPORT

CHAPTER 12

DEATH IN DALLAS

O n November 22, 1963, President John Kennedy and the First Lady, Jacqueline Kennedy, arrived at Love Field, Texas, shortly before noon on Air Force One. As the plane taxied down the runway, Kennedy turned to an aide and said, "Here we are in Dallas, and it looks like everything in Texas is going to be fine for us." President Kennedy and the First Lady emerged from the plane and stood for a moment at the top of the ramp. The crowd below cheered as the couple smiled and waved to their admiring fans. They disembarked from the plane and were immediately greeted by Vice President Lyndon Johnson and his wife, Ladybird. The president and his wife walked along a fence which was lined with people waiting to shake hands with the new arrivals. Jackie carried a bouquet of red roses that Ladybird had given her. Mrs. Kennedy stepped inside the presidential limousine that was awaiting them. She sat down in the back seat and the president followed her, sitting to her right. Mrs. Kennedy placed the bouquet of roses on the seat directly to her right. Governor John Connally of Texas and his wife, Nellie, sat in front of the Kennedys.

Not everyone at Love Field that afternoon was as warm and friendly as those reaching out to shake the president's hand or at least catch a glimpse of him. There were those holding banners with words like "YOU'RE A TRAITOR," and "YANKEE GO HOME."

There was not a cloud in the sky that day. The sun was intense and so Jackie pulled out a pair of sunglasses and put them on. Her husband glanced over at her, looking slightly surprised. He seemed a little annoyed as he explained to her, "Jackie, take those off. The people have come to see you." Jackie agreed to remove the sunglasses and placed them back inside her handbag.

As the president's motorcade headed toward the city of Dallas, the crowds became larger and more boisterous. The motorcade slowed to about 12 miles an hour. Agent Lawson noticed some children standing directly ahead of the motorcade. They were holding a large sign which read, "Please, Mr. President. Stop and shake our hands." As the president's car approached the children, he told his driver, agent Bill Greer, to pull up to the children. "Bill, stop here," Kennedy ordered. "Call these people over and I'll shake their hands."

The crowd raced toward the president. Kennedy stood and leaned over the side of the car and began shaking each of the children's hands. He laughed as the children shouted with excitement. Jackie, however, remained seated and smiled at the children. She looked a little uneasy as the car became totally surrounded by the adoring fans. The president motioned to his driver to move on. As Greer pulled away from the crowd, he noticed the president wince as he sat back down into his seat. Greer knew Kennedy was wearing his back brace, but evidently it was not enough to alleviate the excruciating pain he felt.

The motorcade continued traveling through downtown Dallas. The agents scanned thousands of people standing along the motorcade route. People hung from the windows of skyscrapers as they looked down at the motorcade below them. Some others made sounds with noise makers in an apparent attempt to attract the president's attention.

Dave Powers and Ken O'Donnell, two of Kennedy's top advisors, were amazed at the number of people who came out to welcome the president. Just three years earlier during the 1960 election, the crowds were not as large or appreciative. They estimated that at least one hundred and fifty thousand people used their lunch time to greet the popular president and his lovely wife. This boded well for a president seeking re-election in 1964.

For no apparent reason, a young boy broke past the crowd and ran toward the president's limousine scream-ing, "Slow down! Slow down!" Agent Jack Ready imme-diately leaped off the running board and ran toward the boy and shoved him to the curb. The force of the boy hit-ting the curb caused several onlookers to fall. Agents were trained to make snap decisions like this quite frequently, even though they might be criticized later by the president. It was a risk any agent was willing to take.

Finally, the motorcade continued on the parade route.

As the motorcade approached downtown Dallas, the crowds grew much larger. The motorcade turned off the main street onto Houston Street. They were now one block from the Texas Book Depository. Mrs. Connelly turned and said, "We will soon be there." Jackie recalled that it was very hot that day. She noticed a tunnel in the distance and thought how much cooler it would be once they were inside it.

Agent Clint Hill, the man in charge of the First Lady's safety, noticed that the crowds were getting thinner near the end of Main Street. The safety of the president and his wife would become easier now that there were less people to deal with. Just as the president's car turned right onto Houston Street, the number of people standing along the road diminished even more. Clint Hill looked over to his right and saw the sign for the Stemmons Freeway. The motorcade would soon be moving quickly and out of harm's way.

Directly ahead of the motorcade stood a seven-story building. It was just an old brick building with the words TEXAS SCHOOL BOOK DEPOSITORY over a section of it. Atop the roof of the building was a yellow Hertz billboard with a huge digital clock embedded in it. The agents noticed nothing unusual about the building. There were a number of open windows scattered throughout the side of the building facing the motorcade. But this had been a normal occurrence along the route.

As the three lead motorcycles turned left onto Elm Street, Chief Curry calculated that the president would soon be arriving at his destination, the Trade Mart. Bill Greer was relieved that no significant incidences occurred along the route from Love Field to Dealey Plaza. Fortunately, the crowds remained relatively friendly and cordial.

Just as the president's limousine turned off of Houston Street and onto Elm Street, Mrs. Connally turned to the president and said, "You certainly can't say that the people of Dallas haven't given you a nice welcome." The president agreed with the sentiment. At this very point, the president's car moved very slowly and the crowds grew noticeably thinner.

Suddenly, there was a loud cracking sound. The First Lady recalled later that it sounded like one of the motorcycles had backfired. Bill Greer also thought the sound was caused by backfire or a blowout from one of the motorcycles. Agent Ready thought it sounded like a firecracker. Agent Paul Landis, however, believed the sound was rifle fire. He looked ahead and saw the president turn his head to the right where the sound appeared to have come from. He looked up at the Texas Book Depository but didn't notice anything suspicious. He quickly looked over to his left at the grassy knoll and noticed nothing unusual.

Agent Clint Hill heard another loud snap that appeared to come from the right and behind the president's car. As he turned around, he noticed the president lunging forward while raising both hands to his neck. The president slumped to his left toward the First Lady. Jackie noticed that her husband had a quizzical expression. Hill immediately jumped off the running board of the car behind the president's and ran toward the president's limousine.

Kellerman shouted to the driver, Bill Greer, "Let's get out of here! We are hit!" He shouted another order into the radio: "Lawson, this is Kellerman. We're hit. Get us to the nearest hospital. Quick!"

A third shot hit the president in the head. Jackie

screamed, "They've killed my husband, they've shot his head off! I have his brain in my hand." Jackie got up out of her seat and started to crawl on top of the trunk. Clint Hill was afraid Jackie might get hit by a sniper and so he lunged on top of the trunk and managed to push her onto the back seat.

Agent Clint Hill's body was spread over the trunk of the president's car. He glanced at the president's wounds and was repulsed by what he saw. A section of Kennedy's head was missing, his head was drenched in his own blood and his eyes were fixated. Lying on the seat next to the president was a piece of his head with hair on it. The president appeared dead to him. Mrs. Kennedy was trying to comfort her husband saying, "Jack, Jack, what have they done to you?"

Governor Connally suddenly felt pain down the right side of his back. His shirt was drenched in his own blood. He had heard what Mrs. Kennedy thought was a motorcycle backfiring, but he was sure they were rifle shots and nothing else. He knew this because he was an avid hunter.

Connally cried out, "My God, they're going to kill us all."

His wife, Nellie, pulled him toward her in order to protect him from further injury.

When Abraham Zapruder, one of several witnesses filming the president that day, saw Kennedy slump toward Mrs. Kennedy, he thought the president must have been joking around by pretending to have been shot.

One of the spectators in the crowd was Howard L. Brennan. His testimony to the Warren Commission as to what he witnessed that fateful day would become highly significant. Brennan, aged forty-five, was a family man and worked as a steamfitter. Only a short distance from the corner of Elm and Houston, he stood on a low white wall so that he could see over the people gathering in front of him.

While waiting for the motorcade to arrive, he occasionally looked up at the Texas Book Depository. He spotted three black individuals leaning out one the windows on the fifth floor. They were laughing and enjoying each other's company. Just above them, he noticed a young man behind a window that was partially open. He noticed the man held a rifle, but amazingly, thought nothing of it. Brennan thought to himself that the man "is just sitting there, waiting to see the same thing I'm going to see, the president." The gunman was a mere forty yards from where Brennan stood.

Brennan wasn't the only bystander to notice the man in the sixth floor window. Ronald Fisher and Robert Edwards, two county auditor clerks, observed the man as well. "Look at that guy there in that window," Edwards told his friend. "He looks like he is uncomfortable." They observed that the man did not appear to move at all. He seemed frozen and unemotional. He may have even been lying down and facing the window. The two were unsure. Something didn't seem quite right.

Amazingly, no law officer claimed to have noticed a man situated behind the sixth story window holding what appeared to be a rifle with a telescopic lens. He was visible to several people standing and waiting for the president's motorcade to arrive. Someone who did notice the figure in the window was Arnold Rowland. He and his wife had been waiting below the Depository since 12:14 p.m. Curiously, a police officer stood just a few feet away from the Rowlands, but the couple didn't think to warn the policeman about this unusual circumstance. Even though he supposedly told his wife he thought the man might be a Secret Service sniper, he could have confirmed this information with a law enforcement officer.

Mrs. Carolyn Walther and Mrs. Pearl Springer watched from a point opposite from the Texas Book Depository. Mrs. Walther later testified she witnessed a man at an end window near the top of the building. She saw the man holding a rifle. He was pointing it downward toward where the president's motorcade would soon be arriving. Mrs. Walther was convinced she saw another man accompanying the man holding the rifle.

Why the assassin did not attempt to shoot the president at only four hundred feet away while Kennedy was on Houston Street and facing the Texas Book Depository remains a mystery. Kennedy would have been clearly in the gunman's crosshairs dead on. Perhaps the gunman feared that a missed shot would cause the driver to speed away to safety so that no other shots could be fired in time. Then again, secret service agents might have spotted the gunman instantly after the missed first shot because they would have been facing the Texas Book Depository.

But there was a more compelling reason why the gunman decided to wait for the president's car to slowly turn onto Elm. The president's head and back would have been exposed for a long enough time, allowing the gunman to get off several shots. And there was no escape route. The agent driving the president's car could not make a sudden U-turn on Elm Street in order to avoid further danger to the president. The only feasible option, albeit a bad one, was to continue driving toward the underpass. Unfortunately, this would allow more time for the gunman to reload and get off more shots.

The Hertz clock had just clicked 12:30 p.m. A sixteen year old schoolboy, Amos Lee Euins, waved at the president, and the president waved back. Amos suddenly looked up at the Depository. He noticed what appeared to be a piece of pipe sticking out of one of the windows. He looked back at the president's car one last time.

Suddenly, there was a loud, cracking sound. Brennan thought it sounded like a firecracker. He thought the sound was caused by a firecracker or a motorcycle backfiring. There could be no other possible explanation. Tiny bits of asphalt sprayed the air near the rear of the president's car. Mrs. Donald S. Baker noticed that the fragments shot straight up into the air. James Tague's cheek was showered with many of those fragments.

Roy Kellerman thought he heard the president say something like, "My God, I'm hit!" Bill Greer, the driver, turned to his right and noticed that the president had been hit. As he studied the president's face, the car began veering slightly from right to left. Both Greer and Hill had not yet reacted to what had just transpired. Everything had happened so quickly.

Seconds later, a second shot was fired. Standing twenty feet away Charles Brehm and his son watched in horror as the president's face grimaced. They stared in disbelief as Kennedy raised his hands up to his throat. The second shot was not fatal by any means. A 6.5 millimeter bullet allegedly had ripped through the back of the neck, touched the right lung, ripped through his windpipe and then exited at his throat. The bullet entered Connally's back, chest, right wrist, and left thigh. It was at this exact time when Connally started to turn to his right in the direction of where he thought the rifle blast came from. Immediately after turning, he felt as if someone had punched him hard in the back. Blood oozed out of his wound and he began to pass out.

Secret Service agent Glen Bennett looked right at the president when the second shot was fired. He saw the shot hit Kennedy "about four inches down from the right shoulder." Bennett shouted, "He's hit!" Agent Hickey grabbed for his Colt AR-15 assault rifle and pointed in the direction where he thought the shots came from.

A third shot was fired. Howard Brennan watched again as the gunman let off another shot aimed at the presidential limousine. Brennan turned his head away from the gunman and toward the front of the motorcade to see what had been hit. His view was obstructed by part of a concrete peristyle.

Meanwhile, Zapruder continued to film this horror scene. Just about the time the president's limousine passed him, Zapruder watched in stupefied amazement as Kennedy's head exploded and pieces of his skull shot high into the air.

Zapruder yelled, "They've killed him, they've killed him!" as he continued to film the slain president lying lifeless next to his wife.

Special Agent Roy Kellerman, who was sitting in the front seat, saw brain matter shooting above his head. He heard Mrs. Kennedy shout, "What are they doing to you?"

Howard Brennan jumped off the stone wall to avoid being shot. He looked up at the sixth floor window and saw the gunman pull the rifle back away from the window. The gunman disappeared from Brennan's sight. But Brennan wasn't the only witness to see the gunman in the window. Bob Jackson, a press photographer, saw a rifle barrel being slowly withdrawn from the window. Malcolm Coach, a WFAA-TV cameraman saw "about a foot of a rifle" being pulled away from the same window. It was too late to film the gunman.

Agent Hill yelled to the lead car, "To the hospital, to the hospital!" Hill, who was still stretched across the top of the trunk, turned his head toward Agent Landis who was behind him and gave him a thumb's down sign. This meant that something bad had just happened to the president.

Officer Marrion Baker, certain that the shots came from the direction of the Book Depository, rushed toward the front of the building. The building supervisor noticed the officer and followed him up the front stairs leading into the depository. Baker asked Truly, the building supervisor, where the stairway was that lead to the roof. Truly showed the officer the stairway. They tried to use the freight elevators, but they did not work. They decided instead to take the stairs.

When Baker reached the second floor, he looked through the window of a door and saw a man walking away. Baker opened the door and yelled for the man to stop. "Come here," he shouted. The man turned around and walked toward the officer. He appeared perfectly calm. Baker at this point had his gun drawn on the man. Truly, realizing the officer was no longer behind him, ran down to the second floor where he heard voices.

Truly noticed the officer pointing his gun at one of

the employees who worked at the book depository. That employee's name was Lee Harvey Oswald. Oswald did not appear nervous or afraid. Baker turned to Truly and asked him if he knew the man he had stopped. Truly told Baker that the man worked at the depository. The officer turned away from Oswald and ran toward the stairwell with Truly close behind. They were both headed toward the roof.

As Oswald walked past Mrs. Robert A Reid, an employee at the book depository, she told him, "The president has been shot." She heard Oswald mumble a reply, but could not make out what he had said. She also felt it was somewhat peculiar that he was even in the vicinity where she worked because he normally never passed that way. She noticed him walk toward the front entrance to the building.

Baker and Truly finally reached the roof. Baker ruled out any attempt to shoot from the roof because the parapet was too high to shoot over. He climbed the Hertz sign and determined there was no way a shooter could get off any shots without falling.

In the meantime, the president's limousine rushed toward Parkland Hospital. There was hardly any movement in the back seat of the president's car. Governor Connally had by this time lapsed into unconsciousness. His wife thought he might be dead. The First Lady sobbed over her fallen husband. She cried over and over again, "He's dead – they've killed him." The presidential limousine pulled up to Parkland Hospital's emergency entrance. No hospital personnel greeted the secret service men. Agent Kellerman shouted to agents that had just arrived after him, "Go get us two stretchers on wheels!" Kellerman noticed that

Connally began to show signs of consciousness and assured him that he would survive the attack. "Governor, don't worry. Everything is going to be all right."

Dave Powers rushed toward the president's car. Jackie turned to Powers and said, "Dave, he's dead." Powers noticed that the president's eyes had a dead, vacant stare and that the left eye was bulging from its socket. Vice President Lyndon Johnson was quickly escorted into the building. Jackie was still covering her husband with her body when she was informed that the president needed to be moved. She did not budge, only replying that there was no need to move the president.

Connally tried to get out of the way so that the president could be moved, but in the process he collapsed in pain. He moaned, "My God, it hurts." Connally was lifted onto a gurney and was rushed inside the hospital by hospital attendants. Jackie was again asked by the agents to move so that the president could be carried into the hospital. "I'm not going to let go of him," she replied. When she was told again by Agent Hill to move, she replied, "No, Mr. Hill. You know he's dead. Let me alone." Agent Hill believed Jackie did not want her husband moved because the gruesome nature of the president's wounds would be revealed. He covered the president's head and upper torso with his jacket. Jackie finally released her husband, and the president was rushed into the hospital.

Lawson leaped from the lead car and made his way through to the emergency room corridor. He saw an orderly desperately trying to push two gurneys by himself down the hallway to the emergency entrance doorway. Why weren't these gurneys already outside? Chief Curry had ordered the Dallas police headquarters to call Parkland Hospital to have them ready. Lawson pulled the gurneys away from the orderly and wheeled them down the corridor himself.

The president was wheeled into Trauma Room One where Dr. Charles Carrico was waiting. Although he was only twenty eight years old, he had witnessed two hundred gunshot wounds at Parkland. He examined the president and noticed that his color was "blue white, ashen." The color indicated to him failing blood circulation. There were also no obvious voluntary movements. Although his eyes were open and staring, the pupils were dilated. The doctor detected a very faint heartbeat.

After noticing a gaping hole, shredded scalp and brain tissue, the doctor attempted to restore the president's breathing and circulation. He inserted a endotracheal tube down the throat for adequate air passage. Dr. Perry took over from Dr. Carrico and quickly examined the president's condition. He noticed that the president was struggling to breath. The respirator was hooked up and began pumping fresh air into the president's lungs. His breathing, however, was determined to be inadequate. Dr. Perry made a large incision in the president's throat and a tube was inserted into the windpipe. Another incision was made in the president's chest and a tube was inserted to drain any possible accumulation of blood in the chest cavity.

The president's personal physician, Admiral George Burkley, stepped into the operating room and studied the president's condition. He was convinced that the president could not be saved no matter what the doctors did. He stepped out into the corridor and noticed that Jackie was sitting on a chair, looking totally devastated. She asked that she be allowed to see her husband before he died. A supervising nurse told her she could not be permitted in the operating room. Burkley suggested to Jackie that she take a sedative. She refused the offer and continued to demand that she be with her dying husband. The Admiral, feeling very sorry for the First Lady, ushered her into the trauma room. She handed Dr. Jenkins a piece of the president's brain tissue. Evidently, she had been holding onto the tissue for quite some time. Then she slowly dropped to the floor and prayed.

Bobby Kennedy was on the phone from Washington, D.C. He wanted to speak with Agent Hill to find out what was going on. "What's going on down there?" Bobby asked. Clint Hill told Bobby that shots were fired during the final stages of the motorcade in Dallas. "The president is very seriously injured. They're working on him now. Governor Connally was hit, too." Bobby asked Hill about the seriousness of the president's condition. Clint Hill could not tell Bobby all that he knew. He could not tell him that he had witnessed his brother's head explode, emitting brain matter and blood. "It's as bad as it can get," Clint Hill blurted out to Bobby.

Vice President Johnson was advised by the Secret Service to fly back to Washington, D.C. immediately. It was determined to be the safest place for Johnson. Johnson disagreed with this notion. "It would be unthinkable for me to leave President Kennedy's life hanging in the balance," he explained. He was concerned about how it would look to be flying back in Air Force One while the president was still fighting for his life. In fact, he wasn't even the president at that moment. Johnson asked for advice from Kenneth O'Donnell and Dave Powers about what to do. They both agreed that Johnson should fly back to Washington on Air Force One immediately.

In the meantime, Oswald had boarded a bus on Elm Street. The bus passed by the area where the assassination took place just moments before. The bus got stuck in traffic and so Oswald asked the driver for a transfer ticket and got off.

Swarms of law enforcement officers surrounded the front entrance of the Texas Book Depository. Brennan was again questioned about whom he saw leaning out of a window on the sixth floor of the book depository. The information Brennan offered to Inspector Sawyer was relayed to a police dispatcher. "The wanted person in this is a slender white male about thirty. Five foot ten. A hundred and sixty-five. And carrying a – what looked like – a 30-30 or some type of Winchester."

Oswald got into a cab driven by William Whaley, a former navy gunner who had fought at Iwo Jima. Oswald told the driver he wanted to go to Five Hundred North Beckley Street. After driving for about two and a half miles, Oswald asked the driver to pull over so he could get out. Strangely, Oswald asked to be let out at the 700 hundred block, not the 500 hundred block of North Beckley. Oswald paid the driver the ninety five cent fare and tipped him five cents. The cabbie was not impressed with his tip and drove off.

At 1:00 p.m. at Parkland Hospital, Dr. Kemp Clark examined the president for a pulse. Sadly, he determined there was no pulse. An external heart massage was administered to the president. Suddenly, a pulse could be felt in the president's neck and in the femoral artery in the leg. But hope quickly faded when they noticed that the cardiotachyscope showed absolutely no signs of cardiac activity. President Kennedy was pronounced dead.

The president's wounds were classified as a four-plus injury, the absolute worst case scenario in which no one survives. Although Kennedy arrived at Parkland Hospital still breathing, he was realistically dead on arrival. Dr. Clark signed the death certificate which indicated the president died from massive head trauma. Dr. Jenkins removed the intravenous lines and disconnected the monitoring leads from Kennedy's body. Mrs. Kennedy walked over to her dead husband and gently kissed him through the sheet covering the president.

The president was administered the last rites of the church by Father Oscar Huber. Because the president was dead, he was not given the longer version of absolution normally provided to those who are dying and not yet deceased. After the priest completed the last rites, Admiral Burkley questioned Father Huber about the shortness of the ritual. As nurses continued to clean up the president's blood and brain tissue, Father Huber began reciting the Lord's Prayer and Hail Mary.

After the conclusion of the extended version of the last rites, Mrs. Kennedy slowly sat down on a chair while two priests conveyed to her their deepest sympathies. Father Huber walked over to the First Lady and said, "I want to extend my sympathy and that of my parishioners." The First Lady thanked him and asked that he pray for her husband. Father Huber tried to assure Mrs. Kennedy that he was certain the president's soul had not yet left the body. "This was a valid last sacrament," he assured her.

As Father Huber was about to leave, a Secret Service agent told him, "Father, you don't know anything about this." Waiting for them outside was a large group of reporters. Father Huber was asked by a *Time* magazine reporter if the president was in fact dead. "He's dead, all right," Huber replied.

At about 1:08 p.m., Officer Tippit spotted a man that fit the description of the suspected assassin. That man was Lee Harvey Oswald. The suspect was walking on the right side of the street in front of the officer. He decided to tail the suspect. While Tippit followed Oswald, he tried unsuccessfully to reach the police dispatcher for more detail on the description of the alleged assassin.

Witnesses noticed the squad car stop suddenly. and saw a man walk over to the car. The man was seen leaning over on the passenger side of the squad car and talking to the officer through the open window. The man had his hands inside each of the pockets of his jacket. Tippit slowly got out of the squad car, but he did not have his hand on his revolver. As the officer walked around the front side of the car, his eyes looking toward the ground instead of the suspect, Oswald took two steps back, pulled a gun out and shot the officer. The officer grabbed his stomach and fell to the ground. Oswald immediately ran from the scene, stopped suddenly, and fired one more shot at the officer's head.

Oswald spotted one of the witnesses to the shooting. The witness, Mrs. Markham, was standing across the street when the murder took place. Afraid she might be the next victim, the witness fell to her knees and covered her face with both hands. Seconds later, she looked over her hands and saw the killer run off.

Mrs. Markham began screaming, "He killed him! He killed him!" as she pointed toward Oswald. Another witness overheard Oswald saying to himself, "Poor damn cop" or "poor dumb cop." The witness wasn't sure.

Ex-marine Ted Callaway spotted Oswald holding a gun straight up in the air. Callaway yelled over at Oswald, "Hey, man, what the hell is going on?"

Oswald slowed down, muttered something, and quickly walked on. Other witnesses saw the killer reloading his pistol and then stuffed it under his belt. Mrs. Markham ran over to the fallen officer to see if she could help. She heard what she thought might be death gasps coming from the officer.

"Somebody help me!" she screamed in despair.

No one responded to her pleas for several minutes.

Frank Cimino had heard what sounded like four gunshots. He bolted out the front door to see what was going on. Mrs. Markham yelled over to him, "Call the police!"

Cimino saw that Tippit had been shot in the head and the officer's gun was lying next to him.

At about 1:22 p.m., Deputy Constable Seymour Weitzman found what appeared to be the murder weapon inside the Texas Book Depository. It was hidden beneath some boxes. Found within the sniper's nest was a long, brown paper bag. Detectives determined that the bag may have been used to conceal the weapon as it was brought into the building.

The manager of Hardy's Shoe Store, Johnny C. Brewer, had been listening to loud police sirens for several minutes before a young white male entered the lobby of his store. His hair was messed up and he appeared to be breathing heavily. He also looked out of sorts. Brewer thought it odd that the man kept his back to the street instead of wondering what the sirens were all about.

Once the police cars took off in another direction, the man walked out onto the sidewalk and began walking in the direction of the Texas Theater. That day the theater was showing *Cry of Battle* and *War Is Hell*. Van Heflin's name appeared between both movie titles.

Brewer grew suspicious and started walking in the direction of the strange man. He saw the man slip past the ticket taker and duck inside the movie theater. Brewer walked inside the theater, approached the concession stand employee, and asked if he had seen anyone enter recently. He replied that he had been busy and did not see anyone.

After finishing their search inside the movie theater, Brewer and the ticket taker walked up to the box office and informed Mrs. Postal that it was too dark to see anyone. Postal told the two men that she would call the police while they covered the exit doors. Moments later, police squad cars pulled up to the theater and policemen rushed into the building. All the house lights were turned up. Brewer stood on the stage to get a good look at the audience. Just as the lights came on he spotted the suspect immediately. The man sat about seven rows from the back of the theater in the center. The man jumped out of his seat and headed to the aisle on his right. He sat down again, this time in a seat three rows from the back.

Brewer pointed out the man to police officers. So as not to alert the suspect, officers approached two men sitting up front and searched them for weapons. They continued, however, to keep the suspect in sight. As officers continued walking up the aisles, Officer McDonald, standing with his back to the man, suddenly spun around and ordered the startled man to his feet. The man rose to his feet and raised his hands. He was searched for weapons.

Resigned to his new circumstances, the man said, "Well, it's all over now." He struck one of the officers in the head, knocking him backward into the seats. The officer got back on his feet and lunged toward his assailant and the two ended up on the floor with the man on top of the officer. The man was holding the officer with one hand while he tried reaching for something near his waistband with his other hand. Officer Hutson grabbed the man around the neck and pulled him off of McDonald. Officer Walker grabbed hold of the man's left hand while Officer McDonald grabbed the man's right hand. Apparently, the suspect had been reaching for his pistol with his right hand. Somehow, the suspect was able to free his right hand and attempted to grab the pistol.

Someone yelled, "Look out! He's got a gun!"

At this instant, the man pointed the gun directly at McDonald. The officer grabbed the pistol's cylinder to keep it from turning so no bullet could fire. More officers joined in trying to yank the gun out of the man's hand. An officer commanded the man to let go of the gun.

"I can't," the suspect yelled back.

Finally, one of the officers yelled out, "I've got it!"

The man was quickly cuffed. He pleaded for the officers not to hit him any more and threatened to issue a complaint about police brutality. The man was asked to reveal his name, but he refused to provide it.

As the suspect was being led away by police, he screamed in protest, "They're violating my civil rights!"

An angry mob screamed, "That's him! Murderer! Hang him! Give him to us, we'll kill him!"

Oswald complained that the cuffs were too tight and so an officer tightened them some more. "They're actually a little loose," the officer declared.

As the suspect was being driven to police headquarters, he was asked to provide his name again. The suspect remained silent. He also refused to provide his address. While one of the officers reached into the suspect's pocket to retrieve a wallet, the man asked why he was being treated like a criminal.

"What is this all about? I know my rights. Why am I being arrested? The only thing I've done is carry a pistol in a movie," he claimed.

When the suspect was told that a police officer had been killed recently, he acted surprised.

"I hear they burn for murder," the man replied.

Officer Walker responded ominously with, "You might find out."

The suspect shot back defiantly with, "Well, they say it just takes a second to die."

A library card was found inside the man's wallet. The name, Lee Oswald, was indicated on the card. But then another name, A.J Hidell, was found in another section of the wallet. When asked which of the two names was his, the prisoner refused to speak. Throughout all the questioning, the suspect had not shown any indication of guilt. He remained cool.

The squad car carrying the suspect pulled into a garage located beneath City Hall. The police headquarters was located inside the building. The officers rushed the suspect inside and took an elevator up to the third floor. They took him to the Homicide and Robbery Bureau where they began questioning him. Detective Elmer Boyd asked the suspect how he got a black eye.

The prisoner replied, "Well, I struck an officer and the officer struck me back, which he should have done."

Captain Fritz, chief of the Homicide and Robbery Bureau, asked the suspect to provide his full name. The man replied, "Lee Harvey Oswald."

Fritz's interrogation tactics involved casual conversation. This would hopefully allow the prisoner to lower his guard so that eventually he would say things he normally would not confess under harsh treatment. Fritz asked Oswald about his employment at the book depository and how he got the job. Oswald answered all his questions.

Asked about the name, "Hidell," Oswald replied that it was a name he "picked up in New Orleans."

Oswald denied owning a rifle. He admitted owning a shotgun, however, while he and his wife lived in Russia several years earlier. He revealed that he was a secretary for an organization called Fair Play for Cuba. He became irritated when asked about whether he ever contacted the Soviet Embassy.

"Yes, I contacted the Soviet embassy regarding my wife. And the reason was because you've accosted her twice already!"

When Oswald was asked if he had ever been to Mexico City, be vehemently denied ever having been there. Oswald was asked where he was when the president was shot. He replied that he was having lunch on the first floor of the book depository. When he left work that day he went to his room on Beckley Street, changed his trousers, grabbed his revolver, and headed to a movie theater. Someone asked him why he took his gun to the movies. He said he felt like taking it.

"You know how boys are when they have a gun," Oswald joked. "They just carry it."

Oswald again denied shooting Officer Tippit. Asked about what he did in the Soviet Union for three years, he claimed he worked in a radio electronics factory. Suddenly, the subject changed and Oswald was asked why he left the book depository after the shooting. He explained that he felt there was nothing more to do at the depository due to all commotion after the shooting.

"Did you shoot the president?"

"No, I emphatically deny that," Oswald replied. "I haven't shot anybody."

After he was asked several more questions, he grew belligerent.

"I don't care to answer any more questions," he warned.

Oswald was led out of the Homicide and Robbery office and taken to a corridor swarming with reporters and photographers.

"Did you kill the president?" someone yelled at him.

"No sir," Oswald replied. "Nobody charged me with that."

Oswald was taken to a holdover room where he was searched. Detective Boyd found several live rounds of .38

ammunition in his front pocket. The detectives were surprised no one had bothered to conduct a complete search
of the suspect.

"I just had them in my pocket," Oswald explained.

Several minutes later, Oswald was ordered to stand in
a police lineup. After Mrs. Markham fingered Oswald as
the man who shot Officer Tippit, she fainted. Meanwhile,
the police were busy examining Oswald's belonging in the
room he had been renting. Among some of the items found
in the room were several James Bond books, a pair of binoc-
ulars, a city map of Dallas, and a certificate of Undesirable
Discharge from the marines. The detectives threw many of
Oswald's belongings in some pillow cases and rushed back
to police headquarters.

At around 6:00 p.m., Air Force One touched down
at Andrews Air Force Base in Maryland. Robert Kennedy
ran up the ramp and quickly headed toward the rear of
the plane. He was in a hurry to be with Jackie so he could
comfort her. Shortly afterwards, the nation's new leader,
President Lyndon Baines Johnson, stood in front of Air
Force One and delivered a solemn message to America and
the world. "This is a sad time for all people," Johnson began.
"We have suffered a loss that cannot be weighed. For me it
is a deep personal tragedy. I know the world shares the sor-
row that Mrs. Kennedy and her family bear. I will do my
best. That is all I can do. I ask for your help – and God's."

Many of the nation's former statesmen expressed their
anguish to a grief-stricken nation. Harry S. Truman was so
shaken by the nation's tragedy, he could not issue a statement. Eisenhower felt repulsed and angry by the assassination. He referred to the shocking event as an "occasional

psychopathic thing." General Douglas McArthur was quoted as saying, "The president's death kills something inside me." Adlai Stevenson stated that "All men everywhere who love peace and justice and freedom will bow their heads."

A little after seven in the evening, Oswald was told by Judge Johnston that he was being arraigned for the murder of Officer J.D. Tippit. Oswald shouted back, stating that he could only be arraigned in a courtroom and not a police station. "The way you're treating me, I'd might as well be in Russia," Oswald snarled at the judge. The judge responded by advising Oswald of his rights to remain silent and denied Oswald bail.

Another lineup was scheduled to take place in the assembly room in the basement of City Hall. Three other men were handcuffed together along with Oswald. Two were prisoners and the other man was the jail clerk. Oswald once again took the second position from the left. Barbara and Virginia Davis were two of the witnesses who would be asked to identify the killer of Tippit. Howard Brennan would also partake in trying to identify the killer. Brennan was upset to learn that he was the only person to have reportedly seen Oswald in the sixth floor window of the book depository. He was afraid that he may be putting his family in danger by identifying Oswald as the assassin.

Brennan told Sorrels that he might not be able to make a positive identification of the killer. But he also admitted seeing Oswald under arrest. "I don't know if I can do you any good or not because I have seen the man that they have under arrest on television." He was clearly afraid and uncertain about being involved in this horrific event that had been thrust upon him. Brennan asked if he could view the lineup from about the same distance as when he witnessed the shooter. Sorrels assured him that he would witness the lineup from in back and in front of the room.

The handcuffed men were led onto the stage. Barbara Davis was the first witness to react to the men standing in the lineup. "That's him," she announced to the police officers. "The second one from the left." She had fingered Oswald. She became even more positive after viewing Oswald's profile. She was sure that this was the man who crossed her front yard the day of the killing. Virginia Davis agreed with her sister-in-law that Oswald was indeed the man who had run from the murder scene. The noose was now tightening around Oswald's neck.

Howard Brennan was the next witness to speak. Remarkably, the only person to have reportedly seen Oswald just moments before the nation's leader was murdered claimed that he could not make a positive identification. "I cannot positively say," he proclaimed. When pressed, Brennan finally admitted that perhaps the man second from the left looked like the man he saw in the window.

"He looks like him. But the man I saw wasn't disheveled like this fella," Brennan claimed. Sorrel was noticeably upset by Brennan's reaction to the police lineup.

Immediately after the lineup, Oswald was taken to Captain Fritz's office for more questioning. Before reaching the office, he told reporters that, 'I'm just a patsy!" He blamed his predicament on his stay in the Soviet Union.

During another interrogation session, Oswald remained calm as he answered questions tossed at him by the detectives. He rarely hesitated to answer any of the questions. He was told by Captain Fritz that he himself knew he killed the president. Oswald denied the charge emphatically. When told that the president was in fact dead, Oswald replied heartlessly, "Yeah, well, people will forget that in a few days and there will be another president."

Around 11:00 p.m., Chief Curry, DA Wade, and Captain Fritz agreed to meet with reporters. They informed the press that there had been no confession by Oswald. When pressed on what physical evidence they were holding Oswald on, the officers refused to provide information. They only admitted that the gun played an important part of the evidence. They informed the press that the evidence being used against Oswald was not strong, but sufficient.

David Brinkley, anchor for a major news broadcast, summed up the mood of the nation when he stated on NBC national television that, "We are about to wind up, as about all that could happen has happened. It is one of the ugliest days in American history. There is seldom any time to think anymore, and today there was none. In about four hours we had gone from President Kennedy in Dallas, alive, to back in Washington, dead, and a new president in his place. There is really no more to say except that what happened has been just too much, too ugly, and too fast."

The reporters in the assembly room were allowed access to the alleged assassin of the president. Oswald tried to answer questions, but several reporters from the back shouted for him to speak louder.

"Well, I was questioned by a judge; however, I protested at that time that I was not allowed legal representation..." I really don't know what this situation is about. Nobody has told me anything except that I am accused of murdering a policeman. I know nothing more than that and I do request someone to come forward to give me legal assistance."

When asked if he had killed the president, Oswald replied nervously, "No. I have not been charged with that. In fact, nobody has said that to me yet. The first thing I heard about it was when the newspaper reporters in the hall asked me that question." When told by a reporter that he was indeed charged with the murder of the president, Oswald seemed surprised. He pursed his lips as if annoyed or stunned, but he did not respond. Oswald was led away from the reporters by two of the detectives. A reporter asked Oswald how he hurt his eye. He did not respond. When asked the same question again, he replied, "A policeman hit me."

Oswald was taken to the fifth floor and placed in a maximum security cell, number F-2. He was separated from the other prisoners. The two adjacent cells to his were empty. No one was taking any chances with Oswald's safety. The twelve-by-twelve cell was comprised of four bunk beds, a sink, a toilet, and a water fountain.

Abraham Zapruder was approached by a *Life* magazine representative for the purpose of buying the film from him. Zapruder played the shocking film for the representative. After the film ended, Zapruder was offered $15,000 for the rights. Zapruder hesitated and so the representative offered him a higher figure. And so it went until Zapruder heard the right figure. $50,000.

Oswald was again questioned by Captain Fritz. Oswald denied having ever owned a rifle or of having been a member of the Communist Party. Oswald admitted, however, that he had purchased a pistol seven months earlier. When asked where he purchased the gun, he refused to answer any more questions related to guns without seeing a lawyer first. Not surprisingly, Oswald adamantly refused to submit to a polygraph test.

Oswald was escorted to the Homicide and Robbery office for more questioning. As he was led past the throng of reporters, he took advantage of the nearby microphones to lodge a complaint about not being allowed to take a shower. Apparently, he was trying to build elicit sympathy from the newsmen so they could report the news to the world.

After a few minutes of casual banter designed to make Oswald feel less guarded, Oswald was asked some serious questions. Oswald was reminded that just yesterday he stated that he had never owned a gun. He agreed with that assessment. Fritz pulled out a black and white photo showing Oswald apparently holding a rifle in one hand and a pistol in the other.

"I'm not going to make any comment about that without the advice of an attorney," Oswald snapped back.

Oswald refused to even admit that his face was in the photograph. He insisted it was a fake. He finally admitted it was his face, but the body was not his body. He claimed that a rifle had been superimposed in his hand. He added that he had never seen the photo. When told that the photo was found among his possessions, he simply denied that it was ever owned by him.

Chief Curry was asked by reporters if there were plans to move Oswald that evening. He informed the press that Oswald would probably be moved the next morning, most likely around 10:00 a.m. Curry assured the reporters that they wouldn't miss anything the next morning. He also assured them that Oswald's life was not in any danger, even though he had informed the world where Oswald would be at 10:00 a.m. Sunday morning.

On Sunday morning, Oswald was brought down to the basement to begin his transfer from City Hall to the county jail. Someone noticed that the prisoner was wearing a white tee-shirt with nothing over it. Oswald was offered a black sweater to wear, which he accepted. Surprisingly, Oswald refused to wear a hat which would have helped hide his identity during the transfer. This could have played a key role in what was about to occur. It was decided that there would be two cars parked in the basement. One would be a decoy and the other would transport Oswald to the county jail. The plan was created so that the chances of Oswald being murdered would be lessened substantially.

Secret Service agent Sorrels advised Captain Fritz not to move Oswald to the county jail at a time made known to the public. He further advised that he should instead move the prisoner at around three or four in the morning. Fritz agreed with Sorrels, but understood that Chief Curry "wants to go along with the press and not try to put anything over on them."

Meanwhile, Oswald was in Fritz's office with his hands cuffed in front of him. A detective slipped part of another set of handcuffs through Oswald's cuff on his right wrist and slipped the other half of the cuff on his left wrist. The detective advised Oswald to hit the floor if anything went wrong. Oswald told the detective he was being "melodramatic."

Detectives Leavelle and Graves stepped out of the elevator. Oswald was in between the two men while Lieutenant

Swain and Captain Fritz walked in front of the three men. Reporters became excited, shouting, "Here he comes!"

As the two detectives and Oswald walked toward a white sedan, the glare of television lights momentarily blinded them. The two detectives became upset when they realized the sedan was not where it should have been. It was farther away from the jail room than it should have been and reporters were in the way.

Suddenly, someone rushed from the crowd toward Oswald. He was holding a pistol in his right hand. Leavelle recognized him almost immediately. Detective Billy H. Combest shouted to the man, "Jack, you son of a bitch, don't!" It was too late. The man fired at Oswald, hitting him in the torso. Oswald let out a cry "Ohhh!" He grabbed his stomach while his face expressed deep anguish. *NBC News* correspondent, Tom Pettit, shouted to the world saying, "He's been shot. He's been shot. Lee Oswald's been shot." The world had just witnessed the first live murder in television history.

Detectives Leavelle and Graves wrestled with the man while trying to grab the pistol from him. Graves shouted at the shooter, "Turn it loose! Turn it loose!" Graves finally twisted the revolver out of the man's hand. Suddenly, several detectives knocked Ruby down to the concrete floor. Ruby shouted, "I hope I killed the son of a bitch."

Tom Pettit continued shouting above the noise. "There's absolute panic, absolute panic here in the basement of the Dallas Police Headquarters...pandemonium has broken loose here!"

Reporters surrounded the detectives who were piled on top of Ruby. Captain Talbert shouted at them to get back. He grabbed several reporters and pulled them away from the detectives holding Ruby. This was now a crime scene and they were in the way. Oswald was dragged back to where he was taken before the shooting. The jail cell seemed the only safe haven now. The handcuffs were removed from his wrists as he moaned in anguish.

The gunman was on the floor of the jail office when Captain Talbert arrived to see who the culprit was. When asked who he was, Ruby blurted out, "Oh, hell! You guys all know me. I'm Jack Ruby!" It was apparent that many of the men surrounding Ruby knew exactly who he was. He was the owner of the Carousel Club, a popular strip bar.

One of the detectives examined Oswald's wound. He discovered that the entry wound was in the lower left part of his chest. The surrounding area of the wound was purple. He felt for an exit wound and found that the bullet was lodged just inside the skin. There didn't appear to be much loss of blood.

A young medical student arrived at the jail office after 11:00 a.m. He checked Oswald's pupils and noticed they were slightly dilated. He examined the victim further and found he was unable to detect any vital signs such as a pulse or breathing. He attempted to get a heartbeat by massaging Oswald's sternum.

Four minutes after the shooting, an ambulance arrived to take Oswald to Parkland Hospital, the same hospital President Kennedy had died in just two days earlier. Oswald appeared lifeless as they placed his body on a stretcher and wheeled it toward the waiting ambulance.

A nearby reporter described the scene to the world. "Here is young Oswald now. He is being hustled in, he is lying flat, to me he appears dead. There is a gunshot wound in his lower abdomen. He is white. His head is back. He is out-unconscious! Dangling-his hand dangling over the edge of the stretcher."

The ambulance left City Hall and headed toward Parkland Hospital. Oswald was given oxygen while an attendant massaged Oswald's sternum. The patient appeared dead. Suddenly, Oswald started pulling the resuscitator cup away from his mouth and attempted to stop the attendant from massaging his chest.

The ambulance finally arrived at the entrance to the hospital. Oswald was rushed to Trauma Room Two. Two of the doctors who tried to save President Kennedy's life were on hand to try and save his alleged assassin's life. Dr. Perry quickly examined Oswald's vital signs to determine his condition. The patient had no blood pressure and an infrequent heartbeat. Detective Leavelle informed Dr. Perry that he wanted the bullet as evidence. The bullet was still lodged under Oswald's skin in the back. Someone dislodged the bullet from behind the skin and presented it to the detective.

Dr. Shires, the chief of surgery at Parkland Hospital, realized that Oswald had practically no chance of surviving the shooting because he had lost too much blood. He perceived that the twenty minutes since the shooting was too long a time to survive the loss of blood from such a wound. There was also the matter of internal bleeding that Oswald may have sustained. The press was informed that Oswald was in critical condition and therefore he was going to be operated on immediately. No further information was provided.

In the meantime, Sorrels, head of the Secret Service in Dallas, wanted to interview Ruby. He was interested in determining if Ruby knew Oswald and whether or not they were accomplices in the assassination of President Kennedy. He decided not to warn Ruby about his rights to remain silent because he felt it might cause Ruby not to reveal everything he knew about Oswald. Sorrels felt it was extremely important to determine if there was a link between Oswald and Ruby.

Ruby informed Sorrels that his real name was Rubinstein. He had changed his name legally soon after arriving in Dallas. Ruby informed the agent that he owned the Carousel Club and the Vegas Club. When asked why he shot Oswald, Ruby explained that he liked John and Jackie Kennedy a great deal. He further explained that he even closed his businesses for three days while he was in a state of grief. He wanted to spare Jackie the anguish of sitting through a trial and reliving that fateful day in Dallas.

"I guess I just had to show the world that a Jew has guts," he explained.

"Was anyone involved with you in the shooting of Oswald?" Sorrels asked Ruby.

"No," Ruby replied.

When asked if he knew Oswald prior to the shooting, Ruby replied, "No. There is no acquaintance or connection between Oswald and myself."

Shortly before noon, at Parkland Hospital, Dr. Malcolm Perry and chief surgeon Tom Shires conducted a laparotomy on Oswald's abdomen. They discovered that the wound was very substantial. Oswald's abdomen was filled with over three quarts of blood. They frantically worked to remove as much blood as possible. The liver, spleen, pancreas, and part of one kidney were damaged by the bullet. Over the next hour they managed to curtail the major bleeding points. When Oswald's blood pressure improved dramatically, the doctors became hopeful that perhaps Oswald's life might be saved after all.

Just before 1:00 p.m., the operating team discussed how best to proceed with the operation. By clamping the aorta in order to stop any more blood loss, blood would be prevented from flowing into the kidneys. If this situation continued much longer, it could prove fatal to Oswald. It was decided that this major artery would be repaired immediately.

Suddenly, one of the doctors noticed that Oswald's pulse rate dropped from 85 to 40. In a matter of seconds there was no pulse at all. Dr. Perry immediately massaged Oswald's heart so that it might begin pumping blood on its own. Up to 700 volts of electricity were injected into Oswald, but without any discernible effect. Dr. Jenkins decided any further measure would be fruitless. Oswald was pronounced dead at 1:07 p.m.

After Oswald expired, the Secret Service needed to find a safe place for the Oswald family. An agent told Robert Oswald, brother of Lee Harvey, "All we need is to have one more of you killed."

A decision was made to hold a private ceremony for Lee Harvey Oswald. He was buried in Rose Hill Cemetery, just outside Fort Worth, Texas. Secret Service agents accompanied the Oswald family in order to ensure their safely. Lee Harvey Oswald had no friends and so his casket had to be carried to the gravesite by reporters covering the story. After the twenty minute ceremony, the Oswald's were led away by Secret Service agents. Bulldozers plowed dirt atop the casket and filled up the hole. Two policemen were ordered to watch the gravesite for an indefinite amount of time.

President John Fitzgerald Kennedy's death shocked a nation so profoundly that it never really recovered. It had lost a young leader destined for greatness. It has been argued that the assassination of this promising leader was felt more deeply than the grief that was felt over the loss of Lincoln, Garfield and McKinley. The loss of Lincoln, horrible as it was, was numbed somewhat by the bloodiest war America ever faced. FDR's death was tempered by the jubilation over the impending victory the allies were to experience in 1945.

Kennedy's sudden and unexpected death was an altogether different matter. Kennedy was a young husband married to a wife whom America was infatuated with. He had a young daughter, Caroline, and a boy, affectionately known as John John. President Kennedy had certainly made mistakes, but he also rose to the occasion when needed, as in the case of the Cuban Missile crisis and the Nuclear Test Ban Treaty. He pressed for equal rights for all of the nation's citizens, not just for some.

Perhaps the nation's greatest loss was the realization that Kennedy exuded so much hope for all its citizens. Americans have consistently rated Kennedy as one of our greatest presidents. In fact, Kennedy has the highest public approval rating for all presidents since 1963. Historians have not been so kind, however. According to them, Kennedy did not provide any great legislative victories. His response to the civil rights movement was lukewarm and he had mixed results when it came to foreign affairs. Historians could not in good conscience rank him anywhere near the top of a presidential ranking.

Author Thomas Reeves explained in his book, *A Question of Character*, that Kennedy may have suffered from scandalous leaks in his second term had he lived. His alleged involvement with mobster Sam Giancana could have led to impeachment hearings had they been disclosed. Seymour Hirsh, in his book, *The Dark Side of Camelot*, explained that Kennedy's womanizing may have caught up with him, putting him "just one news story away from cataclysmic political scandal."

Overshadowing the criticism of Kennedy as just an average chief executive has been the American public's admiration and adoration of the 32nd president. The public has had a tendency to dismiss much of the allegations against Kennedy as pure gossip. And even if any of these allegations were true, Kennedy, according to the public, should not be judged by his failings as a leader, but what he accomplished and set out to accomplish.

What the public sees in Kennedy is perhaps something that cannot be measured in simple terms. He was sincere in his conviction that America had entered a "new frontier," where nothing was impossible. He used the space program as a means of focusing on what could be accomplished in our lifetime. Kennedy's youthful good looks, humor and charm affected Americans deeply like no other American leader. People wanted to believe in his unbridled optimism.

Of all the Kennedys, Bobby was perhaps the most deeply moved by the assassination. The night of the assassination, he sat alone in the Lincoln bedroom and asked God why this had to be. What was the sense of it? For what purpose was such a great leader, friend, and brother's life snuffed out in one brief instant? Was a life that had such promise and accomplishment to end so tragically? To what end, God? "The innocent suffer – how can that be possible and God be just?" Bobby asked himself over and over again.

Many theories exist in an attempt to explain the reasons behind the assassination. Bobby Kennedy, for example, had been suspected of being involved in assassination plots against Fidel Castro. According to one source, Bobby privately thought that factions of the mob or Cuban exiles may have been behind the killing of his brother.

Lyndon Johnson initially thought that Kennedy's death was in direct response to the killing of South Vietnamese leader Diem in 1963. Later, he concluded that Castro's boys killed Kennedy. He told an advisor that "President Kennedy tried to get Castro, but Castro got Kennedy first." Johnson told a reporter, "We had been operating a damned Murder Inc. in the Caribbean."

For political reasons, Johnson kept quiet about his suspicions of who may have been behind Kennedy's murder. He didn't want America's dirty laundry to be seen by the nation's citizens, or for that matter, the rest of the world. He was concerned that if the true cause of Kennedy's death ever got out, the threat of nuclear war could become a reality.

The public perception of President Kennedy's greatness has grown stronger through the ages. There are perhaps more books written about him and his times than any other president with the possible exception of Abraham Lincoln. The American citizenry consistently ranks Kennedy among the top five presidents.

Ever since the Warren Commission Report was made public in September of 1964, it has been called into question by scores of investigators and perhaps people who just wanted to make a name for themselves. Many theories have come forward since the very day President Kennedy was gunned down in Dallas. David Lifton, in his highly respected and highly controversial book, *Best Evidence*, theorized that Kennedy was secretly taken to Walter Reed Hospital instead of Bethesda Hospital, which was the official destination of Kennedy's body. Supposedly, this would allow Walter Reed doctors to perform surgery on Kennedy's head so that it would appear the shots came from the back instead of the front. Dallas surgeons had reported that the shots all came from the front of Kennedy's head.

The public's belief that there was a conspiracy has steadily grown through the years. A highly respected book, *Case Closed*, written by attorney Gerald Posner, criticizes many of the conspiracy theories popular at the time. But this book failed to convince enough of the public that Oswald acted alone. Partly influenced by Oliver Stone's film, *JFK*, more than two thirds of the American people believe Oswald did not act alone in the assassination of President Kennedy.

CHAPTER 13

THE WARREN COMMISSION REPORT AND ITS CRITICS

On November 29, 1963, President Lyndon Baines Johnson created the President's Commission on the Assassination of President John F. Kennedy by Executive Order No 11130. The Commission was directed to evaluate all the relevant facts related to the assassination of President Kennedy and the murder of Lee Harvey Oswald, presumably the president's assassin. In President Johnson's own words, he charged the Commission "to satisfy itself that the truth is known as far as it can be discovered, and to report its findings and conclusion to him, to the American people, and to the world." On September 27, 1964, the Commission finally provided the president with its findings. On November 23, 1964, the public was provided with reportedly all the evidence the Commission had seen.

There were several reasons why the president believed a commission needed to be established as soon as possible.

Chief among them was the fact that it was virtually impossible to determine who was behind Kennedy's assassination through the judicial system because Lee Harvey Oswald, the only suspect, was dead. Alternative methods of procedure were considered, such as a court of inquiry and an investigation by a grand jury in Dallas County, Texas. Both Houses of Congress even contemplated the possibility of holding congressional hearings in order to get to the bottom of the assassination. Congress feared that a foreign or domestic conspiracy may have been behind the assassination. President Johnson, sensing that rival investigations and hearings might cause more harm than good, decided that a Commission directed by him would be the best alternative.

President Johnson selected Chief Justice of the United States Earl Warren as Chairman of the Commission. Johnson also selected U.S. Senator Richard B. Russell, a Democrat from Georgia, and U.S. Senator John Sherman Cooper, a Republican from Kentucky to serve on the Commission. From the House of Representatives, Johnson elected Hale Boggs, Democrat from Louisiana, and Gerald R. Ford, Republican from Michigan. From the private sector, Johnson chose two attorneys whom had served former presidential administrations, Allen W. Dulles, former Director of the CIA and John J. McCloy, former president of the International Bank for Reconstruction and Development.

The Commission's first meeting was held on December 5, 1963. The Commission believed that they needed to conduct its own thorough investigation and not accept at face value findings and conclusions from Federal and State agencies. Because there were many rumors floating around that a conspiracy could be a real possibility, the Commission was charged with investigating possible suspects other than Oswald. On December 13, 1963, the Senate Joint Resolution 137 was enacted by Congress, giving the Commission the power to issue subpoenas. The Commission was also given the power to provide immunity to anyone who may seek the Fifth Amendment.

A large staff would be required to carry out the assignment the Commission had been ordered to accomplish. On December 16, 1963, former Solicitor General of the United States, J. Lee Rankin, was sworn in as the Commission's general counsel. Over the course of the next several weeks, additional staff members with impressive legal backgrounds were selected from the Department of Justice, the Internal Revenue Service, the Defense Department and the State Department. Additionally, representatives from the city of Dallas joined the investigative body of the Commission.

On December 9, 1963, the Federal Bureau of Investigation provided to the Commission a five-volume report summarizing its findings as to what occurred during and immediately after the assassination of President Kennedy and Lee Harvey Oswald. The Commission carefully examined the report and requested the Federal Bureau of Investigation to submit the investigative documentation supporting its summary. The first detailed reports were provided to the Commission on December 20, 1963. Two days earlier, the Secret Service handed over a report on the security measures that were taken before President Kennedy's trip to Dallas. Also included was a document reflecting what the Secret Service agents witnessed on November 22, 1963. Several days later, the State Department issued a report covering Oswald's defection in 1959 to the Soviet

Union and his subsequent return to the United States in 1962. In early January, 1964, the Texas Attorney General issued to the Commission some investigative documents on the assassination of Kennedy and Oswald's murder.

A huge job lay ahead for the Commission's staff. As each report was provided to the Commission, the staff began reviewing and organizing all the investigative material. The staff determined what the relevant points were pertaining to each document and categorized items that still required further investigation before a conclusion could be drawn from the facts presented. Moreover, the Commission requested all relevant information related to the assassination of President Kennedy, Oswald's murder, and all pertinent facts about Jack Ruby from various Federal government agencies and commissions.

As the Commission reviewed all the material provided to them, they continuously requested more investigative reports from Federal and State investigative agencies. The Federal Bureau of Investigation and the Secret Service were given the responsibility of executing statement requests from key witnesses. They also examined all physical evidence relevant to the assassination of the president and Oswald's murder. In addition to Federal agencies, the Commission requested experienced experts from State and local governments to help with the investigation.

Beginning on November 22, 1963, the Federal Bureau of Investigation and the Secret Service combined forces for the purpose of conducting interviews with people who may have relevant information related to the events that took place in Dallas between the 22nd and the 24th of November. By September 11, 1964, over 26,000 interviews had taken place, and over 3,000 reports were submitted to the Commission by both agencies. In the end, over 30,000 pages would be issued to the Commission by the FBI and the Secret Service.

To supplement the enormous amount of investigative material received, the Commission held formal hearings in which sworn testimony from key witnesses of the assassination of President Kennedy was disclosed during the procedures. Beginning on February 3, 1964, the Commission and its staff had listened to the testimony of 552 witnesses. Not all the witnesses, however, gave open testimony at a formal hearing. 61 witnesses provided sworn affidavits, and 2 gave statements. The witnesses that did appear before the Commission or the Commission's legal staff were allowed the presence and the advice of an attorney. Each witness had the right to object to any question asked of them and to make a statement after he or she had been interrogated.

The Commission's function was to uncover all relevant facts related to President Kennedy's assassination. Because the prime suspect, Lee Harvey Oswald, had been murdered, the procedures followed by the Commission could not resemble those of a criminal court proceeding. The United States has never allowed provisions for a posthumous trial. Had Oswald survived the shooting at the hands of Jack Ruby, then a trial governed by the American standards of justice would have been initiated. Since Oswald had been murdered, there would be no adversary proceeding against him. The Commission's primary purpose, therefore, was that of a fact gathering body that would hopefully lead to a conclusion supported by the evidence accumulated by all the investigative agencies working for the Commission.

Included in the process of gathering information was the necessity of examining hearsay and other forms of information not held admissible in a court of law. The Commission was mindful of the fact that because hearsay was admissible as a source of information, fairness to the alleged assassin, Lee Harvey Oswald, might be compromised. So on February 25, 1964, Walter E. Craig was requested to participate in the investigation for the purpose of advising the Commission whether or not he felt the whole procedure conformed to the principles of the American justice system.

The published works comprised of 26 volumes for a total of over 17,000 pages. The body of work included 15 volumes of testimony and 11 volumes of exhibits. Some of the testimony was deemed too graphic and so it was stricken from the published text. One example of this involved Mrs. Kennedy's reference to the wounds of her husband. Bracketed within part of her testimony are the words, "reference to wounds deleted."

The original deadline for the Warren Commission Report was June 1, 1964. Most of the staff members in charge of investigating the assassination had not even concluded their work. Lee Rankin, the commission's general counsel, appointed several more people to help speed up the process of writing the report. Revisions of reports already completed had to be implemented as well, causing further delays. For example, Arlen Specter's report justifying the single bullet theory had to be revised because the credibility of the theory was held in question.

On September 28, 1964, The Warren Commission report was finally submitted for the entire world to see. There were a total of eight chapters in the report. The first chapter provided a summary of the events that occurred on November 22, 1963 and November 24th, 1963, in Dallas, Texas. It provided the Commission's conclusion of what exactly occurred and also its recommendations on how to improve the effectiveness of the Secret Service. The second chapter dealt with a detailed account of what transpired on November 22, 1963 in Dallas. Basically, it examines the planning of the trip to Dallas, the route the motorcade took from Love Field to Dallas, the assassination of President Kennedy, and the ordeal at Parkland Hospital where doctors tried desperately to save the president's life. The third chapter dealt with where the Commission believed the gunshots came from, the number of shots and their trajectory, and the president's wounds. The fourth chapter focused on Oswald's movements before, during, and after the assassination. The fifth chapter examined Oswald's capture and detainment by law enforcement officers and his subsequent murder. Chapter six revealed the Commission's findings on Oswald's background and possible connection with Jack Ruby in the assassination of President Kennedy. Chapter seven goes into more detail about Oswald's shadowy background and chapter eight concerns itself with the protection of President Kennedy by the Secret Service on the day of the assassination.

The following conclusions were reached by the Commission. The three shots that were fired at President Kennedy came from a window on the sixth floor of the Texas School Book Depository in Dallas, Texas. One bullet entered President Kennedy's back, exited out his throat, and caused wounds to Governor Connally. Lee Harvey Oswald killed President Kennedy and wounded Governor

Connally. Shortly after President Kennedy's assassination, Oswald shot and killed Dallas Police Patrolman J.D. Tippit. Shortly after Tippit's murder, Oswald was captured inside a movie theater after he resisted his arrest. As far as the evidence showed, Lee Harvey Oswald and Jack Ruby were not part of any conspiracy to murder President Kennedy. Lee Harvey Oswald acted entirely alone in the assassination of President Kennedy.

The Warren Commission Report drew harsh criticism soon after it was released to the public. One of the first critics of the report was Edward Jay Epstein. His book, *Inquest: The Warren Commission and the Establishment of Truth*, blasted the Commission on the way it performed its duties. According to Epstein, the goals of the Commission were suspect from the beginning. Chief Justice Earl Warren stated that "the purpose of this Commission is, of course, eventually to make known to the president, and to the American public everything that has transpired before the commission." Johnson, however, emphasized to Warren how important the nation's prestige was to the rest of the world. Another prominent member of the Commission was concerned that America might look like a banana republic if a conspiracy was behind the assassination of President Kennedy. Epstein, therefore, believed that the Commission may have been too worried about how America looked to the rest of world if evidence of a conspiracy came to light. This concern might compromise the investigation and the whole truth might never see the light of day.

According to Epstein, important and highly significant evidence of an additional assassin garnered by the FBI was never provided to the Commission. The FBI was informed by a Mrs. Eric Walther in December, 1963, that she witnessed a man in a white shirt standing in the window of the Texas School Book Depository. He had blond hair and he was holding a rifle. Mrs. Walther was quoted as saying, "Almost immediately after noticing this man with the rifle and the other man standing beside him, someone in the crowd said "Here they come...." The FBI interviewed a second witness, Arnold Rowland, who reportedly saw a man standing just inside a window on the sixth floor and holding a high-powered rifle. According to Epstein, the FBI provided the commission with Mrs. Walter's testimony, but the report was never reviewed.

Epstein attacked the famous single bullet theory that had been vigorously championed by Arlen Specter. The single bullet theory attempted to explain how only one gunman could have been solely responsible for the murder of President Kennedy. The Zapruder film became an essential piece of evidence used in determining whether or not one assassin was involved in the assassination.

Leaving the Zapruder evidence aside for the moment, there was one key issue Epstein found disturbing. To begin with, according to Epstein, the FBI summary and subsequent reports detailing its research in connection with the autopsy claimed that the first bullet that struck Kennedy did not exit out the front of his body. The FBI report stated that "Medical examination of the president's body had revealed that the bullet entered his back and penetrated to a distance of less than a finger length." This suggested that no path of the bullet causing the wound in the president's back was ever considered. This report therefore was significantly inconsistent with subsequent reports from various sources that the first bullet to strike the president exited out the front of Kennedy's body.

But the main argument against the single bullet theory rested with analysis of the Zapruder film itself and live-fire tests conducted by the FBI using Oswald's own Mannlicher-Carcano rifle. Three marksmen attempted to fire three shots at a target in the shortest time possible. None of the marksmen were able to fire three shots quickly in succession in less than 6 seconds. Indeed, it took 9 seconds for one of the marksmen to fire off all three shots. After careful analysis of the Zapruder film, it was determined that 5.6 seconds had elapsed between the time the first shot was fired and the last shot that killed Kennedy. All of the test shots fired were above and to the right of the target. The distance from the sixth floor window of the Texas Book Depository and Kennedy's head was a thousand yards, whereas the target the marksmen fired at was only fifteen yards away. The assassin would not only have to be a superior marksman, he would have to quickly take into account the deficiency of the telescopic sight. All this would need to be performed while pulling off a major assassination under tremendous pressure.

Epstein called into question the Commission's decision to assign most of the fact-finding of the assassination to only one individual, namely Arlen Specter. This was a daunting assignment for even a committee of individuals whose task it was to get to the bottom of the murder a world leader. The assignment of major responsibilities to only one man caused Specter to drastically limit his scope of his investigation. According to Epstein, Specter spent eight days in Dallas and interviewed only two people, Jack

Ruby and a grassy knoll witness. Amazingly, his short stay in Dallas would be Specter's entire field investigation of "the basic facts of the assassination." In Epstein's view, it was impossible for one individual to effectively conduct a major investigation and determine what the truth is without some oversight.

Epstein argued that the Commission took it upon itself to assign almost all the investigation fieldwork to other government agencies instead of creating its own investigative body. Government agencies, according to Epstein, have their own agenda which may not coincide with what is best for the American people. They constantly need to be mindful about the conclusions they draw and how it may affect funding from Congress. The need to protect its image so that it could enjoy power and prestige could compromise the investigation. Providing the public with embarrassing and potentially illegal activity could well jeopardize an agency's existence.

Another early critic of the Warren Commission report was Mark Lane. He had written a book called *Rush to Judgement* in which he condemned the Commission's conclusions as patently false. He argued that shots had been fired from the front of the motorcade, not from the back as the Warren Commission claimed. He also argued that the authorities were trying to cover up what actually occurred before, during, and after the assassination. Lane stated in his book that several witnesses strongly believed that shots had been fired from the general vicinity of the grassy knoll at Dealey Plaza and not from the Texas Book Depository. He provided quotes from press releases published in Dallas newspapers the morning after the assassination. He reported that two Dallas physicians who were with Kennedy in the emergency room stated that the wound in the front of Kennedy's neck was indeed an entrance wound. Lane provided published dispatches from the *New York Times* reporting that Dallas authorities thought Kennedy was struck from the front while the limousine he was riding in was still on Houston Street and not on Elm. They were attempting to explain the neck wound in relation to where Oswald allegedly fired from. Lane also revealed that *Life* magazine ran an article claiming that Kennedy turned to acknowledge someone in the crowd and therefore exposed the front of his neck to the rear of the limousine he was riding in.

Lane pointed out repeatedly that the earliest accounts explaining the throat wound differed dramatically from the subsequent accounts as reported by the Warren Commission report. The early accounts in the newspapers revealed that the Dallas doctors thought the throat wound was an entry wound. The Commission simply dismissed earlier statements made by the Dallas doctors as either mistaken judgments or misquotes. The implication of an entry wound in the throat meant that a gunshot had to have been fired at the president somewhere in the vicinity of the grassy knoll. This flew in the face of the theory that one gunman fired at the president from behind. Even more curious was the fact that James J. Humes, who was with Kennedy during the autopsy, admitted to destroying certain preliminary draft notes relating to "Naval School Autopsy Report A63-272."

A staggering number of books have been published over the past several decades regarding the assassination of President John F. Kennedy, and there seems to be no end in sight. As long as the majority of the public believes there was a conspiracy to murder the president, there will always be a market for books about this horrific event. Everything related to the assassination of Kennedy and the murder of Oswald seems to have been brought into question. Books and articles have been written about alleged intimidation of witnesses, ignored testimony of key witnesses, the alleged suspicious nature of key witnesses deaths, confiscation by police of film capturing the assassination, claims of suppressed documents suggesting more than one gunman was involved in the assassination, tampering of the president's body to hide evidence of a conspiracy, and claims of a doctored photograph of Oswald supposedly holding the assassin's rifle shortly before the killing.

The assassination of President John F. Kennedy will probably remain a mystery for several generations to come. Indeed, the solution to who really killed the president and why he was gunned down may never be solved. Many of the key witnesses who were there that fateful day in Dallas have since passed away and the memories of those who are still alive are probably less clear now. When the Warren Commission Report was released to the world in September 1964, its purpose was to explain to the nation what exactly happened on that fateful day in Dallas. For many, however, it created more questions than it purportedly answered. In a way, according to many critics, a second tragedy occurred in that the report did not seriously deal with the possibility of a conspiracy.

Shortly after the assassination of President John F. Kennedy, newly sworn-in President Lyndon B. Johnson spoke before a special joint session of Congress and said these words.

"All I have I would have given gladly not to be standing here today. The greatest leader of our time has been struck down by the foulest deed of our time. Today, John Fitzgerald Kennedy lives on in the immortal words and works that he left behind. He lives on in the mind and memories of mankind. He lives on in the hearts of his countrymen."

BIBLIOGRAPHY

Bingham, Howard L. and Max Wallace. *Ali's Greatest Fight.* UK: M. Evans, 2000

Blaine, Gerald with Lisa McCubbin. *The Kennedy Detail.* New York: Gallery Books, 2010

Bugliosi, Vincent. *Four Days In November.* New York: W.W. Norton & Company, 2007

Carlin, Peter. *Paul McCartney: A Life.* New York: Simon & Schuster, 2009

Carson, Clayborne, ed. *The Autobiography Of Martin Luther King, Jr.* New York: Warner Books, 1998

Chambers, Paul G. *Head Shot.* New York: Prometheus Books, 2012

Dallek, Robert. *An Unfinished Life: John F. Kennedy.* New York: Back Bay Books, 2003

Dundee, Angelo with Bert Randolph Sugar. *My View From The Corner.* New York: McGraw Hill, 2008

Garrow, David J. *Bearing The Cross: Martin Luther King, Jr. And The Southern Christian Leadership Conference.* NewYork: Vintage Books, 1986

Karnow, Stanley. *Vietnam: A History.* New York: Viking Penguin, 1983

King, Jr., Martin Luther. *Why We Can't Wait.* New York: Harper Collins, 1963

Langguth, A.J. *Our Vietnam: The War, 1954-1975.* New York: Simon &Schuster, 2000

Lifton, David S. *Best Evidence: Disguise And Deception In The Assassination Of John F. Kennedy.* New York: Dell Publishing Co.,Inc.,1980

Maclear, Michael. *The Ten Thousand Day War, Vietnam: 1945-1975.* New York: Avon Books, 1981

Manchester, William. *The Death of a President: November 1963.* New York: Harper & Row, 1967

Norman, Philip. *Shout! The Beatles in Their Generation.* New York: Fireside, 1981

Pacheco, Ferdie, M.D. *The 12 Greatest Rounds Of Boxing: The Untold Stories.* Toronto: Sport Classic Books, 2003

Remnick, David. *King Of The World.* New York: Vintage Books, 1998

Spitz, Bob. *The Beatles: The Biography.* New York: Little, Brown And Co., 2005

Stark, Steven D. *Meet The Beatles.* New York: Harper Collins, 2005

Washington, James M., ed. Martin Luther King, Jr., *I Have A Dream: Writings & Speeches That Changed The World.* New York: HarperOne, 1986